The New Finance

Regulation and Financial Stability

The New Finance
Regulation and Financial Stability

Franklin R. Edwards

THE AEI PRESS

Publisher for the American Enterprise Institute
WASHINGTON, D.C.
1996

To order call toll free 1-800-462-6420 or 1-717-794-3800. For all other inquiries please contact the AEI Press, 1150 Seventeenth Street, N.W., Washington, D.C. 20036 or call 1-800-862-5801.

Library of Congress Cataloging-in-Publication Data

Edwards, Franklin R., 1937–
 The new finance: regulation and financial stability/Franklin R. Edwards.
  p. cm.
 Includes bibliographical references and index.
 ISBN 0-8447-3988-X (alk. paper)—ISBN 0-8447-3989-8 (pbk.: alk. paper)
 1. Banks and banking—Deregulation—United States. 2. Banking law—United States. 3. Financial institutions—United States. 4. Mutual funds—United States. 5. Monetary policy—United States. 6. Collateralized banking. I. Title.
HG2491.E39   1996
332.1'0973—DC2   96-14226
                                                          CIP

THE AEI PRESS
Publisher for the American Enterprise Institute
1150 17th Street, N.W., Washington, D.C. 20036

Contents

PREFACE   xi

1 INTRODUCTION   1

2 BANKING AND FINANCIAL INTERMEDIATION   4
     The Economics of Financial Intermediation   4
     Banks and Banking Regulation in the United States   6
     Economic Forces Underlying Recent Changes in Financial
         Intermediation   7

3 THE DECLINE OF TRADITIONAL BANKING AND THE RISE OF
NONBANK FINANCIAL INTERMEDIARIES   10
     The Decline of Traditional Banking in the United
         States   11
     Why Is Traditional Banking in Decline?   12
     The Erosion of Bank Profitability   35
     How Have Banks Responded?   38
     The Decline of Traditional Banking Is a Global
         Phenomenon   42
     Recent Changes in Historical Perspective   47
     Nonbank Intermediaries as Money Managers: Implications
         for Securities and Derivatives Markets   53
     Conclusion   59

4 ALTERNATIVE VIEWS OF THE DECLINE OF BANKING: PUBLIC POLICY
IMPLICATIONS   60
   The Excess Capacity Theory 60
   The Regulatory Burden Theory 61
   The Theory of Declining Bank Uniqueness 63
   Public Policy Concerns 70

5 MUTUAL FUNDS AND FINANCIAL STABILITY   73
   Fear of a Mutual-Fund-Induced Financial Collapse 76
   Depositor Runs versus Shareholder Runs 82
   Will Commercial Paper Defaults Cause a Run on
      MMMFs? 86
   Will Mutual Fund Redemptions Destabilize Stock and
      Bond Markets? 88
   Can the Federal Reserve Still Be Effective as Lender of Last
      Resort? 91
   Proposals to Extend Bank Regulation to Mutual Funds:
      The Parallel Banking System Proposal 94
   Mutual Funds and Derivatives: Lessons from Recent
      Events 96
   Conclusions and Policy Implications 97

6 THE CHANGING STRUCTURE OF FINANCIAL INTERMEDIATION AND
THE EFFECTIVENESS OF MONETARY POLICY   100
   Does a Stable Relationship Still Exist between Money and
      Economic Activity? 101
   Can the Federal Reserve Still Control the Supply of
      Money? 108
   Proposals to Expand the Coverage of Legal Reserve
      Requirements 110
   Alternative Views of the Monetary Transmission
      Mechanism 111
   Assessing Monetary Policy Effectiveness in the 1990s 115
   Evidence from Large-Scale Econometric Models 118
   Conclusions and Policy Implications 119

7 OTC DERIVATIVES MARKETS AND FINANCIAL FRAGILITY   120
How Would a Derivatives-Induced Systemic Crisis
     Occur? 123
Sources of Risk 125
Banks 135
Conclusions and Recommendations 144

8 FINANCIAL REGULATION FOR THE 21ST CENTURY: PROPOSALS FOR
REFORMING BANK REGULATION   148
The Current Regulatory Structure: Rationale and
     Deficiencies 151
Improving the Current System of Bank Regulation 163
Collateralized Banking 167
Conclusions and Implications for Regulatory Reform 172

9 CONCLUSION   177

NOTES   183

BIBLIOGRAPHY   199

INDEX   211

ABOUT THE AUTHOR   221

TABLES
3-1   Assets Held by Financial Intermediaries,
      1900–1994 14
3-2   Relative Shares of Total Financial Intermediary Assets,
      1900–1994 15
3-3   Distribution of Household Financial Assets,
      1982–1994 22
3-4   Net Flows of Household Financial Assets,
      1982–1994 24
3-5   Amount of Outstanding Commercial Paper,
      1980–1994 29
3-6   Outstanding U.S. Credit Market Debt Owed by
      Households and Nonfinancial Business,
      1980–1994 30

3-7   Finance Companies' Balance Sheet, 1980–1994 32

3-8   Bank Profit Margins, 1980–1992 43

3-9   Assets of Open-End Investment Companies throughout the World, 1988–1993 44

3-10   Growth of Institutional Investors, 1980–1990 46

3-11   Noninterest Income of Banks in Selected Industrial Countries, 1981–1992 48

3-12   Net Loan-Loss Provisions of Banks in Selected Industrial Countries, 1981–1992 50

3-13   Changes in U.S. Institutional Equity Ownership, 1981–1990 54

3-14   Aggregate U.S. Purchases and Sales of Foreign Securities, by Geographic Region, 1980–1994 56

3-15   Notional/Contract Amounts for Financial Derivatives Worldwide by Individual Product Type as of End of Fiscal Year, 1989–1993 57

4-1   Selected Data for Commercial Banks, 1980–1994 65

4-2   Commercial Banks' Balance Sheet, 1950–1994 66

4-3   Nonfinancial Company Borrowing, 1970–1994 69

5-1   Money Market Funds' Balance Sheet, 1980–1994 78

5-2   Mutual Fund Holdings as a Percentage of Total Securities Outstanding 79

6-1   Turnover Rates on Bank Deposits and Taxable Money Market Mutual Funds, 1980–1994 102

6-2   Components of Money Supply, 1950–1994 105

7-1   Fifteen Major U.S. OTC Derivatives Dealers and Their Notional/Contract Derivatives Amounts, 1992 and 1994 122

7-2   U.S. Federal Regulatory Oversight of OTC Derivatives Activities of Financial Institutions and Financial Institution Affiliates as of April 1994 133

7-3   Notional Amount of Off-Balance-Sheet Derivatives Contracts of the Twenty-five Commercial Banks and Trust Companies with the Most Off-Balance-Sheet Derivatives Contracts, March 31, 1995 136

7-4   Notional Amount of Off-Balance-Sheet Derivatives Contracts Held for Trading by the Nine Commercial Banks and Trust Companies with the Most Off-Balance-Sheet Derivatives Contracts, March 31, 1995 139

7-5   Derivatives Trading: Contribution to Total Trading
       Income, 1993 and 1994 140
7-6   Credit Exposures of the Twenty-five Commercial
       Banks and Trust Companies with the Most Off-
       Balance-Sheet Derivatives Contracts, March 31,
       1995 142
8-1   Major Episodes of Bank Insolvencies, 1974–1995 150

FIGURES

3-1   Commercial Banks' Share of Total Nonfinancial
       Borrowing, 1960–1994 12
3-2   Thrifts' Share of Total Nonfinancial Borrowing,
       1960–1994 13
3-3   Banks' Private Domestic Checkable Deposits,
       1950–1994 16
3-4   Growth of Pension Plans' Assets, 1960–1994 17
3-5   Holdings of Corporate Equity, 1966–1991 18
3-6   Demographic and Portfolio Shifts, 1945–1993 18
3-7   Households' Investment in Pension and Mutual Funds,
       1945–1994 19
3-8   Average Annual Net Acquisition of Mutual Fund
       Assets by Type, 1960–1994 20
3-9   Bank Checkable Deposits and Money Market Mutual
       Funds, 1959–1994 21
3-10   Net Flows of Household Financial Assets as a
       Percentage of Net Acquisition of All Financial
       Assets, 1982–1994 27
3-11   Foreign Banks' Share of the U.S. Market,
       1975–1992 35
3-12   Return on Equity and Assets for Commercial Banks,
       1960–1994 36
3-13   Share of Noninterest Income in Total Income for
       Commercial Banks, 1960–1994 37
3-14   Return on Equity and Assets for Commercial Banks,
       Excluding Noninterest Income, 1960–1994 37
3-15   Number of Bank Failures, 1960–1994 38
3-16   Commercial Real Estate Loans as a Percentage of
       Total Commercial Bank Assets, 1960–1994 39
3-17   Loan-Loss Provisions Relative to Assets for
       Commercial Banks, 1960–1994 39

3-18   Net Interest Margins for Commercial Banks, 1960–1994 40

5-1   Ratio of Money Market Mutual Funds to Banks' Checkable Deposits, 1959–1994 74

5-2   Composition of Money Market Mutual Fund Assets, January 1995 77

5-3   Bond Mutual Fund Net Redemptions, 1994–1995 90

6-1   Ratio of GDP to M1, 1969–1995 103

6-2   Ratios of Money Market Mutual Funds to M1 and M2, 1959–1994 106

6-3   Ratio of GDP to M2, 1969–1995 106

6-4   Three-Month Treasury Bill Rate, 1972–1995 107

6-5   Ratio of M1 to Monetary Base, 1969–1995 108

6-6   Ratio of M2 to Monetary Base, 1969–1995 109

6-7   Short-Term and Long-Term Daily Interest Rates, February 2, 1990–April 13, 1995 116

7-1   Largest Nine Bank Derivatives Players: Gross Notional Value of Total Derivatives Held, 1995 128

7-2   Credit Exposures from Derivatives and Loans of Seven Largest U.S. Banks as a Percentage of Equity, 1994 129

7-3   Domination of All Commercial Banks by Nine U.S. Banks with Most Derivatives, 1995 135

Preface

I decided to write this book for two reasons. First, I wanted to address the concerns of those who fear that the rapid growth of nonbank financial institutions, like mutual funds, and the proliferation of new financial instruments, like derivatives, are creating a fragile financial climate that will ultimately culminate in a financial meltdown of some kind. A major theme of this book is that those fears are overblown and that the proposed cures for the maladies that have been perceived—additional government regulation of nonbank financial institutions and markets—would be far worse than whatever problems we may have.

The second reason I wrote the book, paradoxically, was that I feared that we are being overly complacent about what is happening in financial markets. Things are indeed happening in financial markets that have substantial policy implications, but no one seems particularly interested in trying to understand what those implications are, or in attempting to figure out what, if anything, needs to be done. Very little thought seems to be going into determining just what kind of financial system and structure we would like to see evolve in the United States. Part of the explanation for that, of course, is the usual one of vested interests not wanting to rock the boat: there might be more to lose than gain by any shake-up. Another is the inability of Congress to deal with any significant matter related to financial institutions in the absence of some kind of financial crisis, such as the implosion of the thrift industry in the 1980s. As the ultimate taxpayer bailout of the thrift industry made abundantly clear, however, that kind of policy paralysis can be very damaging and costly for us. I thought that by writing this book I could at least open up the policy debate by distinguishing what are potentially important issues from those I believe to be unimportant. Along the way, however, as so often happens, I formed some strong opinions about what needs to be done, and in the book I do not spare the reader those opinions.

One of my surprises in writing the book is that I came to believe that the biggest potential problem lay with traditional banks, rather than with either the rapidly growing nonbank financial sectors or with the new technologies and financial instruments that are springing up throughout the world. The metamorphosis of financial markets in the past twenty years has affected banks more than any other financial institution. Depository institutions, and the role of bank deposits in the economy generally, have changed dramatically, and those changes have important implications for how banks are going to operate in the future and for how they should be regulated. Innovations in lending and borrowing technologies and the development of new financial instruments and markets have increasingly enabled both savers and borrowers to bypass banks—either by going directly to capital markets or by replacing banks with the services of nonbank financial institutions.

This new finance has put banks under intense pressure to change what they do to survive. They have sought to expand their activities into new and nontraditional areas and have fought to free themselves from what they perceive to be unnecessary and costly regulation. In the process, I believe, banks everywhere have increased their risk-taking and have become involved in many new activities that are difficult to regulate. My fear is that we are fooling ourselves by thinking that nothing significant has changed—that it is business as usual. That fear also is in no way relieved by the fact that bank regulators appear wedded to the notion that no matter what happens, they can continue to regulate effectively—that banks can continue to expand into more risky and more opaque activities without that expansion's interfering with the effectiveness of prudential regulation.

I remain a skeptic. There are even now real deficiencies in our current system of prudential bank regulation, and those will become painfully evident as the new finance overwhelms financial markets throughout the world. Part of the reason that I wrote this book was to bring those deficiencies to people's attention. In the book I discuss those deficiencies and why they will be difficult to fix. I believe that instead of tinkering with the present system, we need to rethink our entire regulatory system—to make it more compatible with today's competitive and financial market realities. Unless we do so, I fear that the road we are on will lead to still another banking debacle.

The trick, of course, is how to change the system. How do we afford banks greater freedom from regulation without jeopardizing the stability of the banking and financial system? We need to have a regulatory structure that can safeguard the financial system but at the same time put all financial institutions on the same competitive footing. In the book I propose one way of doing that—collateralized banking. Adopting a collateralized banking system would, I believe, allow us to free up banks to compete without jeopardizing the stability of the financial system. Ultimately, we must face the fact that we cannot continue to rely on pervasive and omniscient government regulation to safeguard the financial system. The key is to find ways to make markets work more effectively in containing excessive risk-taking by financial institutions. I believe that adopting some form of collateralized banking can accomplish that goal.

I understand, of course, that many of my conclusions and recommendations are likely to be highly controversial. This is as it should be and must be. The issues are complex, and the vested interests many. It is my hope, however, that my efforts will succeed in stimulating debate about the implications of the transformation sweeping over financial markets, and about the future role and effectiveness of government regulation of financial markets. It is well past the time that such a debate should occur.

Many people and institutions contributed to the writing of this book. The Columbia Business School, my home institution, provided me with an intellectually stimulating environment, which contributed to the book in many subtle ways. The American Enterprise Institute provided me with the opportunity of being a visiting scholar in Washington, D.C., where I benefited from many discussions with informed policy makers and with financial markets scholars and was given the time to complete the manuscript. A number of people also read parts of an earlier draft of the manuscript or commented on my ideas in discussions on many different occasions. I would like to thank, in particular, Richard Aspinwall, Charles Calomiris, Christopher DeMuth, Jacob Dryer, Mark Gertler, Glenn Hubbard, William Haraf, Ed Kane, George Kaufman, Marvin Kosters, Richard Marcis, Allan Meltzer, Rick Mishkin, John Rea, Craig Tyle, and Peter Wallison. Finally, I want to thank all my colleagues on the Shadow Financial Regulatory Committee for stimulating discussions during our meetings on many topics that turned out to be germane to the theme of this book. None of the above, of course, can be held accountable for the opinions that I ultimately formed and for the recommendations contained in the book. Indeed, it is probably accurate to say that none of the above would agree with all of my conclusions. Finally, I wish to thank Xin Zhang and Jimmy Liew, Ph.D. students at the Columbia Business School, and Jianguo Shang of the Investment Company Institute for excellent research assistance, and Leigh Tripoli, my editor at the American Enterprise Institute, for guiding the book to publication.

Franklin R. Edwards
Columbia University

✦ 1 ✦

Introduction

The 1980s were the most revolutionary decade in U.S. financial markets since the free-wheeling 1920s ended in the Great Depression of the 1930s. The collapse of the entire thrift industry necessitated a government bailout in the hundreds of billions of dollars. Traditional commercial banks lost their competitive advantage vis-à-vis other financial intermediaries, and as a consequence suffered an unprecedented loss of market share. Households sharply reduced their direct participation in equity markets; they preferred instead to make their investments through institutions such as mutual funds. Pension funds and mutual funds became financial powerhouses, exerting for the first time power over the managers of some of our largest corporations. The internationalization of financial markets combined with new technologies to create a global trading environment that now closely links events in financial markets in all countries. The use of derivatives and derivatives-linked instruments by financial institutions and corporate end-users in all countries grew explosively.

Underlying all of this are two key trends: an intensifying competitive environment and increased pressure on U.S. regulators to relax restrictions so that U.S. financial institutions (and especially banks) can compete more effectively with each other and with foreign banks. Continuing competitive pressures together with a steady stream of innovations make it likely that in the future financial markets and institutions will have to be completely reshaped to accommodate those innovations and to afford financial institutions much

1

greater freedom to compete. The regulatory barriers that have historically separated and isolated banks from each other and from non-bank financial institutions are rapidly disappearing. We must, therefore, rethink our entire approach to regulating financial markets and institutions.

The current regulatory structure is sadly out of date, and is no longer capable of continuing to protect the financial system from financial excesses that threaten to undermine its stability. The growing frequency of eye-catching losses in financial markets has rightly generated concerns about the speculative excesses of financial institutions as well as the ability of regulators to prevent such financial excesses from cascading into a financial crisis (Kaufman 1994).

Critics of the current system point first to the erosion of restrictions on banks and to the resulting increased risk that banks are taking in the pursuit of higher earnings. In the 1980s deregulation of banking in Norway, Sweden, and Finland led to the collapse of entire banking systems, as banks loaded up on risky loans in an effort to sustain or increase earnings (Llewellyn 1992). Those critics are not alone. A study by the Organization for Economic Cooperation and Development (1992) into the condition of global banking foresees the development of a "fragile" banking industry worldwide. A Bank for International Settlements (Bisignano 1992) study notes, "There is a widespread perception that deregulation and financial innovation have gone hand-in-hand with greater financial instability." Is the United States headed in the same direction?

Outside of banking, critics point to the rapid growth of mutual funds and the potential for a collapse of confidence in mutual funds to precipitate a cascade of selling that ends in a financial crisis (Bleakley 1994; Hale 1994). Still others point to the potentially destabilizing effects of massive speculation by "high-octane" institutional fund managers, as well as to the growing use of financial derivatives to squeeze out the last basis point of return (Kaufman 1993). They worry about the dire consequences that could flow from a major default in derivatives markets (General Accounting Office 1994).

Finally, those concerned about the continuing structural revolution fear that the very forces that have increased the prospect of a systemic crisis in financial markets have also diluted the power of regulators and central banks to deal with such a crisis. They argue, in particular, that structural changes in both U.S. and global financial markets have undermined the effectiveness of central banks and monetary policy—the chief bulwark against financial instability. As they see it, there no longer exist reliable analytical guideposts on which to base monetary policy, and central banks no longer have the power to intervene effectively to prevent financial excesses from snowballing into a full-fledged crisis (Kaufman 1993; Feldstein 1992).

This book has three purposes. The first is to describe the fundamental changes that are occurring in financial markets and to identify the economic, political, and market forces responsible for those changes. The second is to explore the implications of those changes for regulatory policy. Of particular concern is whether the changes that are occurring are making the financial system more susceptible to a financial crisis or meltdown. The third is to determine whether changes in the current regulatory system need to be made, and, if so, what those changes should be. A major conclusion of the book is that the current regulatory system is becoming increasingly costly and ineffective and needs to be substantially changed if we are to continue to maintain the efficiency and stability of our financial markets. After examining alternative proposals for reforming the current system, I argue that there does exist a simpler regulatory structure that would both lower regulatory costs and be more effective at protecting us against financial excesses.

✦ 2 ✦

Banking and Financial Intermediation

$\mathbf{B}$anks have long been the centerpiece of the financial systems in the United States and elsewhere because of their critical role in financing commercial enterprises and in providing "liquidity." As a consequence, governments in all countries have made the stability and integrity of the banking system a central public policy concern. In the United States, to ensure that stability, the federal government has insured bank deposits since the 1930s and has subjected banks to intensive prudential regulation. This chapter examines the economic role of financial intermediaries in general and the central role of traditional commercial banks in the intermediation process.

The Economics of Financial Intermediation

Banks and other financial intermediaries fulfill two basic economic functions: they facilitate the savings-and-investment process, and they provide liquidity to the economy, most notably in the form of money or transaction balances. As middlemen between savers and investors, financial intermediaries issue claims on themselves, known as secondary or indirect securities (such as demand deposits or insurance policies) in exchange for the savings of surplus economic units (mostly households). They then loan those funds to borrowers and take in return the primary securities (promissory notes, mortgages, stocks, and bonds) issued by deficit units (such as business firms). In the

4

absence of financial intermediaries, the savings-and-investment process would have to be done through direct financing—the primary securities issued by deficit units would have to be directly purchased and held by surplus units in their original, unadulterated form.

Financial intermediaries increase both savings and investment and enhance economic growth because they offer significant advantages vis-à-vis direct financing. First, they lower transactions costs by relieving lenders and borrowers of the burden of having to seek out their opposites—investors having to find savers to back their projects and savers having to find suitable investments. Second, they transform the primary securities issued by deficit units into more attractive savings (or financial investment) vehicles for surplus units.

A major obstacle to saving is that savers frequently do not want to hold the primary securities that deficit units (or firms) want to issue. Firms, for example, customarily wish to use long-term loans to finance long-term investment projects that take years to pay off, while savers wish to purchase primarily short-term or liquid securities to limit their risk. Financial intermediaries resolve such conflicts by issuing to savers short-term liquid claims on themselves and using the funds they obtain to acquire less liquid claims on borrowers (or firms). Stated another way, intermediaries transform the primary assets issued by investors into indirect securities that savers find more attractive. Banks, for example, issue demand and savings deposits to savers while acquiring illiquid term loans and mortgages with distant maturities. Thus, financial intermediaries increase savings and investment in an economy both by lowering transactions costs and by transforming primary assets into claims on financial intermediaries that are more attractive assets for savers to hold.

Another key function of intermediaries has been to provide liquidity services to facilitate economic transactions and interchange. Banks, in particular, have traditionally provided money in the form of deposits redeemable on demand at par value (checkable deposit accounts). While other ways of providing money exist (through, for example, the issuance of government fiat or government-sponsored fund-transfer systems), checkable deposits issued by banks have proven to be among the most efficient ways of providing liquidity. Size and diversification advantages have enabled banks to be efficient providers of liquidity services. By pooling the funds of many savers, they have been able to acquire large diversified portfolios of primary securities (assets with different maturities, different credit risks, and so forth), which have enabled them to meet the liquidity demands made on them by depositors while still holding sizable quantities of illiquid assets.

Finally, because financial intermediaries enjoy economies of scale in the collection and use of information, they both lower the cost of capital to firms by reducing the required risk premiums and improve the allocation of financial resources. By specializing in the use of certain kinds of information—for example, by lending to certain industries—intermediaries can make more informed judgments about the risks associated with a particular loan or project, or about the future prospects of a borrower. Further, because of their superior information and size, intermediaries have the ability to extract more information from borrowers on a continuing basis and to be better monitors of borrowers. Those benefits are passed through to savers and investors in the form of lower risk premiums and a lower cost of capital. Also, to the extent that intermediaries are better informed about the prospects of potential investment projects, savings are allocated more efficiently— savings flow to projects with the greatest expected returns.

Banks and Banking Regulation in the United States

The financial structure in the United States is a product of our unique political, cultural, and economic history, all of which came together in the 1930s to create by legislative decree a highly segmented financial system. Reforms enacted in the 1930s were motivated largely by the collapse in the stock market in 1929 and by the depression that followed. While interpretations differ as to the causes and effects of those cataclysmic events, they unquestionably occupied center stage in the thinking of financial reformers at the time.

Four significant themes emerge from the legislative reforms adopted during the 1930s. First, commercial banks, as the main providers of money and liquidity to the economy, were seen as key, or unique, financial intermediaries, requiring special protections. The widespread failure of banks and the concurrent economic depression during the 1930s undoubtedly encouraged such a view. Second, legislation discouraged large size among financial institutions, especially banks. Branch and affiliate operations were restricted, and severe restrictions were imposed on banks' activities. Third, banking and securities activities were viewed as particularly incompatible and, if intermingled, a threat to economic stability. Finally, to reduce speculative activity and make security markets more efficient, legislation required issuers of public securities to disclose more information and imposed curbs on the provision of credit for speculative purposes.

The main result of those reforms was to create a rigid and segmented financial structure. Banks were supposed to do certain things, savings institutions other things, and life insurance, pension funds, and investment companies still other things. Such a segmented structure, it was believed, would ensure both the stability of the financial system and its continued contribution to the growth of the economy.

Regulation sought to achieve financial stability in two ways. First, it insulated banks from competition. Only banks were permitted to provide demand deposits, and they were not permitted to compete with one another by paying interest on those deposits. That ensured banks a steady flow of cheap funds—demand deposits. Interest rate ceilings on savings and time deposits (Regulation Q) similarly prevented banks from competing with one another by paying higher interest rates. In addition, geographical restrictions on where banks could have offices prevented competition from banks outside a bank's immediate area. The result was to create a banking system of many thousands of small banks operating in competitively insulated markets. That system was reinforced by entry restrictions that carefully controlled the formation of new banks, even in locales that were underbanked—where additional competition would not be destabilizing. By limiting competition, banks were made more profitable, and the number of bank failures kept to a minimum.

Second, regulation limited the freedom of banks to take risks. Banks were required to maintain specified levels of capital, were prohibited from making certain kinds of loans and from extending more than a certain amount of credit to specified borrowers, were prevented from engaging in securities activities (such as the underwriting of stocks and bonds) or from holding corporate stocks and bonds in their own portfolios, and were prohibited from engaging in other activities viewed as excessively risky, like the underwriting of insurance. Thus, by limiting the ability of banks to take risks and insulating them from competition, regulation sought to guarantee the soundness of banks and the stability of the financial system, as well as the uninterrupted flow of credit to business enterprises.

Economic Forces Underlying Recent Changes in Financial Intermediation

In recent years new economic forces have swept through financial markets and have caused major changes in the way financial intermediaries operate. While changes have occurred virtually everywhere and in all phases of the business, we can trace them to three fundamental factors: macroeconomic changes that resulted in more sophisticated and demanding customers, financial innovations that broke down barriers to competition, and the internationalization of financial markets.

Significant macroeconomic changes occurred over the past three decades. The long period of price and interest rate stability that followed the Great Depression and later World War II ended in the 1960s. The result was higher and more volatile inflation rates, which led to higher and more volatile interest rates. Savers became sensitized to yield differences and aggressively sought higher yields wherever they could find them. As a result, banks and other financial intermediaries were forced to pay higher yields to retain funds and to attract new funds.

Second, innovations in both information and communications technologies began to break down what were heretofore natural barriers to competition. The ability to retrieve, store, process, manipulate, and transmit large masses of data at low cost made it easier for financial institutions to offer new products and enter new markets to compete for customers. Also, the increased speed and lower cost of communicating and transmitting data over large geographical areas eliminated geographical distances as an obstacle to competition. Institutions were able to collect and service deposits (and other funds) from distant savers as easily as they could from local savers, and they could make loans to distant borrowers as easily as to local borrowers.

Third, the growing internationalization or globalization of markets (both financial and nonfinancial) that accompanied the end of capital controls and the institution of flexible exchange rates further increased competition. U.S. financial institutions were forced to compete with foreign financial institutions, often for corporate borrowers who had been their clients for decades. That competition was particularly wrenching because many foreign institutions were governed by different rules and regulations that sometimes gave them a competitive advantage. Thus, with globalization came not only head-to-head competition between U.S. and foreign financial institutions but direct competition between U.S. and foreign regulatory systems.

Internationalization also created a regulatory loophole that prevented the enforcement, or undercut the effectiveness, of key U.S. regulations. For example, with capital free to flow to the highest yields, wherever that may be, the imposition of deposit rate ceilings in the United States became unenforceable and counterproductive. The gigantic Eurodollar market is a case in point. That market was largely the creation of unwise and misdirected U.S. regulations during the 1960s—many of which no longer exist.

Those economic changes had two key effects: they intensified competition among financial intermediaries and between financial intermediaries and primary security markets, and they undercut the effectiveness of traditional regulation. In particular, as competitive pressures mounted, regulatory barriers impeding the ability of firms to respond to those competitive pressures had to be abandoned. In some cases regulation simply became ineffective; in others it distorted the flow of funds and destabilized markets. As a result, regulators increasingly abandoned outdated regulatory restrictions in favor of unimpeded competition. Much of this book is motivated by the public policy concerns that have arisen because of the revolutionary changes that have taken place in financial markets. The next chapter describes in greater detail the transformation that has occurred in financial markets during the 1980s and 1990s.

✦ 3 ✦

The Decline of Traditional Banking and the Rise of Nonbank Financial Intermediaries

The business of banking historically has been making long-term loans with funds raised by issuing short-dated deposits, with most of a bank's profits coming from the spread between the lending and deposit rates. For more than two centuries banks in the United States were the main repository of households savings and the primary source of credit for businesses. They occupied the central role in the intermediation of credit. In the 1980s and 1990s all that has changed. Innovations in financial markets have allowed many borrowers to bypass banks entirely, and newly developed nonbank financial intermediaries have invaded the traditional turf of banks by taking their customers and undercutting their profitability. During those two decades banks have seen their share of traditional financial intermediation steadily eroded as nonbank financial intermediaries have provided better substitutes for traditional banking services and as innovations in financial markets have enabled business borrowers to directly access credit markets for their funds. In response, banks have sought to enhance their competitiveness through mergers and consolidations, by extending their geographical reach in search of new customer bases, and by expanding the activities they engage in and

10

the services they provide. Increasingly, banks also have turned to making riskier loans and to engaging in nontraditional activities in an effort to maintain their profitability.

This chapter describes the changes that have taken place in financial intermediation and in U.S. financial markets. It examines, in particular, the declining role of traditional banking in financial intermediation, both in the United States and in foreign countries, and the forces responsible for that development. In addition, it discusses how banks have responded to the intensified competitive environment. Later chapters examine several key policy issues raised by the decline of traditional banking.

The Decline of Traditional Banking in the United States

In the United States the importance of commercial banks as a source of funds to nonfinancial borrowers has shrunk dramatically. In 1974 banks provided 35 percent of those funds; today they provide around 22 percent. (See figure 3-1.) Thrift institutions (savings and loans, mutual savings banks, and credit unions), which can be viewed as specialized banking institutions, also have suffered a similar decline in their market share of nonfinancial borrowing, from over 20 percent in the late 1970s to below 10 percent in the early 1990s. (See figure 3-2.)

Another way of viewing the declining role of banking in traditional financial intermediation is to look at the size of banks' balance-sheet assets relative to those of other financial intermediaries. Commercial banks' share of total financial intermediary assets fell from around the 40 percent range from 1960 through 1970 to below 30 percent by the end of 1994. (See tables 3-1 and 3-2.) Similarly, the share of total financial intermediary assets held by thrift institutions declined from around 20 percent from 1960 through 1980 to below 10 percent by 1994 (Edwards 1993b). Finally, from 1980 to 1993 the number of U.S. banking organizations declined by 32 percent, from 12,363 to 8,415 (Wheelock 1992).[1]

Recent studies of the decline of banking have correctly pointed out that by itself a decline in market share measured in terms of total financial intermediary assets may not necessarily indicate that the banking industry is in decline (Boyd and Gertler 1993, 1994; Kaufman and Mote 1994). Those studies argue that, by ignoring the earnings generated by the off-balance-sheet activities of banks, the decline of banking may be overstated and the role of banks in the provision of financial

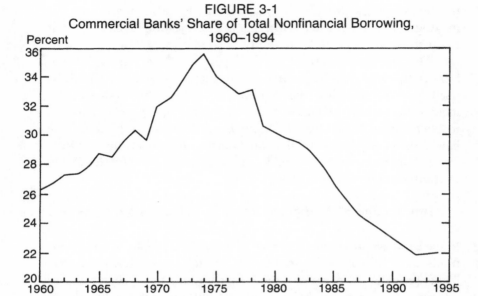

FIGURE 3-1
Commercial Banks' Share of Total Nonfinancial Borrowing,
1960–1994

services broadly defined may be understated.[2] In recent years banks have increasingly turned to off-balance-sheet (fee-generating) activities to maintain profitability. Many such activities, however, are not those commonly associated with *traditional* banking in the United States (for example, broker-dealer activities) and do not involve financial intermediation in its traditional sense—the transformation of assets. Thus, the declining share of intermediary assets held by banks is a better indicator of the declining role of traditional banking in financial intermediation than is the general profitability of banks as institutions. Further, the declining role of traditional banking in financial intermediation, rather than the survival of the banking industry per se, gives rise to the policy questions examined in this book.[3]

Why Is Traditional Banking in Decline?

Fundamental economic forces have led to financial innovations that have both diminished the cost advantage that U.S. banks once had in acquiring funds and undercut their competitive position in loan markets. As a result, U.S. banks have lost market share and have suffered a secular erosion in profitability, notwithstanding the resurgence of bank profitability in recent years.

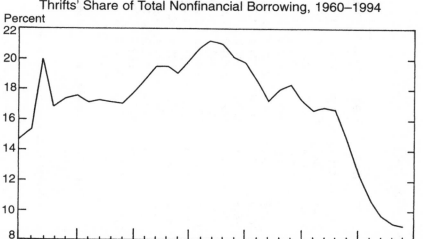

FIGURE 3-2
Thrifts' Share of Total Nonfinancial Borrowing, 1960–1994

Diminished Advantages in Acquiring Funds (Liabilities). Until 1980 deposits were a cheap source of funds for U.S. banking institutions (commercial banks, savings and loans, mutual savings banks, and credit unions). Banks were subject to deposit rate ceilings that restricted them from paying interest on checkable deposits, and Regulation Q limited them to paying specified interest rate ceilings on savings and time deposits. For many years those restrictions worked to the advantage of banks because a major source of their funds was checkable deposits (which in 1960 and earlier years constituted over 60 percent of total bank deposits). The zero interest cost on those deposits resulted in banks' having a low average cost of funds.

That cost advantage did not last. The rise in inflation beginning in the late 1960s led to higher interest rates and made investors more sensitive to yield differentials on different assets. The result was the so-called disintermediation process, in which depositors took their money out of banks paying low interest rates (on both checkable and time deposits) and purchased assets with higher yields.

Restrictive bank regulations also created an opportunity for nonbank financial institutions to invent new ways to offer bank depositors higher rates. Nonbank competitors were not subject to the deposit rate ceilings that restricted banks and did not have the costs associated with having to hold non-interest-bearing reserves and to pay deposit insurance premiums. A key development was the creation

TABLE 3-1

Assets Held by Financial Intermediaries, 1900–1994

(dollars in billions)

	1900	1912	1922	1929	1939	1949	1960	1970	1980	1990	1993	1994
Commercial banks[a]	10.0	21.8	47.5	66.2	66.3	155.3	256.3	570.1	1,481.7	3,338.6	3,896.1	4,161.7
Thrifts	2.9	5.0	9.4	17.3	17.5	36.8	118.8	273.5	860.0	1,574.7	1,310.4	1,307.7
Savings and loans[b]	0.5	1.0	2.8	7.4	5.4	14.5	71.5	176.2	792.4	1,357.7	1,029.5	1,013.1
Mutual savings[b]	2.4	4.0	6.6	9.9	11.9	21.5	41.0	79.3	NA	NA	NA	NA
Credit unions	NA	NA	0.0	0.0	0.2	0.8	6.3	18.0	67.6	217.0	280.9	294.6
Insurance companies	2.2	5.6	11.2	23.0	35.2	73.6	142.0	250.8	646.3	1,900.7	2,425.7	2,557.4
Life insurance	1.7	4.4	8.7	17.5	29.2	59.6	115.8	200.9	464.2	1,367.4	1,784.9	1,887.9
Other insurance	0.5	1.2	2.5	5.5	6.0	14.0	26.2	49.9	182.1	533.3	640.8	669.5
Pension and trust	3.0	7.0	18.3	32.0	42.2	95.2	57.8	170.7	701.0	2,449.5	3,601.0	3,579.1
Personal	3.0	7.0	18.0	30.0	35.0	50.0	NA	NA	NA	NA	NA	NA
Private	NA	NA	0.0	0.5	1.0	6.0	38.1	110.4	504.4	1,629.1	2,449.8	2,356.4
Public	0.0	0.0	0.3	1.5	6.2	39.2	19.7	60.3	196.6	820.4	1,151.2	1,222.7
Investment companies	NA	NA	0.1	3.0	1.6	3.3	17.0	49.2	138.2	1,100.5	1,985.2	2,068.3
Mutual fund	NA	NA	NA	NA	NA	NA	17.0	46.8	61.8	602.1	1,426.3	1,463.0
Money market[c]	NA	NA	NA	NA	NA	NA	NA	2.4	76.4	498.4	558.9	605.3
Finance companies	NA	NA	NA	2.6	3.0	6.4	27.6	64.0	204.8	610.9	653.7	741.7
Total	18.1	39.4	86.5	144.1	165.8	370.6	619.5	1,378.3	4,032.0	10,974.9	13,872.1	14,415.9

a. FDIC-insured commercial banks and trust companies.

b. Beginning in 1993, a new series, savings institutions, was created that statistically combined savings and loan associations and mutual savings banks. Consequently, we report them as statistically combined beginning in 1980.

c. Money market mutual fund data start in 1974.

Sources: 1900–1949, *Financial Intermediaries in the American Economy since 1900*; 1960–1990, Flow of Funds Accounts, *Federal Reserve Bulletin*, March 8, 1995.

TABLE 3-2
Relative Shares of Total Financial Intermediary Assets, 1900–1994
(in percent)

	1900	1912	1922	1929	1939	1949	1960	1970	1980	1990	1993	1994
Commercial banks[a]	55.2	55.3	54.9	45.9	40.0	41.9	41.4	41.4	36.7	30.4	28.1	28.9
Thrifts	16.0	12.7	10.9	12.0	10.6	9.9	19.2	19.8	21.3	14.3	9.4	9.1
Savings and loans[b]	2.8	2.5	3.2	5.1	3.3	3.9	11.5	12.8	19.7	12.4	7.4	7.0
Mutual savings[b]	13.3	10.2	7.6	6.9	7.2	5.8	6.6	5.8	0.0	0.0	0.0	0.0
Credit unions	0.0	0.0	0.0	0.0	0.1	0.2	1.0	1.3	1.7	2.0	2.0	2.0
Insurance companies	12.2	14.2	12.9	16.0	21.2	19.9	22.9	18.2	16.0	17.3	17.5	17.7
Life insurance	9.4	11.2	10.1	12.1	17.6	16.1	18.7	14.6	11.5	12.5	12.9	13.1
Other insurance	2.8	3.0	2.9	3.8	3.6	3.8	4.2	3.6	4.5	4.9	4.6	4.6
Pension and trust	16.6	17.8	21.2	22.2	25.5	25.7	9.3	12.4	17.4	22.3	26.0	24.8
Personal	16.6	17.8	20.8	20.8	21.1	13.5	0.0	0.0	0.0	0.0	0.0	0.0
Private	0.0	0.0	0.0	0.3	0.6	1.6	6.2	8.0	12.5	14.8	17.7	16.3
Public	0.0	0.0	0.3	1.0	3.7	10.6	3.2	4.4	4.9	7.5	8.3	8.5
Investment companies	0.0	0.0	0.1	2.1	1.0	0.9	2.7	3.6	3.4	10.0	14.3	14.3
Mutual fund	0.0	0.0	0.0	0.0	0.0	0.0	2.7	3.4	1.5	5.5	10.3	10.1
Money market[c]	0.0	0.0	0.0	0.0	0.0	0.0	0.0	0.2	1.9	4.5	4.0	4.2
Finance companies	0.0	0.0	0.0	1.8	1.8	1.7	4.5	4.6	5.1	5.6	4.7	5.1

a. FDIC-insured commercial banks and trust companies.

b. Beginning in 1993, a new series, savings institutions, was created that statistically combined savings and loan associations and mutual savings banks. Consequently, we report them as statistically combined beginning in 1980.

c. Money market mutual fund data start in 1974.

Sources: 1900–1949, *Financial Intermediaries in the American Economy since 1900*; 1960–1990, Flow of Funds Accounts, *Federal Reserve Bulletin*, March 8, 1995.

FIGURE 3-3
Banks' Private Domestic Checkable Deposits, 1950–1994

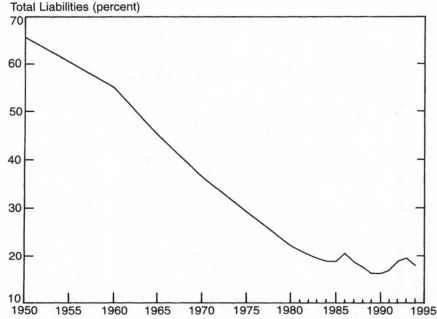

of money market mutual funds (MMMFs). MMMFs offered bank depositors check-writing services similar to banks' while paying a higher interest rate on their funds. Not surprisingly, as a source of funds for banks, low-cost checkable deposits declined dramatically; they fell from 55 percent of bank liabilities in 1960 to under 20 percent in 1994. (See figure 3-3.)

The growing disadvantage of banks in raising funds led to their supporting legislation in the 1980s to eliminate Regulation Q ceilings on time deposits and to allow checkable deposits that paid interest (NOW accounts). Although those changes helped to make banks more competitive in their quest for funds, it also meant that their cost of funds rose substantially, which reduced their historical cost advantage.

In the competitive struggle for the savings of households that ensued, pension funds and investment companies came up big winners during the 1980s. As shown in table 3-2, their share of intermediary assets grew from 20 percent in 1980 to almost 40 percent in 1994, and that growth shows no sign of abating. By pooling funds from a large number of investors and purchasing a diversified port-

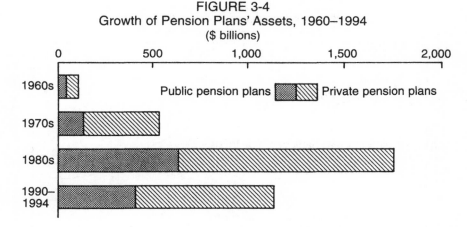

FIGURE 3-4
Growth of Pension Plans' Assets, 1960–1994
($ billions)

folio of assets, pension and mutual funds provide individual investors with a low-cost way of holding highly diversified (and, in the case of mutual funds, liquid) portfolios of stocks, bonds, and mortgage-backed securities. They also make available to investors, particularly small investors, professional portfolio management.

Pension fund growth during the postwar period has been due to increased pension coverage—both in the private and public sectors—and to the increasing value of the assets held by pension funds. During the 1980s and 1990s all types of pension funds grew rapidly. (See figure 3-4.) In addition, federal tax policy, which permits the deduction of employers' contributions and the deferral of taxes on both employees' contributions and earnings on pension fund assets, has been a major stimulant to pension fund growth. As a consequence, pension funds have become the dominant institutional player in the stock market; they hold more than 25 percent of all corporate stock outstanding. (See figure 3-5.)

The growth of pension funds and mutual funds has also been fueled by demographic shifts. By the early 1980s most "baby boomers" were in their thirties and began to shift from more liquid assets (such as savings deposits) into investments promising a higher long-term yield—stocks and bonds. Figure 3-6 shows the close association between the age-composition of the population and the percentage of household assets invested in stocks and bonds. As workers age and begin preparing for retirement, they save more and are willing to make investments with higher expected yields over a longer investment horizon, despite a greater risk of short-run volatility. A similar demo-

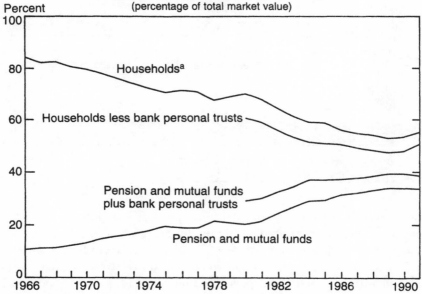

FIGURE 3-5
Holdings of Corporate Equity, 1966–1991
(percentage of total market value)

a. Includes households' holdings through bank personal trust accounts.
Source: *Flow of Funds*, Federal Reserve System.

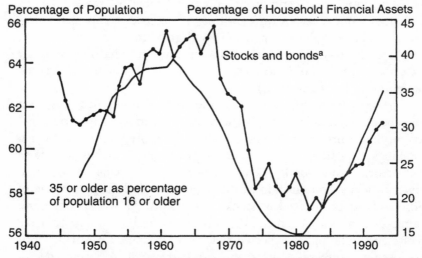

FIGURE 3-6
Demographic and Portfolio Shifts, 1945–1993

a. Portfolio is total equity, credit market instruments, and bond and equity mutual funds
held by households as a percentage of total household financial assets.

FIGURE 3-7

Households' Investment in Pension and Mutual Funds, 1945–1994

Percentage of Household Financial Assets

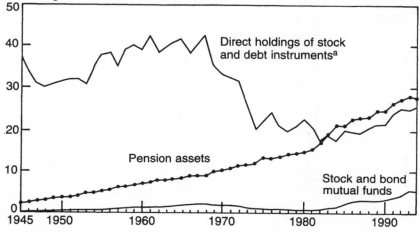

a. Assets that households hold directly rather than indirectly through financial intermediaries, such as mutual funds.

graphic trend resulted in a shift into stocks and bonds in the 1950s as
well, but what distinguishes the 1980s and the 1990s from the 1950s
is that in the later period households exhibited a strong preference for
making those investments indirectly through financial intermediaries—
pension and mutual funds. In the 1950s and 1960s households invested directly in stocks and bonds, even though stock and bond mutual
funds were available. Now they hold those investments indirectly
through pension and mutual funds, because they prefer to place their
funds in the hands of professional money managers. (See figure 3-7.)

Mutual funds also have grown rapidly. In the 1950s and 1960s
that growth was due almost entirely to savings flowing into equity
mutual funds. Equity funds offered investors a way to hold a diversified, professionally managed stock portfolio, and a booming stock
market did the rest. In the 1970s disappointing stock market performance caused investors to seek other investments. The mutual fund
industry responded by creating money market mutual funds and a
wide variety of bond or fixed-income funds. During the 1970s and
1980s the growth of mutual funds came primarily from the expansion of money market mutual funds and, to a lesser extent, bond
funds. Those funds offered savers an attractive alternative to savings
deposits in banks and thrifts, which until the early 1980s were con-

FIGURE 3-8
Average Annual Net Acquisition of Mutual Fund Assets by Type,
1960–1994

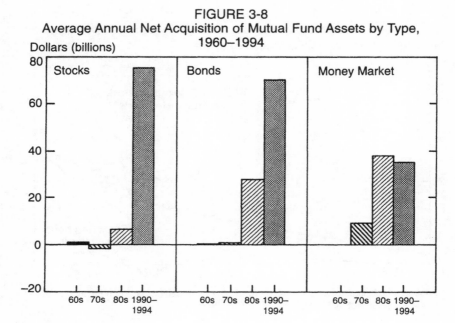

strained by interest rate ceilings. In the 1990s all types of mutual funds have experienced substantial growth. (See figure 3-8.)

By 1994 MMMFs had grown to $605 billion, up from $76 billion in 1980. (See table 3-1.) In 1980 MMMF shares constituted only 7.2 percent of total commercial bank deposits; by 1994 that figure had grown to 56 percent. Further, from 1978 to 1994 MMMF shares as a percentage of commercial bank checkable deposits rose from virtually nothing to almost 70 percent (Gorton and Pennacchi 1992a). (See figure 3-9.)

The sharp growth of both pension and mutual funds is also evident when viewed in terms of household assets. (See table 3-3.) In 1982 pension and mutual fund assets amounted to 20.5 percent of total household financial assets; by 1994 that figure had jumped to over 35 percent. In contrast, deposits in financial intermediaries—banks and thrifts—constituted 23.6 percent of total household financial assets in 1982 but only 15.3 percent in 1994. Mutual fund assets alone soared from 7 percent of household liquid financial assets in 1982 to over 14 percent in 1994.

The growth of nondepository intermediaries is even more pronounced when viewed in terms of the annual flows of household assets. (See table 3-4.) From 1982 to 1994 pension and mutual funds

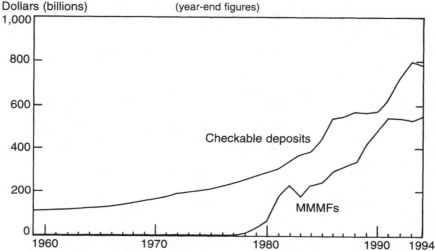

FIGURE 3-9
Bank Checkable Deposits and Money Market Mutual Funds,
1959–1994

alone accounted for about 67 percent of the net growth of households' total financial assets. In addition, mutual funds accounted for about 36 percent of the net growth of households' liquid financial assets during that period, and 49.7 percent of that growth during the last five years of the period. In contrast, depository intermediaries accounted for 36.8 percent of the growth of households' liquid financial assets from 1982 through 1994, and only 19.3 percent of the growth in households' total financial assets. (See table 3-3 and figure 3-10.)

Those structural changes manifest two major developments in financial markets. First, households have become highly sensitive to the relative returns and risks associated with different financial assets and are increasingly putting their savings in assets that offer them the best risk-adjusted returns. Second, the segmentation of financial markets is rapidly disappearing. The opportunities available to small savers are now very similar to those available to large savers. Through pension and mutual funds, small savers can hold portfolios of all kinds of fixed-income securities as well as diversified stock portfolios, which in the past were available only to the wealthy. Nor does geography any longer constrain savers and investors. The flow of savings and investment has few natural barriers. Funds flow across national borders as readily as between different areas of the United States.

TABLE 3-3
Distribution of Household Financial Assets,[a] 1982–1994
($ billions)

	1982	1983	1984	1985	1986	1987	1988	1989	1990	1991	1992	1993	1994
Bank and thrift deposits													
Checkable deposits and currency	319	332	331	348	436	431	449	443	449	511	635	713	722
Small time and savings deposits	1,249	1,436	1,574	1,690	1,784	1,829	1,940	2,002	2,069	2,021	1,957	1,888	1,883
Large time deposits	160	158	231	222	206	248	281	289	260	194	147	128	148
Total bank and thrift deposits	1,728	1,926	2,137	2,260	2,426	2,508	2,670	2,735	2,778	2,726	2,738	2,729	2,752
Credit market instruments													
U.S. government securities													
Savings bonds	68	72	74	80	93	101	110	118	126	138	157	172	180
Other Treasury issues	153	197	236	226	188	189	256	227	323	268	304	331	497
Agency issues	16	10	34	44	31	71	134	183	199	194	237	199	407
Total U.S. government securities	237	279	345	350	312	360	499	527	648	600	699	702	1,084
Tax-exempt securities	122	157	184	257	242	322	375	431	448	483	449	433	403
Corporate and foreign bonds	25	28	31	31	60	62	38	61	95	105	107	142	198
Open-market paper	21	42	41	99	93	115	146	137	131	96	103	71	60
Total credit market instruments	406	506	601	737	708	860	1,059	1,156	1,322	1,284	1,357	1,349	1,745
Corporate equities	905	1,028	951	1,210	1,399	1,383	1,514	1,828	1,717	2,469	2,810	3,088	2,913
Security credit	18	21	22	35	44	39	41	53	62	87	76	103	108

Miscellaneous assets	87	103	104	132	150	175	191	206	224	234	251	264	281
Mutual fund shares													
Equity, bond, and income MF shares	57	88	106	192	318	352	370	435	452	592	734	972	968
Money market MF shares	180	149	193	195	231	253	269	346	374	383	341	331	352
Total mutual fund shares	238	237	298	387	549	606	639	781	826	975	1,075	1,303	1,320
Total household liquid financial assets	3,382	3,820	4,113	4,762	5,276	5,571	6,114	6,759	6,930	7,775	8,308	8,835	9,119
Mutual fund assets as a % of total household liquid financial assets	7.0	6.2	7.3	8.1	10.4	10.9	10.5	11.5	11.9	12.5	12.9	14.7	14.5
Other (nonliquid) financial assets													
Mortgages	122	121	112	125	115	172	179	190	177	162	166	177	187
Life insurance reserves	233	241	246	257	274	300	326	354	380	406	433	468	488
Pension fund reserves	1,261	1,500	1,870	2,032	2,411	2,615	2,861	3,401	3,484	4,138	4,516	4,975	5,061
Investment in bank personal trusts	264	293	306	358	404	414	444	515	522	608	630	681	656
Equity in noncorporate business	2,060	2,110	2,095	2,134	2,199	2,306	2,423	2,582	2,529	2,444	2,412	2,422	2,485
Total nonliquid financial assets	3,940	4,265	4,629	4,906	5,404	5,807	6,232	7,043	7,093	7,759	8,157	8,723	8,878
Total household financial assets	7,322	8,085	8,742	9,668	10,680	11,378	12,346	13,802	14,023	15,534	16,465	17,558	17,997
Mutual fund assets as a % of total household financial assets	3.2	2.9	3.4	4.0	5.1	5.3	5.7	5.9	6.3	6.5		7.4	7.3
Pension and mutual fund assets as a % of total household financial assets	20.5	21.5	24.8	25.0	27.7	28.3	28.3	30.3	30.7	32.9	34.0	35.8	35.5

a. Includes households, personal trusts, and nonprofit organizations.

Sources: Federal Reserve Board, Flow of Funds Accounts; calculations by the Investment Company Institute, Washington, D.C.

TABLE 3-4
Net Flows of Household Financial Assets[a], 1982–1994
($ billions)

	1982	1983	1984	1985	1986	1987	1988	1989	1990	1991	1992	1993	1994
Net flows													
Bank and thrift deposits													
Checkable deposits and currency	21.0	13.2	-0.9	16.9	87.9	-4.3	19.0	-5.6	5.4	62.0	123.8	78.1	8.9
Small time and savings deposits	122.5	187.2	138.2	115.3	98.6	52.5	93.9	64.0	66.3	-45.4	-64.7	-68.8	-5.2
Large time deposits	-12.3	-2.5	73.6	-9.7	-15.7	41.8	33.0	7.0	-28.5	-68.6	-46.5	-19.3	19.9
Total bank and thrift deposits	131.2	197.9	210.9	122.5	170.8	90.0	145.9	65.4	43.2	-52.0	12.6	-10.0	23.6
Credit market instruments													
U.S. government securities	6.7	38.6	74.9	14.9	-36.3	47.3	132.3	65.5	127.0	-34.9	100.9	5.2	358.9
Tax-exempt securities	29.6	34.7	27.6	72.2	-15.8	80.1	39.7	55.6	17.7	34.9	-34.8	-15.8	-29.6
Corporate and foreign bonds	-0.8	2.5	-6.0	-0.8	33.9	18.3	-21.8	-17.2	38.0	10.3	-4.8	26.2	58.5
Open-market paper	-4.2	17.9	-1.6	58.4	-5.8	3.3	31.3	-9.0	-8.3	-34.8	5.2	-37.7	-19.7

Total credit market instruments	31.3	93.7	94.9	144.7	-24.0	149.0	181.5	94.9	174.4	-24.5	66.5	-22.1	368.1
Corporate equities	-24.1	-22.6	-66.8	-111.2	-103.9	-102.6	-92.6	-109.1	-21.7	-33.8	43.8	-33.1	-89.0
Security credit	3.1	2.7	1.0	13.5	9.0	-5.8	1.8	12.3	9.2	24.6	-11.0	26.6	5.2
Miscellaneous assets	7.1	15.5	1.3	28.3	17.2	25.1	16.4	14.9	18.2	9.6	17.0	13.1	17.1
Mutual fund shares													
Equity, bond, and income MF shares	3.4	26.9	20.2	75.5	120.0	56.9	14.1	36.0	37.7	115.1	146.5	187.0	76.6
Money market MF shares	31.5	-31.2	43.3	2.3	35.7	22.0	15.9	76.8	28.6	8.7	-41.8	-10.7	20.8
Total mutual fund shares	34.9	-4.3	63.5	77.8	155.7	78.9	30.0	112.8	66.3	123.8	104.7	176.3	97.4
Total household liquid financial assets	183.5	282.9	304.8	275.6	224.8	234.6	283.0	191.2	289.6	47.7	233.6	150.8	422.4
Mutual fund assets as a % of total household liquid financial assets	19.0	NM^b	20.8	28.2	69.3	33.6	10.6	59.0	22.9	259.5	44.8	116.9	23.1
Other (nonliquid) financial assets													
Mortgages	10.3	-0.4	-0.3	16.9	-4.2	27.2	15.2	-0.2	-17.2	-15.1	4.1	10.5	10.2
Life insurance reserves	7.2	8.0	5.2	10.7	17.5	26.0	25.3	28.8	25.7	25.7	27.3	35.2	20.1
Pension fund reserves	170.9	168.2	157.2	271.7	289.1	201.3	132.3	321.2	165.1	360.3	249.7	309.2	113.9

(Table continues)

TABLE 3-4 (continued)

	1982	1983	1984	1985	1986	1987	1988	1989	1990	1991	1992	1993	1994
Investment in bank personal trusts	−1.9	3.2	15.1	10.2	18.1	13.2	2.2	19.6	29.7	16.1	−7.1	1.6	4.6
Equity in noncorporate business	−82.9	−76.5	−72.3	−58.6	−34.6	−70.0	−23.5	−25.8	−28.3	−3.3	18.4	−10.2	−44.8
Total nonliquid financial assets	103.6	102.5	104.9	250.9	285.9	197.7	151.5	343.6	175.0	383.7	292.4	346.3	104.0
Total household financial assets	287.1	385.4	409.7	526.5	510.7	432.3	434.5	534.8	464.6	431.4	526.0	497.1	526.4
Mutual fund assets as a % of total household financial assets	12.2	NMb	15.5	14.8	30.5	18.3	6.9	21.1	14.3	28.7	19.9	35.5	18.5
Pension and mutual fund assets as a % of total household financial assets	71.7	42.5	53.9	66.4	87.1	64.8	37.4	81.2	49.8	112.2	67.4	97.7	40.1

a. Includes households, personal trusts, and nonprofit organizations.
b. NM = not meaningful.
Sources: Federal Reserve Board, Flow of Funds Accounts; calculations by the Investment Company Institute, Washington, D.C.

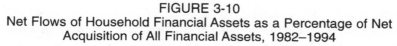

FIGURE 3-10
Net Flows of Household Financial Assets as a Percentage of Net
Acquisition of All Financial Assets, 1982–1994

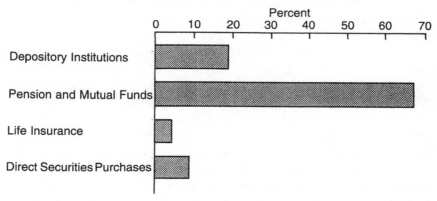

The changes that have occurred also are irreversible because they are economically motivated and technologically driven. The 1980s were to financial markets what World War II was to labor markets. World War II and its aftermath made women a major component of the labor force and set in motion an irreversible trend that resulted in profound changes in the economy and in society. While not everyone found that to his liking at the time, it was a fact of life. People who believe that the changes in financial markets that occurred during the 1980s can be undone or rolled back are as naive as those who in the late 1940s believed that they could return to a prewar society.

Diminished Income (or Lending) Advantages. Banks also have experienced a deterioration in the income advantages they once enjoyed on the asset side of their balance sheets. The growth of nonbank competitors, the commercial paper market, the junk bond market, and the increased securitization of assets have combined to undercut the historical advantage that banks have had in providing credit.

Improvements in information technology, which have made it easier for households, corporations, and financial institutions to evaluate the quality of securities, have made it easier for business firms to borrow directly from the public by issuing securities. Instead of going to banks to finance short-term credit needs, many businesses now borrow through the commercial paper market. In 1980 commercial paper issued by nonfinancial companies amounted to $28.0 billion—about 6 percent of banks' commercial and industrial loans. By 1994 that figure had jumped to $139.2 billion, 16.7 percent of banks' commercial and industrial loans. (See table 3-5, line 5, and table 3-6, line 4(a).) In addition, in 1980 banks accounted for 30.8 percent of the total debt owed by nonfinancial businesses. By 1994 the share of firms' indebtedness held by banks had declined to 21.4 percent. (See table 3-6, line 4(b).)

The growth of money market mutual funds also helped undercut banks. MMMFs have created a ready market for commercial paper because they are required to hold liquid, high-quality, short-term assets. Finance companies capitalized on the growth of MMMFs by issuing commercial paper for much of their funding during the 1980s and then using those funds to expand their lending at the expense of banks. (See table 3-5.) From 1980 to 1994, when the commercial paper market grew from $121.6 billion to $600.1 billion, MMMFs acquired about 60 percent of the commercial paper issued by finance companies (Post 1992). As a consequence, finance companies were able to acquire funds on a competitive basis and were able to compete directly with banks for many of the business customers that banks traditionally served.

The pattern of lending by finance companies during the 1980s can be seen in table 3-7. First, they sharply reduced consumer lending and expanded mortgage lending. Second, although the proportion of business loans in their portfolios did not change appreciably, before the 1980s those loans were made largely by "captive" finance companies to affiliates and customers of their parent companies. In the 1980s, however, finance companies increasingly made general business loans, in direct competition with banks (Remolona and Wulfekuhler 1992). In 1980 finance company loans to businesses amounted to only 19.2 percent of banks' commercial and industrial loans. By 1994 that figure had jumped to over 40 percent. (See table 3-6, lines 2(a) and 4(a).)

Banks themselves aided business firms in bypassing them by providing back-up lines of credit and guarantees to firms issuing commercial paper, including finance companies. One consequence of Penn Central Railroad's 1970 default on $83 billion of its commercial paper was that banks began to provide commercial paper issuers with guarantees and back-up lines of credit, on which banks earned a fee. Although it is difficult to know exactly what portion of the commercial paper issued by finance companies is backed by bank guarantees or lines of credit, it has been reported that over 90 percent of the paper issued by the fifteen largest finance companies is backed by banks

TABLE 3-5
Amount of Outstanding Commercial Paper, 1980–1994

	1980	1981	1982	1983	1984	1985	1986	1987	1988	1989	1990	1991	1992	1993	1994
A. Amounts Outstanding ($ billions at year end)															
All issuers	121.6	161.1	161.8	183.5	231.7	293.9	326.1	373.6	451.8	521.9	557.8	528.1	545.1	553.8	600.1
Financial															
companies[a]	86.6	107.6	109.2	125.2	145.5	187.8	225.9	258.6	316.1	351.7	365.6	347.9	360.4	367.2	419.4
Bank related	25.9	33.0	34.6	38.0	44.1	46.4	43.1	44.6	44.4	48.8	30.1	24.3	20.4	25.6	31.6
Finance															
companies	60.1	74.1	74.2	86.2	99.2	138.3	178.4	207.5	263.7	286.1	303.2	283.8	291.6	289.2	325.5
Nonfinancial															
companies[b]	28.0	42.7	37.6	36.8	58.5	72.2	62.9	73.8	85.7	107.1	116.9	98.5	107.1	117.8	139.2
B. Shares of Total Outstanding (in percent)															
All issuers[c]	100.0	100.0	100.0	100.0	100.0	100.0	100.0	100.0	100.0	100.0	100.0	100.0	100.0	100.0	100.0
Financial															
companies	71.2	66.8	67.5	68.2	62.8	63.9	69.3	69.2	70.0	67.4	65.5	65.9	66.1	66.3	69.9
Bank related	21.3	20.5	21.4	20.7	19.0	15.8	13.2	11.9	9.8	9.4	5.4	4.6	3.7	4.6	5.3
Finance															
companies	49.4	46.0	45.9	47.0	42.8	47.1	54.7	55.5	58.4	54.8	54.4	53.7	53.5	52.2	54.2
Nonfinancial															
companies	23.0	26.5	23.2	20.1	25.2	24.6	19.3	19.8	19.0	20.5	21.0	18.7	19.6	21.3	23.2

a. Commercial banking, funding corporations, finance companies, real estate investment trusts, and asset-backed security issuers.
b. Excluding foreign issuers in the United States.
c. Subclassifications do not sum to 100% owing to omitted issuers.
Sources: Flow of Funds Accounts, *Federal Reserve Bulletin*, March 8, 1995; D'Arista and Schlesinger (1992).

TABLE 3-6
Outstanding U.S. Credit Market Debt Owed by Households and Nonfinancial Business, 1980–1994
($ billions)

	1980	1981	1982	1983	1984	1985	1986	1987	1988	1989	1990	1991	1992	1993	1994
Total Credit Market Debt Owed by:															
Households	1,391	1,500	1,568	1,733	1,951	2,243	2,504	2,771	3,074	3,380	3,614	3,785	4,002	4,294	4,646
Nonfinancial businesses[a]	1,487	1,658	1,801	1,981	2,294	2,576	2,889	3,148	3,400	3,637	3,752	3,709	3,710	3,749	3,885
1. Outstanding finance company credit to consumers															
(a) Amount	79	88	93	104	112	132	151	154	155	145	139	126	122	116	135
(b) Percentage of total debt owed by households	5.7	5.9	5.9	6.0	5.7	5.9	6.0	5.6	5.1	4.3	3.8	3.3	3.0	2.7	2.9
2. Outstanding finance company credit to businesses															
(a) Amount	89	99	100	113	138	159	177	214	245	270	294	293	296	295	336
(b) Percentage of total debt owed by nonfinancial businesses	6.0	6.0	5.6	5.7	6.0	6.1	6.1	6.8	7.2	7.4	7.8	7.9	8.0	7.8	8.6

3. Outstanding bank loans to individuals															
(a) Amount	180	184	191	214	259	296	321	338	371	385	387	372	366	400	461
(b) Percentage of total debt owed by households	13.0	12.2	12.3	13.3	13.2	12.8	12.2	12.1	11.4	10.7	9.8	9.1	9.3	9.9	
4. Outstanding commercial and industrial loans of U.S. banks															
(a) Amount	458	512	533	564	623	665	732	732	771	820	815	786	777	768	832
(b) Percentage of total debt owed by nonfinancial businesses	30.8	30.9	29.6	28.5	27.2	25.8	25.3	23.2	22.7	22.5	21.7	21.2	20.9	20.5	21.4

a. Includes farm, nonfarm, noncorporate sectors, and nonfinancial corporate businesses.

Source: Federal Reserve Board, Flow of Funds Accounts.

TABLE 3-7
Finance Companies' Balance Sheet, 1980–1994

	1980	1981	1982	1983	1984	1985	1986	1987	1988	1989	1990	1991	1992	1993	1994
								($ billions)							
Total financial assets	204.8	230.9	242.7	270.4	306.1	365.3	421.3	484.0	534.6	571.2	610.9	633.9	637.2	653.7	741.7
Checkable deposits and currency	4.7	4.8	4.9	5.1	5.2	5.5	5.9	6.5	7.3	8.3	9.4	10.6	11.9	12.3	12.7
Credit market instruments	181.4	204.1	212.3	237.6	273.3	319.7	362.4	409.9	448.0	468.6	497.6	484.9	486.6	482.8	549.6
Mortgages	13.8	16.8	18.7	20.5	23.8	28.6	34.2	42.2	47.3	53.8	65.5	65.8	68.4	71.7	79.0
Consumer credit	78.9	87.8	93.2	103.7	111.7	132.4	151.0	154.0	155.3	144.6	138.6	126.2	121.6	116.5	134.8
Other loans (to business)	88.7	99.4	100.4	113.4	137.8	158.7	177.2	213.8	245.3	270.2	293.6	292.9	296.5	294.6	335.7
Miscellaneous assets	18.7	22.0	25.5	27.8	27.6	40.1	53.1	67.6	79.4	94.3	103.9	138.4	138.8	158.6	179.4
Total liabilities	181.9	206.2	216.3	241.6	274.7	329.7	382.2	438.9	477.9	503.3	534.5	556.5	569.4	582.3	667.1
Credit market instruments	126.9	141.6	144.9	159.7	183.6	224.3	275.9	299.1	323.0	350.4	374.4	393.0	389.4	390.5	440.8
Corporate bonds	65.5	68.9	77.0	81.0	90.5	105.3	131.6	141.2	147.0	162.7	178.2	191.3	195.3	206.0	235.1
Bank loans	13.8	15.5	16.5	18.3	20.0	16.4	20.0	22.9	23.9	27.0	31.0	42.3	37.6	25.3	21.2
Open-market paper	47.6	57.2	51.4	60.5	73.1	102.7	124.3	135.0	152.1	160.7	165.3	159.5	156.4	159.2	184.6
Taxes payable	0.2	0.1				0.1	0.1	0.2	0.3	0.4	0.6	0.7	0.8	0.9	1.0
Miscellaneous liabilities	54.8	64.5	71.4	81.8	91.0	105.3	106.2	139.6	154.6	152.5	159.5	162.7	179.2	190.9	225.3
Foreign direct investments in U.S.	0.4	0.4	0.4		1.9	1.4	3.6	3.5	2.7	9.3	4.6	11.6	13.9	21.5	30.1
Investment by parent	24.4	16.5	23.2	28.1	36.9	52.5	60.0	50.0	36.8	35.2	37.5	34.5	37.8	42.7	50.7
Other	29.9	48.0	47.8	53.6	52.1	51.4	42.6	86.2	115.2	107.9	117.4	116.6	127.5	126.7	144.6

(percent)

Total financial assets ($ billions)	204.8	230.9	242.7	270.4	306.1	365.3	421.3	484.0	534.6	571.2	610.9	633.9	637.2	653.7	741.7
Checkable deposits and currency	2.3	2.1	2.0	1.9	1.7	1.5	1.4	1.3	1.4	1.5	1.5	1.7	1.9	1.9	1.7
Credit market instruments	88.6	88.4	87.5	87.9	89.3	87.5	86.0	84.7	83.8	82.0	81.5	76.5	76.4	73.9	74.1
Mortgages	6.7	7.3	7.7	7.6	7.8	7.8	8.1	8.7	8.8	9.4	10.7	10.4	10.7	11.0	10.7
Consumer credit	38.5	38.0	38.4	38.4	36.5	36.2	35.8	31.8	29.0	25.3	22.7	19.9	19.1	17.8	18.2
Other loans (to business)	43.3	43.0	41.4	41.9	45.0	43.4	42.1	44.2	45.9	47.3	48.1	46.2	46.5	45.1	45.3
Miscellaneous assets	9.1	9.5	10.5	10.3	9.0	11.0	12.6	14.0	14.9	16.5	17.0	21.8	21.8	24.3	24.2
Total liabilities ($ billions)	181.9	206.2	216.3	241.6	274.7	329.7	382.2	438.9	477.9	503.3	534.5	556.5	569.4	582.3	667.1
Credit market instruments	69.8	68.7	67.0	66.1	66.8	68.0	72.2	68.1	67.6	69.6	70.0	70.6	68.4	67.1	66.1
Corporate bonds	36.0	33.4	35.6	33.5	32.9	31.9	34.4	32.2	30.8	32.3	33.3	34.4	34.3	35.4	35.2
Bank loans	7.6	7.5	7.6	7.6	7.3	5.0	5.2	5.2	5.0	5.4	5.8	7.6	6.6	4.3	3.2
Open-market paper	26.2	27.7	23.8	25.0	26.6	31.1	32.5	30.8	31.8	31.9	30.9	28.7	27.5	27.3	27.7
Taxes payable	0.1	0.0	0.0	0.0	0.0	0.0	0.0	0.1	0.1	0.1	0.1	0.1	0.1	0.2	0.1
Miscellaneous liabilities	30.1	31.3	33.0	33.9	33.1	31.9	27.8	31.8	32.3	30.3	29.8	29.2	31.5	32.8	33.8
Foreign direct investments in U.S.	0.2	0.0	0.2	0.0	0.7	0.4	0.9	0.8	0.6	1.8	0.9	2.1	2.4	3.7	4.5
Investment by parent	13.4	8.0	10.7	11.6	13.4	15.9	15.7	11.4	7.7	7.0	7.0	6.2	6.6	7.3	7.6
Other	16.4	23.3	22.1	22.2	19.0	15.6	11.1	19.6	24.1	21.4	22.0	21.0	22.4	21.8	21.7

Note: Data are for all finance companies including retail captive finance companies.

Source: Flow of Funds Accounts, *Federal Reserve Bulletin*, March 8, 1995.

(D'Arista and Schlesinger 1993, 14–17). Those fifteen companies account for about 40 percent of the total commercial paper issued by finance companies. It seems likely that most commercial paper issued by small finance companies would have a bank guarantee as well. Thus, a safe assumption is that almost all commercial paper issued by finance companies is backed by a bank guarantee or line of credit.

The ability to securitize assets also has made nonbank financial institutions more formidable competitors in mortgage and consumer credit markets. Advances in information and data processing technology have enabled nonbank competitors to originate loans, transform them into marketable securities, and sell them to obtain more funding with which to make more loans. Computer technology has eroded the competitive advantage of banks by lowering transactions costs and enabling nonbank financial institutions to evaluate credit risk efficiently through the use of statistical methods. When credit risk can be evaluated using statistical techniques, such as is the case for consumer and mortgage loans, banks no longer have an advantage in making those loans. An effort is now underway in the United States to develop a market for securitized small business loans as well.

Finally, the development of the junk bond market and the increased internationalization of financial markets have further eroded the market share of banks. In the past only Fortune 500 companies were able to raise funds by selling their bonds directly to the public—bypassing banks. Now, even lower-quality corporate borrowers can readily raise funds through access to the junk bond market. Despite predictions of the demise of the junk bond market after the Michael Milken embarrassment, it is clear that the junk bond market is here to stay. Although sales of new junk bonds slid to $2.9 billion by 1990, they rebounded to $16.9 billion in 1991, $42 billion in 1992, and $60 billion in 1993.

Competition from foreign banks, particularly Japanese and European banks, has undercut the competitive position of U.S. banks as well, even in U.S. markets. The success of the Japanese economy and Japan's high savings rate gave Japanese banks access to cheaper funds than were available to American banks. That cost advantage permitted Japanese banks to more aggressively seek out loan business in the United States and resulted in the erosion of U.S. banks' market share. (See figure 3-11.) In addition, foreign banks have been subject to less burdensome regulation than have U.S. banks and have as a consequence enjoyed a competitive advantage over U.S. banks.

FIGURE 3-11
Foreign Banks' Share of the U.S. Market, 1975–1992

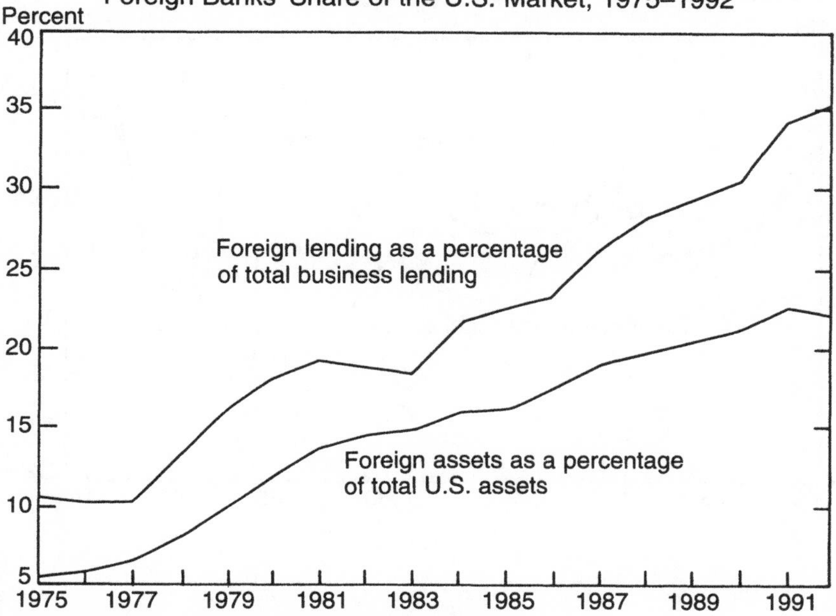

Source: *Statistical Abstract of the United States,* 1990.

The Erosion of Bank Profitability

Not surprisingly, reduced advantages in raising funds and in making loans steadily eroded bank profitability during the 1980s. Two measures of commercial bank profitability, the pretax rates of return on assets and equity, show a trend toward declining profitability during the 1980s. The average before-tax rate of return on equity fell from an average of about 15 percent from 1970 through 1984 to below 12 percent from 1985 through 1991.[4] In the 1990s, however, bank profits improved sharply, helped by the return of a favorable term structure of interest rates. (See figure 3-12.)

Those measures, however, are not good indicators of the profitability of traditional banking because they include profits from the increasingly important nontraditional activities of banks. While there is no way to break out earnings from nontraditional activities, an indicator of the growing importance of such earnings may be the sharp growth that has occurred in banks' noninterest income (fee and trading income). Noninterest income derived from off-balance-sheet activities

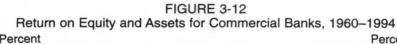

FIGURE 3-12
Return on Equity and Assets for Commercial Banks, 1960–1994

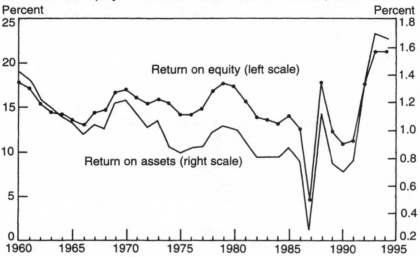

grew from about 19 percent of banks' total income from 1960 to 1980 to almost 35 percent in 1993. (See figure 3-13.) While some of that growth may be attributable to an expansion of traditional fee activities, much of it is probably due to banks' expanding into new activities. A crude way to adjust bank profitability for that new fee income is to exclude noninterest income from total bank earnings. Excluding noninterest income, the pretax return on equity has fallen from plus 10 percent in 1960 to levels that exceeded negative 14 percent in the late early 1990s. (See figure 3-14.) That measure, however, does not adjust for the expenses associated with generating noninterest income and therefore may overstate the declining trend in the profitability of traditional banking. Another indicator of the declining profitability of traditional banking is the fall in the ratio of market-to-book value of bank equity that occurred from the mid-1960s to the early 1980s. This indicates that bank charters became less valuable as income-generating assets during that period (Keeley 1990). Subsequently, during the 1980s and 1990s, that ratio has risen, probably because banks have sharply expanded their nontraditional fee-generating activities and thus restored some of the market value they lost earlier.

FIGURE 3-13
Share of Noninterest Income in Total Income for Commercial Banks, 1960–1994

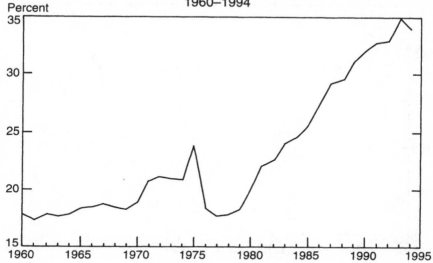

FIGURE 3-14
Return on Equity and Assets for Commercial Banks, Excluding Noninterest Income, 1960–1994

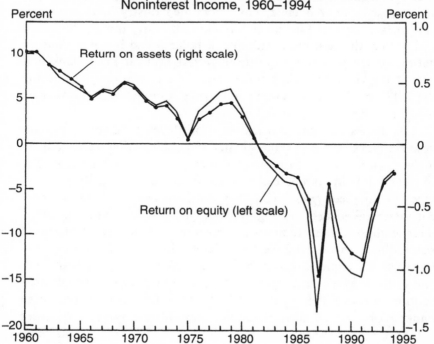

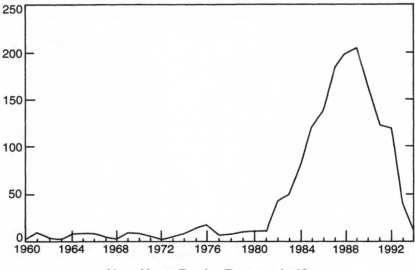

FIGURE 3-15
Number of Bank Failures, 1960–1994

How Have Banks Responded?

A common characteristic of an industry with declining profitability is an increase in the frequency of exit from the industry. Substantial exit has, in fact, occurred in the U.S. banking industry during the 1980s and 1990s, through both widespread failures and industry consolidation via mergers and acquisitions. From 1960 to 1980, bank failures in the United States averaged less than 10 per year, but during the 1980s bank failures soared and rose to more than 200 a year by the late 1980s. (See figure 3-15.)

Banks also sought to maintain profit levels by diversifying into new activities and by taking greater risks. First, they made riskier, higher-yielding loans. In particular, they placed a greater percentage of their funds in commercial real estate loans, historically a riskier type of loan. (See figure 3-16.) They also increased lending to support corporate takeovers and highly leveraged buyouts, and expanded their lending to less creditworthy borrowers. Evidence of increased risk-taking is that during the 1980s banks' loan-loss provisions, relative to assets, climbed substantially to a peak of 1.25 percent in 1987 and remained high until tighter regulation in the 1990s brought that ratio back down. (See figure 3-17.) There is also evidence that large banks took on even more risk, since they suffered larger loan losses

FIGURE 3-16
Commercial Real Estate Loans as a Percentage of Total Commercial
Bank Assets, 1960–1994

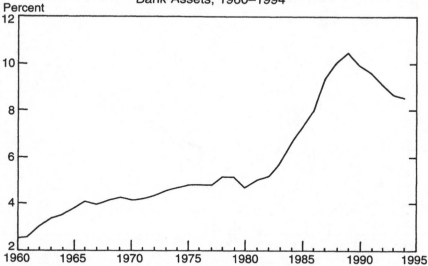

FIGURE 3-17
Loan-Loss Provisions Relative to Assets for Commercial Banks,
1960–1994

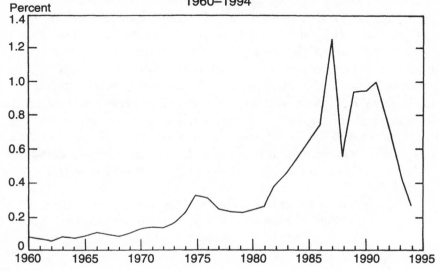

FIGURE 3-18
Net Interest Margins for Commercial Banks, 1960–1994

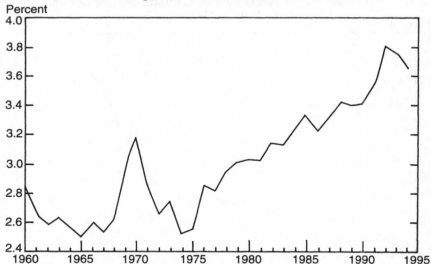

than did smaller banks (Boyd and Gertler 1993). Thus, during the 1980s banks appear to have attempted to maintain their net interest margins (interest income minus interest expense divided by total assets) and overall profitability by taking on greater credit risks.[5] (See figure 3-18.)

The second way banks have sought to maintain profitability is by expanding off-balance-sheet activities, some of which may be quite risky. Figure 3-13 shows that commercial banks clearly did do so during the 1980s and 1990s, doubling the share of their income coming from off-balance-sheet (non-interest-income) activities. That strategy has raised questions about what the proper activities for banks should be, and about whether nontraditional activities might result in banks' taking excessive risk. For example, there is considerable controversy about whether banks should be permitted to engage in unlimited derivatives activities, including being off-exchange (OTC) derivatives dealers. Some have argued that those activities are more risky than traditional banking and could threaten the stability of the entire banking system. (This issue is discussed more fully in chapter 7.)

The United States is not the only country to experience increased risk-taking by banks. Excessive risk-taking has precipitated large losses and widespread bank failures in many countries.[6] For example, banks in Norway, Sweden, and Finland responded to deregulation by dramatically increasing their real estate lending, which was followed by a boom and bust in the real estate sector that resulted in the insolvency of many large banking institutions. Indeed, banks' loan losses in those countries as a fraction of GNP exceeded losses in both the banking and savings and loans industries in the United States. The International Monetary Fund (1993) reports that government (or taxpayer) support to shore up the banking system in Scandinavian countries has been estimated to range from 2.8 to 4.0 percent of GDP, which is comparable to the savings and loan bailout in the United States (which amounted to 3.2 percent of GDP).

Japanese banks also suffered large losses due to riskier lending, particularly to the real estate sector. The collapse of real estate values in Japan left many banks, such as Sumitomo Trust and Banking Company, one of the world's largest, with huge losses. Official estimates indicate that the twenty-one largest Japanese banks are holding over $136 billion of nonperforming loans—loans on which interest payments have not been made for more than six months. Many private analysts think that the amount of their nonperforming loans may be much larger than reported. Japan's banking federation, with the assistance of the government, has set up cooperative arrangements to shore up the banking system.

Both French and British banks suffered from the worldwide collapse of real estate prices and from major failures of risky real estate projects. Olympia and York's failure is a prominent example. Just as in the United States, the loan-loss provisions of British and French banks have risen in the 1990s, although neither banking system appears to be threatened by major bank collapses. In addition, even in countries with healthy banking systems, such as Switzerland and Germany, some banks have run into trouble. Regional banks in Switzerland failed, and Germany's BfG Bank suffered huge losses (DM 1.1 billion) in 1992 and needed a capital infusion from its parent company Credit Lyonnais. In 1995 Credit Lyonnais, after years of bad loans and investments, itself required a government bailout of over $5 billion to save it. Thus, fundamental forces not limited to the United States have caused a decline in the profitability of traditional banking throughout the world and have created an incentive for banks to expand into new activities and to take greater risks.

The Decline of Traditional Banking Is a Global Phenomenon

Traditional banking is in decline in other countries as well. That decline has been the most severe in countries where constraining regulations have created a highly segmented financial structure and prevented banks from responding to the competitive initiatives of nonbank competitors. In all countries, however, technologically driven financial innovation, increased competition, and deregulation threaten sweeping changes in financial markets.

Although it is difficult to make cross-country comparisons because of differences in national accounting conventions, banks appear to be under greater pressure in the United States, the United Kingdom, Australia, and the Scandinavian countries than in continental European countries. Table 3-8, for example, shows a greater decline in bank profitability in the former countries than in most European countries. Banks in continental European countries are less constrained by regulation and may have been better able to respond to the changing market environment by developing new products and diversifying into new activities.

In addition, nondepository financial intermediaries have been growing rapidly in all countries. Mutual funds in foreign countries, for example, have doubled in size since 1988. (See table 3-9.) Further, nondepository intermediaries as a group—life insurance companies, pension funds, and investment companies—have sharply increased their share of household financial assets in all major foreign countries. (See table 3-10.) In some countries banks have been able to participate in that growth via ownership of, or a relationship with, the rapidly growing nondepository financial institutions.

Foreign banks also have had to face increased competition from expanding securities markets. In many foreign countries fundamental economic forces and regulatory reforms have improved the efficiency of securities markets so that they are more attractive alternatives for both savers and business firms seeking funds. Just as in the United States, business borrowers are bypassing banks by issuing securities to raise funds. Further, even in countries where securities markets have not yet grown (such as Australia), banks have nevertheless lost loan business because their best corporate customers have been able to access foreign and offshore capital markets, such as the Eurobond market. In addition, the same forces driving the securitization process in the United States are at work in other countries and have undercut the advantages that banks have traditionally had in providing credit.

TABLE 3-8
Bank Profit Margins, 1980–1992[a]

Countries	1980–1982	1983–1985	1986–1988	1989–1991	1992
United States[b]	0.83	0.78	0.70	0.61	1.30
Japan[c,d]	0.40	0.46	0.60	0.36	0.21
Germany[c,d]	0.50	0.92	0.83	0.83	0.70
France[c]	0.34	0.21	0.28	0.26	0.31
Italy	0.68	0.80	0.98	1.16	1.03
United Kingdom[e]	1.04	0.99	0.64	0.43	0.32
Canada[d]	0.63	0.73	1.02	0.10	0.53
Australia[d]	1.41	NA	1.20	0.85	-0.02
Belgium[d]	0.34	0.42	0.35	0.18	0.23
Finland[f,g]	0.49	0.48	0.53	-0.09	-1.85
Netherlands	0.31	0.63	0.71	0.55	0.53
Norway	0.63	0.8	0.03	-1.81	-1.26
Spain	1.09	0.65	1.05	1.56	1.12
Sweden[h,i]	0.38	0.38	0.77	1.18	0.25
Switzerland	0.65	0.69	0.68	0.61	0.57

a. Ratio of pretax profit to average total assets of commercial banks; the data are not fully comparable across countries.
b. Institutions with assets of U.S. $100 million or more.
c. Large commercial banks.
d. Fiscal years.
e. Before 1984, data only reported to OECD on London clearing banks' group.
f. As of 1984, foreign branches of Finnish commercial banks included in data.
g. As of 1988, data include the Post Office Bank (Postipankki).
h. For 1991, the Foreningsbankernas Bank is not included in data.
i. Includes cooperative banks.

Sources: Bank Profitability: Financial Statements of Banks, 1983–1992 (Paris: OECD, 1994). David Llewellyn, "Secular Pressures on Banking in Developed Financial Systems: Is Traditional Banking and Industry in Secular Decline?" in D. E. Fair and R. Raymond, eds., The New Europe: Evolving Economic and Financial Systems in East and West (Amsterdam: Kluwer Academic Publishers, 1993).

TABLE 3-9

Assets of Open-End Investment Companies throughout the World, 1988–1993
(U.S. $ millions)

	1988	1989	1990	1991	1992	1993
Non-U.S. countries						
Australia[a]	12,180	30,892	29,125	34,543	19,280	24,556
Austria	9,448	12,750	14,324	15,079	15,029	18,174
Belgium	4,538	5,027	4,538	6,067	8,954	15,149
Canada[a]	17,484	20,270	21,483	43,195	52,921	86,567
Denmark	3,317	3,820	3,614	3,729	3,658	4,401
Finland	NA	NA	NA	77	110[b]	NA
France	236,392	295,750	378,826	489,556	447,338	483,327
Germany						
Public	50,870	62,352	71,018	77,266	70,196	78,552
Special	48,992	62,189	74,477	88,942	101,405	129,915[c]
Greece	71	132	936	952	1,018	3,465
Hong Kong	NA	NA	NA	NA	16,351	31,135
India	17,000	NA	12,477	12,669	14,318	31,425
Ireland[a]	4,985	6,715	6,977	7,452	5,905	5,244
Italy	39,488	38,700	41,924	48,823	41,036	64,272
Japan	433,940	408,165	353,528	323,913	346,924	454,608
Korea	21,037	27,584	33,806	37,050	49,183	69,988
Luxembourg	NA	NA	94,559	117,112	182,244	247,804
Mexico	NA	NA	18,410	22,750	16,036[d]	16,036
Netherlands[a]	NA	23,204	24,308	21,340	34,797	48,530
New Zealand[a]	NA	NA	NA	NA	1,062	1,833

Norway	NA	NA	NA	NA	2,722[d]	2,722
Portugal	278	1,308	2,848	6,380	7,925	7,957[c]
South Africa	NA	NA	NA	NA	4,524	4,647
Spain	6,775	7,927	11,996	40,025	54,699	72,058
Sweden	17,460	23,739	21,113	20,779	18,108	24,356
Switzerland	NA	NA	NA	NA	24,304	34,094
United Kingdom[d]	76,705	92,850	91,530	104,394	91,153	131,455
Total non-U.S.	1,000,960	1,123,374	1,311,817	1,462,093	1,631,200	2,092,380
United States						
Long-term	472,297	553,862	568,517	853,000	1,100,100	1,510,100
Short-term	337,954	428,093	498,375	542,500	546,200	565,300
Total U.S.	810,251	981,955	1,066,892	1,395,500	1,646,300	2,075,400
Total world	1,811,211	2,105,329	2,378,709	2,857,593	3,277,500	4,167,780

Note: Comparison of annual total assets across countries is not recommended because of reporting coverage.

a. Approximately 95 percent relates to life insurance–linked funds. The other 5 percent are unit investment trusts. International Financial Service Center funds are not included.

b. As of December 1992.

c. As of September 1993.

d. Fund of fund assets not included.

TABLE 3-10

Growth of Institutional Investors, 1980–1990

(assets as percentage of household financial assets)

Country	Pension Funds and Life Insurance Companies			Collective Investment Institutions			Total		
	1980	1985	1990[a]	1980	1985	1990[a]	1980	1985	1990[a]
United States	17.8	21.1	23.5	2.2	5.0	7.7	20.0	26.0	31.2
Japan	13.8	16.6	20.8	1.8	3.6	5.6	15.6	20.2	26.4
Germany	19.4	24.2	27.1	3.2	4.8	8.1	22.6	29.0	35.1
France	8.0	11.2	14.7	2.7	12.4	21.7	10.6	23.6	36.3
Italy	1.6	0.9	3.2	NA	2.1	2.9	NA	2.9	6.1
United Kingdom	39.9	49.9	53.7	1.6	3.1	4.9	41.5	53.1	58.6
Canada	19.4	23.3	26.7	1.0	1.6	3.0	20.4	24.9	29.7

a. For Italy and United Kingdom, 1989 figures.

Source: Bank for International Settlements, *Annual Report*, 1992.

In all countries banks have changed what they do in response to increased competition. When permitted to do so, they have pursued off-balance-sheet activities as a way of increasing fee income to replace lower income from traditional banking activities. They have expanded their securities, insurance, and trading activities, "securitized" more of their loan portfolio, provided more loan commitments and standby letters of credit, and increased derivatives-market services. Table 3-11 shows that in almost all major foreign countries banks' noninterest income (relative to gross income) has increased.

Finally, there is evidence that banks in other countries have responded to increased competitive pressures by escalating their willingness to take greater risk. Table 3-12 shows that loan-loss provisions have increased in most foreign countries, which indicates the increased willingness of banks to lend to less creditworthy borrowers.

Thus, the decline of traditional banking is a global phenomenon and has put banks under increasing pressure to seek income by diversifying into new activities and by taking greater risk.

Recent Changes in Historical Perspective

During the 1920s and 1930s traditional banks experienced an erosion in market share similar to the 1980s and early 1990s. From 1922 to 1939 banks' share of financial intermediary assets slipped from almost 55 percent to about 40 percent, a fall of nearly fifteen percentage points. (See table 3-2.) Similarly, from 1970 to 1994, the market share of banks fell from 41.4 percent to 28.9 percent, a fall of 12.5 percentage points. (See table 3-2.) The 1922 to 1939 period can also be divided into two distinct subperiods: one of great economic prosperity—from 1922 to 1929—and one of great economic depression—from 1929 to 1939. Even omitting the economically depressed period after 1929, banks' market share fell from 54.9 percent in 1922 to 45.9 percent in 1929, a decline very much like that which occurred from 1980 to 1994. Finally, if thrift institutions are combined with banks, the decline of depository institutions from 1980 to 1994 was even steeper than during the 1920s and 1930s: their combined market share fell by 20 percentage points from 1980 to 1994 versus only 7.9 percentage points from 1922 to 1929 and 15.2 percentage points from 1922 to 1939.

In both the 1920s and the 1980s banks replaced loan income (or interest income) with fee income. In the 1920s they increased fiduciary services and expanded investment banking activities. As corpo-

TABLE 3-11
Noninterest Income of Banks in Selected Industrial Countries, 1981–1992[a]
(percentage of gross income)

	1981	1982	1983	1984	1985	1986	1987	1988	1989	1990	1991	1992
United States												
Commercial banks	23.98	24.61	26.54	24.71	26.57	29.76	30.20	30.08	31.77	32.79	34.28	34.50
Large commercial banks	30.97	30.99	32.96	29.20	30.93	34.13	35.13	34.75	36.80	37.99	39.06	39.12
Japan												
Commercial banks	17.78	13.94	14.68	17.68	21.06	19.69	25.12	25.83	23.84	24.12	10.94	3.89
Large commercial banks	23.79	19.11	18.95	22.77	26.59	24.53	32.23	40.05	37.20	35.94	18.18	6.78
Germany												
Commercial banks	29.11	26.85	24.82	25.94	30.05	29.55	29.83	30.39	36.02	35.68	30.51	30.80
Large commercial banks	28.89	30.29	26.68	27.16	31.15	27.54	30.14	31.43	33.62	34.92	28.73	32.39
France												
Commercial banks and credit cooperatives	16.00	16.18	16.77	13.19	14.08	14.45	17.03	17.01	21.18	20.07	25.83	32.96
Large commercial banks	15.21	15.76	17.02	12.96	15.69	17.20	20.74	20.98	23.84	24.92	28.68	35.81
Italy												
Commercial banks	NA	NA	NA	29.18	31.51	31.88	27.98	27.58	25.74	26.78	26.15	19.97
Large commercial banks	NA	NA	NA	34.56	39.27	38.67	32.79	34.34	29.99	30.13	29.06	22.02
United Kingdom												
Commercial banks	NA	NA	NA	35.60	34.51	36.33	38.17	37.58	39.10	40.09	40.66	41.89
Large commercial banks	27.07	29.35	31.94	33.38	32.48	33.88	35.86	36.33	38.12	39.86	NA	NA
Canada												
Commercial banks	NA	21.61	21.07	22.68	23.71	24.73	28.35	27.39	29.18	30.95	30.10	30.97
Netherlands												
Commercial banks	25.85	23.25	23.51	24.66	25.65	23.92	25.95	27.25	29.37	28.65	29.14	28.63

Sweden												
Commercial banks	29.17	31.11	28.68	30.25	34.95	35.27	28.25	28.77	28.58	26.21	25.18	40.12
Switzerland												
All banks	47.69	44.22	46.49	45.67	47.38	49.35	51.58	47.10	50.87	49.05	50.78	49.93
Large commercial banks	52.57	47.28	47.91	46.65	48.16	49.75	51.34	47.38	50.29	50.93	51.23	50.14
Belgium												
Commercial banks	17.35	21.17	24.48	20.76	23.65	25.82	26.89	29.96	27.42	23.04	24.83	26.24
Luxembourg												
Commercial banks	23.73	18.38	17.49	13.24	19.67	21.37	19.99	24.28	28.23	35.00	26.51	29.19

a. Owing to differences in national accounting practices, the figures in this table should be interpreted with caution. In particular, cross-country comparisons may be less relevant than developments over time within a single country.
Source: Bank profitability: financial statements of banks, 1983–1992, OECD, 1994.

TABLE 3-12
Net Loan-Loss Provisions of Banks in Selected Industrial Countries, 1981–1992[a]
(percentage of gross income)

	1981	1982	1983	1984	1985	1986	1987	1988	1989	1990	1991	1992
United States												
Commercial banks	6.56	9.57	11.06	12.80	14.30	16.34	26.30	11.14	18.90	18.53	18.15	12.75
Large commercial banks	7.23	10.37	12.16	14.02	14.12	15.78	32.31	11.01	22.51	21.36	21.21	14.35
Japan												
Commercial banks	0.83	3.33	2.17	2.26	1.24	2.42	2.16	3.34	3.36	2.37	5.72	10.16
Large commercial banks	1.02	4.73	2.37	2.65	1.07	2.33	2.23	10.37	4.61	3.18	8.70	15.18
Germany												
Commercial banks	15.62	21.89	22.59	15.29	13.44	15.05	13.26	7.77	13.07	16.45	15.03	21.56
Large commercial banks	14.53	20.56	16.26	12.44	8.01	9.53	10.15	3.32	6.13	13.52	10.90	17.46
France												
Commercial banks and credit cooperatives	18.10	20.89	21.58	20.40	19.33	21.30	18.67	18.80	20.87	20.93	22.16	27.78
Large commercial banks	20.64	23.73	24.23	22.81	22.81	25.15	21.02	22.39	23.31	21.78	22.41	20.55
Italy												
Commercial banks	NA	NA	NA	13.16	12.52	12.18	11.12	12.41	11.49	11.65	10.55	14.36
Large commercial banks	NA	NA	NA	11.35	13.60	11.89	10.25	13.89	12.97	13.05	9.73	15.44
United Kingdom												
Commercial banks	NA	NA	NA	14.49	11.68	10.95	30.99	6.19	32.74	20.07	26.30	29.42
Large commercial banks	4.20	10.23	12.34	14.50	10.24	9.32	30.32	3.94	33.07	21.00	NA	NA
Canada												
Commercial banks	NA	14.61	15.24	17.36	17.69	20.57	17.49	13.68	25.56	8.28	11.93	24.81

Netherlands												
Commercial banks	27.37	27.39	19.69	20.45	12.25	10.68	6.13	13.26	12.19	11.78	11.48	11.59
Sweden												
Commercial banks	24.74	19.08	29.91	23.90	26.89	20.94	23.45	27.20	28.64	14.10	18.19	58.60
Switzerland												
All banks	14.75	17.75	18.73	18.72	19.64	19.00	19.06	17.82	18.90	20.70	30.26	31.65
Large commercial banks	13.30	16.70	17.68	18.31	19.44	19.23	18.32	17.78	17.89	17.40	26.40	30.16
Belgium												
Commercial banks	10.40	14.26	14.32	14.29	14.95	14.18	13.93	20.46	23.61	11.54	17.13	20.88
Luxembourg												
Commercial banks	39.09	52.28	56.51	49.90	49.38	46.05	39.66	29.54	32.37	44.06	36.87	33.43

a. Owing to differences in national accounting practices, the figures in this table should be interpreted with caution. In particular, cross-country comparisons may be less relevant than developments over time within a single country.

Source: Bank profitability: financial statements of banks, 1983–1992, OECD, 1994.

rations increasingly went to the equity markets for their financing, large banks were able to capture a piece of that business and retain their corporate relationships by enlarging their underwriting functions. By 1929 nearly all large commercial banks had at least one securities affiliate, which performed a complete range of investment banking functions: they originated new security issues, formed and took part in underwriting syndicates, sold new issues to retail banks and to institutional investors, and participated at the retail level in the distribution of securities to individual investors through a network of branch offices. By the late 1920s, it has been estimated that banks and their securities affiliates handled almost half the total distribution of securities. The growth of personal fortunes in the United States in the 1920s also fueled the growth of banks as active money managers, through trust departments and subsidiaries. A few large banks even began their own mutual funds (or investment trusts as they were then called).

In the 1920s and in the 1980s similar changes in the banking structure occurred as well. The number of banks fell substantially. There was a high rate of bank failures, especially among smaller banks whose profitability diminished. The number of bank mergers also sharply increased, especially among city banks. As a result, concentration in urban banking markets grew appreciably. Finally, there was an upsurge in branch and "chain" (or "group") banking. Those changes occurred then as now in response to an intensified competitive environment.

Finally, in the 1920s pension funds and investment companies grew rapidly, just as in the 1980s. Although those institutions did not become major players until after World War II, their growth in the 1920s was a harbinger of what was to come in the 1980s when open competition replaced protective regulation.

The changes in financial intermediation that occurred during the 1920s took place in an economic environment strikingly similar to that of the 1980s. First, both the 1920s and the 1980s were a time of great international expansion in financial markets. In the 1920s New York became a world financial center. Money freely flowed between countries in search of more attractive yields, and financial institutions built international networks by establishing overseas branches. Second, both periods were marked by considerable macroeconomic instability and policy experimentation. Third, there was tremendous product innovation during both periods, and increased competition among financial institutions greatly weakened traditional customer relationships. Fourth, in both periods banks turned to more expensive sources of funding. In 1920 time deposits in national banks (generally the large banks) were about one-third the level of demand deposits; by 1929 time deposits had become three-fourths as large as demand deposits. Fifth, commercial loans became a less important part of banks' portfolios in both the 1920s and the 1980s. In 1920 loans to business and agriculture, most of which were short-term, accounted for almost half the total earning assets of large urban banks. By 1929 such loans comprised only one-third of their total earning assets. Large corporations then, as now, were able to obtain financing directly by issuing securities, although in the 1920s new equity issues were the main financing vehicle rather than commercial paper and fixed-income securities as in the 1980s.

The 1920s ended with an economic disaster, which caused the U.S. Congress to substantially change the structure of the U.S. financial system for the next fifty years. Currently, U.S. financial markets are once again undergoing substantial change, propelled this time not by legislation but by technologically driven market forces. What the ultimate course of that transformation will be depends critically on the policy decisions we make during the next few years.

Nonbank Intermediaries as Money Managers: Implications for Securities and Derivatives Markets

The shift in household assets from depository institutions to nonbank intermediaries that has accompanied the decline of traditional banking has had effects reaching far beyond banking itself. In particular, mutual funds and pension funds, by becoming major equity owners and institutional fund managers, have been thrust into the position of being able to influence what happens in the boardrooms of all major corporations. In addition, the growing dominance of institutional trading has changed the way that equity markets operate and has been a major factor in the development of both on- and off-exchange derivatives markets.

During the past several decades, households have increasingly placed their money with institutional fund managers. Their direct purchases of stocks and bonds have steadily fallen. From 1982 to 1994 direct purchases of securities accounted for only 10 percent of the net growth of households' financial assets. (See figure 3-10.) Further, households have been net sellers of stock in every year but one (1992) since 1982. (See table 3-4.) In 1952 households' direct holdings of

TABLE 3-13
Changes in U.S. Institutional Equity Ownership, 1981–1990
(percentage of total U.S. market capitalization)

Institution	1981	1986	1990	Change 1981–1990
Private pension funds	15.5	16.7	19.9	4.4
Bank trusts	10.1	10.1	9.2	−0.9
Public pension funds	3.0	2.1	8.3	5.3
Mutual funds	2.5	6.8	7.2	4.7
Insurance companies	5.7	4.8	6.9	1.2
Foundation/endowments	1.2	1.3	1.8	0.6
Total	38.0	44.8	53.3	15.3

Note: See Brancato and Gaughan (1991, table 10). Brancato and Gaughan define *institution* to include pension funds, mutual funds, insurance companies, bank-managed trusts, and foundation and endowment funds. That definition excludes shares owned by investment banks, bankholding companies, and nonbank, nonpension trusts.

stock as a percent of total household financial assets was 32 percent. By 1994 that figure had fallen to 16.2 percent (Sellon 1992). (See table 3-3.) Even more telling, in 1952 households directly held 91 percent of all corporate stock outstanding; in 1991 they held about 50 percent. (See figure 3-5.) During that period the share of total outstanding stock held by pension and mutual funds rose from 3 percent to 34 percent. By 1990 all institutional investors, taken together, held 53.3 percent of the total stock outstanding. (See table 3-13.)

The growing dominance of institutional fund managers has had significant effects on equity markets and has raised a number of important public policy issues. First, trading activity in securities markets has increased substantially, as institutions have sought to outperform one another. In 1975 institutions demanded and obtained a lower institutional commission structure for trades made on equity exchanges. Lower commissions together with a greater emphasis on portfolio performance in turn resulted in a sharp increase in "annual turnover" in equity markets. The typical stock is now held for an average of a little over two years, compared with an average of four years in 1982 and seven years in 1960. The average holding period for institutional investors is less than two years, compared with almost five years for individuals (Froot, Perold, and Stein 1992, table 1). That has raised questions about whether institutional trading is increasing volatility in securities markets and about what effect that institutional trading may be having on the behavior of corporate managers. Has it, in particular, made corporate managers more myopic or short-term-oriented ("Business Bulletin" 1986; Edwards 1993a)?

Second, the growth of institutional trading has led to the fragmentation of equity markets. Spurred by advances in automation and communications technology, institutional traders have demanded low-cost, standardized, trading services as well as specialized, tailor-made services. In response, new trading systems have developed (such as Instinet, Posit, and the Wunsch Auction System), and there has been a substantial increase in "upstairs" or off-exchange trading. Just as the role of traditional banking in financial intermediation has declined, the role of the traditional, regulated exchange in securities markets has diminished. In 1980 the New York Stock Exchange accounted for 85.4 percent of the number of consolidated-tape trades. By 1990 that figure had fallen to 62.2 percent (Stoll 1993).

Third, institutional investors have been a major factor in the surge in the trading of foreign securities since 1980, as well as in the increase in cross-border stock holdings. U.S. purchases and sales of securities abroad grew from $17.9 billion in 1980 to $818.3 billion in 1994, a cumulative annual growth rate of about 30 percent (Grundfest 1990). (See table 3-14.) At the end of 1994, U.S. investors held $148.8 billion in foreign securities, of which approximately 80 percent was held by Employee Retirement Income Security Act pension funds and 13 percent by mutual funds and closed-end country funds (Grundfest 1990). Not surprisingly, the globalization of securities trading has in turn created new tensions and policy debates, such as about whether the U.S. disclosure standards should be applied to foreign firms issuing stock in the United States (Edwards 1993c) or whether uniform world accounting and disclosure standards need to be developed.

Fourth, institutional ownership of securities has fueled the growth of derivatives markets—futures, forwards, options, and swaps—both on and off exchanges. Trading has soared in exchange-traded futures and options contracts on financial instruments (such as U.S. Treasury bonds, Eurodollar time deposits, and stock indexes) and in off-exchange interest rate and foreign currency swaps and forward agreements. (See table 3-15.) Institutional investors are making extensive use of derivatives both to manage risk and to enhance portfolio performance (Remolona 1992–1993).

Lastly, the increasing importance of institutional investors as stockholders has raised a number of corporate governance issues.

TABLE 3-14

Aggregate U.S. Purchases and Sales of Foreign Securities, by Geographic Region, 1980–1994[a]
($ billions)

	1980	1981	1982	1983	1984	1985	1986	1987	1988	1989	1990	1991	1992	1993	1994	1980–1989 AAGR[b] (%)	1989–1994 AAGR[b] (%)	1989 Mkt. Share (%)	1994 Mkt. Share (%)
Canada	6.7	4.9	2.9	5.0	4.4	6.8	9.8	18.9	9.7	10.9	9.8	13.1	14.1	26.5	35.1	5.6	26.4	4.7	4.3
Total Europe	6.9	5.7	6.5	13.7	13.3	21.5	55.3	101.4	75.6	127.9	153.7	156.9	199.2	296.1	442.5	38.3	28.2	55.5	54.1
United Kingdom	2.8	2.9	3.6	6.5	7.8	13.3	32.6	67.9	51.2	80.1	92.9	100.2	134.3	194.9	285.5	45.2	28.9	34.8	34.9
Switzerland	1.6	0.9	0.7	1.8	1.3	1.6	3.2	6.3	5.3	6.5	9.0	8.7	10.3	14.7	22.4	20.4	21.6	3.7	2.7
Other Europe	2.5	1.9	2.2	5.4	4.2	6.6	19.5	27.2	19.1	39.3	51.6	48.0	54.6	86.5	134.6	35.8	27.9	17.5	16.4
Total Asia	3.3	6.5	5.1	9.4	10.6	14.1	30.1	56.7	56.2	75.8	74.6	72.4	77.3	142.7	196.3	41.7	21.0	33.0	24.0
Japan	2.7	5.4	4.3	8.0	9.0	11.6	25.6	47.8	50.4	65.8	61.4	56.4	49.6	78.3	109.9	42.6	10.8	28.6	13.4
Other Asia	0.6	1.1	0.8	1.4	1.6	2.5	4.5	8.9	5.8	10.1	13.2	16.0	27.7	64.4	86.4	36.8	53.6	4.4	10.6
Latin America	0.7	1.1	0.8	1.6	0.9	1.2	3.6	7.1	5.3	9.3	10.3	22.9	34.4	75.6	123.9	33.3	67.8	4.0	15.1
All other	0.3	0.4	0.3	0.8	1.1	2.0	2.7	5.8	4.8	5.4	15.0	29.1	6.5	12.4	20.5	37.9	30.6	2.3	2.5
Total	17.9	18.6	15.6	30.5	30.3	45.6	101.5	189.9	151.6	229.3	263.4	294.4	331.5	553.3	818.3	32.8	28.9	100.0	100.0

a. Defined as aggregate foreign stocks purchased by foreigners plus aggregate foreign stocks sold by foreigners.

b. AAGR (average annual growth rate) is calculated as $(Q_{(t+n)}/[(Q_{(t+n)}/Q_t)(1/n)]-1$.

Source: Office of the Secretary, U.S. Department of Treasury, *Treasury Bulletin*, table CM-V-5, Spring issues.

TABLE 3-15
Notional/Contract Amounts for Financial Derivatives Worldwide by Individual Product Type as of End of Fiscal Year, 1989–1993
($ billions)

Type of Derivative	1989	1990	1991	1992	1993	Percentage of Total 1993	Percentage Increase 1989–1993
Forwards							
Forward rate agreements[a]	770	1,156	1,533	1,807	2,522		
Foreign exchange forwards[b]	2,264	3,277	4,531	5,510	6,232		
Total forwards	3,034	4,433	6,064	7,317	8,754	35	189
Futures							
Interest rate futures	1,201	1,454	2,157	2,902	4,960		
Currency futures	16	16	18	25	30		
Equity index futures	42	70	77	81	119		
Total futures	1,259	1,540	2,252	3,008	5,109	20	306
Options							
Exchange-traded interest rate options	387	600	1,073	1,385	2,362		
OTC interest-rate options	450	561	577	634	1,398		
Exchange-traded currency options	50	56	61	80	81		
Exchange-traded equity options	66	96	137	168	286		
Total options	953	1,313	1,848	2,267	4,127	16	333

(Table continues)

TABLE 3-15 (continued)

Type of Derivative	1989	1990	1991	1992	1993	Percentage of Total 1993	Percentage Increase 1989–1993
Swaps							
Interest rate swaps	1,503	2,312	3,065	3,851	6,177		
Currency swaps	449	578	807	860	900		
Total swaps	1,952	2,890	3,872	4,711	7,077	28	263
Total derivatives[c]	7,198	10,176	14,036	17,303	25,067	100	248
Total derivatives[d]	4,934	6,899	9,505	11,793	18,835		

a. GAO estimated forward rate agreements as of the end of fiscal year 1992 on the basis of methodology the New York Federal Reserve used in computing estimates for year-ends 1989, 1990, and 1991.

b. GAO estimates for foreign exchange forward contracts are from the General Accounting Office (1994, table IV.5). Those also include an unknown amount of OTC foreign exchange options.

c. Does not include complete data on physical commodity derivatives and equity options on the common stock of individual companies. Table IV.2 of the GAO report (1994) shows that seven of the databases contain equity and commodity derivatives that ranged from 1.1 to 3.4 percent of total derivatives notional/contractual amounts.

d. Before including GAO estimates for foreign exchange forwards and OTC options.

Sources: Bank for International Settlements; GAO Report; International Swap Dealers' Association; and the Federal Reserve Bank of New York.

Looking at only the largest 100 American corporations, we see that institutions own, on average, 53 percent of the outstanding stock. Their ownership is much greater in some corporations: 82 percent of General Motors Corporation, 74 percent of Mobil Oil, 70 percent of Citicorp, 86 percent of Amoco, and so forth (Brancato and Gaughan 1991, table 10). Large stock ownership by institutions, especially pension funds, has raised questions regarding the appropriate role of institutions on corporate boards and about how active institutional investors should be in monitoring managerial performance and in replacing underperforming corporate managers (Black 1992a, 1992b; Roe 1994).

Conclusion

The revolution in financial markets during the 1980s and early 1990s has been unlike anything that has occurred since the 1920s and 1930s. An intensified competitive environment coupled with an erosion of protective regulations resulted in a significant decline in the importance of traditional banking relative to nonbank financial intermediaries, especially mutual funds and pension funds. In addition, a steady stream of technological advances and financial innovations gave business borrowers greater direct access to capital markets so that they could bypass financial intermediaries entirely. Banks responded to those pressures by increasing their off-balance-sheet activities and by providing a wider array of nontraditional financial products, such as underwriting, securities, and derivatives market services. In the process, banks as a whole appear to have increased the amount of risk they are willing to bear so as to maintain both their market share and profitability.

✦ 4 ✦

Alternative Views of the Decline of Banking: Public Policy Implications

Views differ about why traditional banking is in decline and about whether that decline creates public policy issues that need to be addressed. Some argue that the decline is the product of a natural evolution toward more efficient financial markets and that government should stay out of the way and allow that evolution to find its logical end. Others argue that the shift toward nonbank financial intermediaries has been artificially induced by outdated, restrictive, and distorting regulations and that government must act quickly both to restore the competitive balance and to maintain financial stability.

This chapter discusses three competing theories that can explain the decline of traditional banking. I call these the "excess capacity," the "regulatory burden," and the "declining bank uniqueness" theories. Although all three theories can explain the decline of traditional banking, they provide different reasons for that decline and suggest different policy responses. The chapter concludes with a discussion of the public policy concerns raised by the decline of traditional banking and the growing role of nonbank financial institutions.

The Excess Capacity Theory

The excess capacity thesis views the decline of traditional banking as the natural result of the erosion of the protective regulation that traditionally has insulated banks from competition. Protective regulation has allowed banks in the past to earn abnormally high profits, which have resulted in overinvestment and the creation of excess capacity in the banking industry.[1] As regulatory protections were stripped away, however, competition intensified and profitability declined to more normal levels. As a consequence, the banking industry was forced into a process of disinvestment to rid itself of excess capacity. Only after that process is completed can a new and sustainable industry equilibrium be achieved.

According to that view, we might expect to observe declining profitability in banking, greater risk-taking by banks as they seek to maintain former profit levels, and a shrinking market share for banks vis-à-vis nonbanking financial intermediaries. The failure rate in banking also should rise as banks exit the industry, and banks should make an intensified effort to diversify away from traditional banking activities and into more profitable nontraditional activities, such as those carried on by investment banks, broker/dealers, and insurance companies. Finally, more competitive markets should intensify pressure on banks to cut costs and to restructure to achieve greater efficiency. As a result, the number of small banks should decline, either because of increased failures or because of widespread industry consolidation, and fewer but larger and more diversified banks should emerge. Once the required industry "shakeout" is completed, banking should settle into a new equilibrium, as a relatively smaller and more efficient industry.

The Regulatory Burden Theory

An alternative view is that banks are in decline only because inequitable and burdensome regulation has disadvantaged them vis-à-vis nonbank competitors. In that view, rather than protect banks from competition, regulation has fated them to a diminishing role by imposing unnecessary costs and restrictions on them. Nonbank financial institutions are not subject either to reserve requirements or to having to pay deposit insurance premiums, both of which raise the cost of funds for banks. Nor are nonbank competitors subject to geographical restrictions and burdensome prudential regulation and supervision, or to "social requirements" such as those imposed by the Community Reinvestment Act of 1977. Thus, instead of protecting banks, regulation has increased their costs and has prevented banks from responding to new competitive forces by diversifying into new products and services.

The growth of finance companies is a good example of how differential regulation can work to the advantage of nonbank competitors. Finance companies make short-term business loans like banks but are virtually unregulated. They do not have reserve or capital requirements, are not subject to loan limits, do not pay deposit insurance premiums, can operate freely anywhere in the country, and are able to engage in unrestricted transactions with parents and affiliates. Finance companies also are not subject either to community lending obligations under the Community Reinvestment Act or to restrictions imposed by the Glass-Steagall Act of 1933, and are free to have insurance company affiliates. Another example is the cost advantage that MMMFs have over banks in raising funds. MMMFs pass that advantage on to finance companies by purchasing the commercial paper that finance companies issue to fund the loans that they make, which further enables finance companies to undercut banks in making loans. Thus, adherents of the regulatory burden thesis argue that the excessive regulatory disadvantages imposed on banks explain their declining market share.[2]

That thesis is difficult to evaluate. Banks have been the recipients of regulatory benefits as well. They have been protected from competition by legally erected entry barriers (chartering and branching restrictions), have been the beneficiaries of government deposit insurance and other government guarantees, and have had access to the Federal Reserve's discount window, all of which have reduced their cost of funds. But the increased regulatory burdens that accompany those governmentally bestowed benefits make it unclear whether on net banks have been subject to a regulatory tax or subsidy.

Recent experience suggests that in the past banks (and other depository institutions) have been net beneficiaries of regulation. The widespread failure of thrifts and banks during the 1980s imposed huge costs on general taxpayers when government insurance funds backing deposits in those institutions proved inadequate (Barth and Bartholomew 1992; Barth, Brumbaugh, and Litan 1992). The government bailout, in effect, is a measure of the accumulated subsidy extended to those institutions in the past. Had either deposit insurance premiums been high enough to accumulate the necessary funds to pay for the bailout or regulation been sufficient to prevent or reduce the losses to taxpayers that occurred, there would not have been a subsidy.

New legislation has begun the process of eliminating that subsidy. The Financial Institutions Reform, Recovery and Enforcement Act of 1989 (FIRREA) and the Federal Deposit Insurance Corporation

Improvement Act of 1991 (FDICIA) raised capital requirements for banks and thrifts, increased insurance premiums, and curtailed the asset and liability powers of thrifts. In addition, those laws required early corrective action by regulators and least-cost resolution of failing banks to prevent troubled institutions from imposing costs on the deposit insurance fund and therefore taxpayers.

Whether that legislation has entirely eliminated the past subsidy to banks or, alternatively, by overregulation has imposed a net tax on banks is unclear. Because banks have traditionally performed a different economic and social role from that of nonbank financial intermediaries, it may be justifiable to impose a different regulatory structure on them, even though the result may be different cost structures that create what appear to be an "unlevel playing field."

The regulatory burden view is that the regulatory balance no longer favors banks, and that if nothing is done to correct that imbalance, traditional banks will become an ever-shrinking part of the financial system. Bank deposits may come to play a role not unlike U.S. savings bonds: repositories for small savers who place an exceptionally heavy weight on a government guarantee.

Both the excess capacity and the regulatory burden theses imply that banking will shrink relative to other financial intermediaries. Depending on which view is accepted, however, the respective policy response is different. The excess capacity thesis implies that the diminishing importance of banking is a natural consequence of efficiency-enhancing technological and organizational innovations and should be allowed to run its course. The regulatory burden thesis implies that the decline of banking has been artificially induced—the unnatural consequence of misdirected and suboptimal government interference with markets—and should be reversed, either by easing the regulatory burden on banks or by increasing the burdens on the nonbank competitors of banks. That is the genesis of calls to extend bank-type regulations, such as reserve requirements, deposit insurance premiums, and Community Reinvestment Act responsibilities, to the nonbank competitors of banks (D'Arista and Schlesinger 1993; Bacon 1993; Starobin 1993).

The Theory of Declining Bank Uniqueness

A third view of the decline of banking is that technological advances and market innovations have eroded the comparative advantage that banks have traditionally enjoyed—or that banks are no longer "special." Economic theories of the banking firm have viewed banks as enjoying a special competitive advantage vis-à-vis other financial institutions that stems from their superior ability to overcome informational obstacles common to the process of financial intermediation.[3] In particular, lenders frequently encounter difficulties in evaluating projects proposed by borrowers and in monitoring the activities of borrowers during the life of a loan. Economists often identify those informational problems by the short-hand expression "asymmetric information," which refers to the informational problems arising from the fact that borrowers almost always possess more information about their businesses than do creditors.

Banks, it is argued, have a lending advantage because of their superior ability to manage informational problems by monitoring borrowers and controlling agency costs through the use of restrictive covenants in lending contracts.[4] In part, that advantage is thought to stem from their ability to exploit information produced as a byproduct of other services they provide. Specifically, in providing liquidity services (or checkable deposits) to borrowers, banks may be in a position to observe the cash flows of their borrowers and thus have a monitoring advantage (Black 1975; Fama 1985; Lewis 1991). That monitoring advantage is probably greatest with respect to small business borrowers, where problems of asymmetric information are particularly severe and where banks commonly provide those firms with unsecured credit.

To the extent that banks do possess a lending advantage, that advantage has undoubtedly diminished in recent years. First, as we have seen, banks have substantially reduced their lending to businesses in favor of increased consumer and mortgage lending, which suggests that they do not have a significant competitive advantage in making information-intensive business loans. As recently as 1986, banks made more business loans than any other kind of loan. By 1994, however, their combined mortgage and consumer loans were more than two-and-a-half times their business (or commercial and industrial) loans.[5] (See table 4-1.) Banks have apparently shifted away from making information-intensive loans and toward making loans that require less extensive (and less costly) evaluation and monitoring—loans that can be standardized, packaged, and sold in secondary markets.

Second, banks have drastically reduced their reliance on checkable deposits, which suggests that those deposits are not particularly valuable to them. Such deposits, once the major source of funds for banks, currently account for less than 18 percent of bank funds. (See table 4-2 and figure 3-3.)

TABLE 4-1
Selected Data for Commercial Banks, 1980–1994

	1980	1981	1982	1983	1984	1985	1986	1987	1988	1989	1990	1991	1992	1993	1994
Number of institutions	14,435	14,415	14,451	14,467	14,472	14,417	14,188	13,703	13,137	12,709	12,343	11,921	11,462	10,958	10,450
Total assets ($ billions)	1,856	2,029	2,194	2,342	2,509	2,731	2,941	2,999	3,131	3,299	3,389	3,431	3,506	3,706	4,011
Equity capital ($ billions)	108	118	129	140	165	169	182	181	197	205	219	232	263	297	312
Net after-tax income ($ millions)	13,974	14,737	14,844	14,932	15,499	17,977	17,412	12,806	24,812	15,575	15,991	17,936	31,987	43,069	44,680
Net operating income ($ millions)	14,443	15,542	15,547	14,867	15,408	16,536	13,905	11,439	23,825	14,605	14,975	14,881	28,634	38,782	45,040
Taxes ($ millions)	4,657	3,873	2,980	4,017	4,721	5,643	5,304	5,424	9,991	9,540	7,704	8,265	14,481	19,838	22,426
Real estate loans to total assets (%)	14.5	14.4	14	14.4	15.4	16.1	14.5	20	21.6	23.1	24.5	24.8	24.8	24.9	24.9
Commercial and industrial loans to total assets (%)	21.1	22.4	23	22.4	22.5	21.2	20.4	19.7	19.2	18.7	18.1	16.3	15.3	14.5	14.7
Agricultural production loans to total assets (%)	1.7	1.7	1.7	1.7	1.6	1.3	1.1	1	1	0.9	1	1	1	1	1
Loans to individuals to total assets (%)	10.1	9.5	9.1	9.6	10.6	11.3	11.4	11.7	12.1	12.2	11.9	11.4	11	11.3	12.1
Number of problem banks	NA	NA	NA	NA	NA	1,098	1,457	1,559	1,394	1,092	1,012	1,016	787	426	247
Assets of problem banks ($ billions)	NA	NA	NA	NA	NA	NA	NA	329	305	188	342	528	408	242	33
Resolutions, commercial and savings banks Number	11	10	42	48	80	120	145	203	221	207	168	127	122	41	13
Total assets ($ millions)	8,189	4,859	11,632	7,027	36,909	8,741	7,643	9,234	52,620	29,396	15,705	63,198	45,447	3,524	1,392
Estimated present value cost $ millions	31	776	1,148	1,419	1,497	1,099	1,725	2,021	6,872	6,123	2,813	6,269	3,960	584	139

Sources: *Statistics on Banking* and *Quarterly Banking Profile* (Washington, D.C.: Federal Deposit Insurance Corporation, various years); James R. Barth and R. Dan Brumbaugh, Jr., "The Changing World of Banking: Setting the Regulatory Agenda," unpublished manuscript, 1993; Federal Reserve Board, Flow of Funds Accounts.

TABLE 4-2
Commercial Banks' Balance Sheet, 1950–1994

	1950	1960	1970	1980	1981	1982	1983	1984	1985	1986	1987	1988	1989	1990	1991	1992	1993	1994
Total financial assets ($ billions)	150	229	517	1,482	1,618	1,731	1,887	2,127	2,376	2,620	2,774	2,952	3,232	3,339	3,443	3,657	3,896	4,162
U.S. government securities (%)	43	28	15	12	11	12	14	12	11	12	12	12	12	14	16	18	19	17
Tax-exempt securities (%)	6	8	14	10	10	9	9	8	10	8	6	5	4	4	3	3	2	2
Corporate and foreign bonds (%)	2	1	1	1	1	1	1	1	1	0	3	3	3	3	3	3	2	2
Mortgage loans (%)	9	13	14	18	18	17	18	18	18	19	21	23	24	25	26	25	24	24
Consumer credit loans (%)	6	12	13	12	11	11	12	12	12	12	12	13	12	12	11	10	10	11
Bank loans (%)	17	26	30	31	32	31	30	29	28	28	26	26	25	24	23	21	20	20
Open market paper (%)	0	0	1	1	1	1	1	1	0	0	0	0	0	0	0	0	0	0
Other (%)	16	14	13	16	17	18	18	19	19	19	18	18	20	18	18	20	21	22

Total liabilities ($ billions)	139	211	485	1,411	1,561	1,699	1,854	2,046	2,279	2,516	2,689	2,890	3,150	3,251	3,363	3,527	3,739	4,028
Private domestic checkable deposits (%)	66	56	36	22	21	20	19	19	21	19	18	16	16	17	19	19	18	
Small time and savings deposits (%)	23	30	37	34	34	36	40	40	39	38	38	40	41	39	37	34		
Large time deposits (%)	3	5	11	19	19	21	15	16	13	14	14	13	12	9	8	8		
Federal funds and security RPs (%)	0	0	1	8	8	8	8	8	8	8	9	8	7	8	8	10		
Other (%)	8	10	15	16	16	16	18	19	22	22	23	23	23	25	27	30		

Note: Commercial banks include U.S.-chartered commercial banks, foreign banking offices in the United States, bank holding companies, and banks in U.S.-affiliated areas.

Sources: Flow of Funds Accounts, Federal Reserve Board; James R. Barth and R. Dan Brumbaugh, Jr., "The Changing World of Banking: Setting the Regulatory Agenda," unpublished manuscript, 1993.

Third, finance companies have sharply increased their role as providers of credit to the business sector, despite not providing any checking (or other deposit) services to borrowers. At year-end 1994, finance company loans to businesses totaled more than 40 percent of banks' commercial and industrial loans. (See table 3-6.) In addition, business borrowers have increased their reliance on finance companies; in 1994 they obtained almost 29 percent of their credit from finance companies. (See table 4-3.) Although finance companies tend to make loans that are secured by accounts receivable, inventory, equipment, and other property—so-called asset-based loans, while banks prefer to make unsecured loans based on a firm's cash flow projections (which generally means dealing with more creditworthy borrowers), it is not clear which of those is more information-intensive. A *Wall Street Journal* article states that asset-based loans require a "nuts-and-bolts knowledge of . . . industries" and "constant monitoring" (Scism 1993). Thus, the recent inroads in business lending made by finance companies suggest that banks may be losing whatever information advantage they once had.

Fourth, foreign banks have become aggressive lenders to U.S. businesses, even though they often do not provide liquidity services to borrowers. Lending by foreign banks to U.S. businesses (both onshore and offshore) as a percentage of total commercial and industrial loans by U.S. banks rose from about 18 percent in 1983 to over 35 percent in 1992. (See figure 3-11.)

Finally, academic research on the question of bank uniqueness, while mixed, generally confirms that banks have lost much of the comparative advantage they once had (James 1987; Osborne and Zaher 1992). Beckette and Morris (1992), after examining bank loan growth in two periods, 1959 to 1976 and 1977 to 1991, conclude that in recent years bank loans have lost much of the "specialness" that distinguished them in the past. Hook and Opler (1993) look at the characteristics of firms that borrow from banks and find little support for the "view that banks provide loans to firms where problems of monitoring and verification . . . are greatest."[6]

Thus, to the extent that banks once had significant informational advantages that gave them a competitive advantage, those advantages have shrunk to seeming insignificance. Although banks are still the only joint providers of liquidity services and nonmarketable (or opaque) business loans, there is no compelling reason to believe that this unique joint-production technology gives them a competitive advantage. The separa-

TABLE 4-3
Nonfinancial Company Borrowing, 1970–1994
(percentage of net funds borrowed)

Type of Instrument	1970	1980	1983	1984	1985	1986	1987	1988	1989	1990	1991[a]	1992	1993	1994
Bank loans														
U.S. banks	16.8	48.7	27.7	27.6	21.5	23.5	5.5	17.2	17.3	-4.0		-41.6	-9.7	38.8
Foreign banks	0.0	2.2	7.8	12.4	5.1	9.2	2.9	11.1	13.7	43.8		17.6	-55.3	2.3
Commercial paper	6.2	6.9	-1.0	11.0	8.6	-4.0	1.0	5.3	11.1	8.7		21.0	24.3	17.8
Finance company loans	0.6	3.7	12.8	9.9	9.9	6.4	17.8	11.3	10.9	16.8		7.1	-12.9	28.7
Asset-backed securities issuers	0.0	0.0	0.0	0.0	0.0	0.0	0.0	0.0	0.3	2.7		5.6	18.7	1.3
Bonds and notes[b]	69.4	66.6	43.7	34.7	62.5	50.3	47.3	46.0	37.9	42.0		165.0	182.3	17.1
Mortgages	3.1	-36.2	1.0	2.4	-4.7	14.1	22.8	9.6	7.1	-3.4		-67.2	-40.0	-4.9
Bankers acceptances and U.S. government loans	3.9	8.1	8.0	2.0	-2.8	0.6	2.7	-0.4	1.5	-6.6		-7.3	-7.5	-1.3
Total	100.0	100.0	100.0	100.0	100.0	100.0	100.0	100.0	100.0	100.0	100.0	100.0	100.0	100.0
Memorandum item														
Total funds raised in credit markets (in billions of U.S. dollars)	18.9	28.5	81.0	197.9	169.2	233.0	164.8	224.5	192.1	111.3	-9.6	40.9	41.2	119.9

a. A net reduction in total debt occurred in 1991; hence, new funds raised are zero.
b. Includes bonds and notes issued abroad by U.S. corporations and tax-exempt bonds issued for the benefits of nonfinancial corporations.
Source: Board of Governors of the Federal Reserve System, Flow of Funds Accounts (Statistical Release Z.7), table F.104 (nonfarm nonfinancial corporate businesses).

ble production of liquidity services and nonmarketable business loans by different financial entities (such as MMMFs and finance companies) does not appear to be inferior to the joint production of those services.[7] Further, to the extent that banks still tend to specialize in making some kinds of loans while nonbank competitors specialize in other types of loans, such specialization may be more an artifact of the current regulatory structure than a manifestation of a natural advantage that banks enjoy.

The decline in the importance of traditional banking may simply be the logical consequence of an evolving financial technology that is rapidly eroding the uniqueness of banks. If so, in the future we can expect to see many different nonbank financial intermediaries' providing the products and services traditionally provided by banks. To survive, banks will have to transform themselves into more efficient and diversified firms.

Public Policy Concerns

Irrespective of the reasons for the decline of traditional banking, the changing role of banks together with the concomitant growth of nonbank financial intermediaries raises important policy issues related to the stability of both financial markets and the economy. First, because banks have come under increased competitive pressure from nonbank competitors and from financial innovation generally, there is a concern that they will take greater risks to maintain earnings and market share. That concern is reinforced by the recognition that banks have had an incentive to take excessive risk because of federal deposit insurance and de facto "too-big-to-fail" policies, which eliminate incentives for depositors to monitor banks and to penalize them for taking excessive risk. As the thrift debacle clearly demonstrated, the combination of deposit insurance, regulatory laxity, and increased competitive pressures can result in insured institutions' engaging in excessive risk-taking, with substantial costs to taxpayers. That fear is compounded by a concern that bank regulation is not so effective as it once was. Rapid changes in telecommunications and electronic technology have spawned a steady flow of innovations that have made it increasingly difficult to monitor banks' activities and to segregate regulated from unregulated activities.

Second, technological change and out-of-date regulation have combined to create an unhealthy competitive imbalance that threatens to destabilize financial markets. Unnecessary restrictions have put banks at a competitive disadvantage vis-à-vis both their nonbank competitors and foreign banks and have restricted their ability to operate more efficiently and more safely by diversifying their activities. Such restrictions also have unnecessarily curbed competition. An example is the Glass-Steagall Act of 1933, which prohibits banks from underwriting, holding, or dealing in corporate securities. Those restrictions put banks at a competitive disadvantage vis-à-vis both securities firms and foreign banks, which are permitted to provide a wide array of securities services. It is now widely accepted that Glass-Steagall restrictions are not necessary to maintain bank soundness or financial stability (Benston 1990; Kroszner and Rajan 1994). Thus, there is an urgent need to revisit the issue of what should be the permissible activities of insured banks.

Third, there is a concern that structural changes have made the financial system more vulnerable to destabilizing runs. In particular, the shift of household assets from insured bank deposits to nonbank institutions like mutual funds represents a de facto reduction in insurance coverage for households. Since the New Deal, federal deposit insurance has been a critical component of the safety net underpinning the financial system. Together with the Federal Reserve's lender-of-last-resort capability, federal deposit insurance was instituted to prevent bank runs and to maintain financial stability. With the shift of households' assets to uninsured institutions like mutual funds, there is a renewed fear that the federal safety net will ultimately be undermined so that financial markets once again will be vulnerable to ruinous runs (Koretz 1994; Kuhn 1993; Wayne 1993). That concern appears to center on the vulnerability of mutual funds to banklike runs. To prevent that from occurring, proposals have been made to extend banklike prudential regulation to mutual funds (D'Arista and Schlesinger 1993).

Fourth, there is a concern that the development and growth of new instruments and markets has outpaced regulation and increased the likelihood of a systemic breakdown. A key focus of that concern is the explosive growth of derivatives markets (futures, forwards, options, and swaps), and the role of banks as dealers in off-exchange (or OTC) derivatives markets. There is a fear that a default by a major bank derivatives dealer could trigger a domino effect ending in a widespread financial collapse.

Finally, the transformation of financial markets has resulted in a proliferation of substitutes for traditional bank liabilities (such as MMMF shares), which some fear has undercut the effectiveness of monetary policy. In particular, financial innovations have blurred the definition of *money* and may be destabilizing the empirical relationships that have existed in the past between the money supply and economic activity. As a consequence, the Federal Reserve may no longer be able to control the supply of money or to achieve its macroeconomic policy objectives.

The challenge to both legislators and regulators is to determine which of those fears represent valid concerns and to determine how to restructure regulation without undermining either financial soundness or the efficiency and innovativeness of financial institutions and markets. The chapters that follow examine those concerns in greater depth. Chapter 8 examines alternative proposals for reshaping regulation to achieve greater efficiency and financial stability.

+ 5 +

Mutual Funds and Financial Stability

In the thirteen-year period from 1982 through 1994, mutual funds captured an impressive 35.8 percent of the net growth of households' liquid financial assets. (See table 3-4.) If just the last five years are taken, a staggering 49.7 percent of the net growth of households' liquid financial assets has found its way into mutual funds. Households have increasingly turned away from bank deposits in favor of holding mutual fund shares. From 1982 to 1994 their holdings of small time and savings deposits as a percentage of their total liquid financial assets declined from 36.9 percent to 20.6 percent, while their mutual fund holdings increased from 7 percent to 14.5 percent. (See table 3-3.)

Mutual funds also have become major suppliers of transactions services. MMMFs, most of which grant check-writing privileges, have grown to almost 70 percent of households' checking deposits in banks and thrifts.[1] (See figure 5-1.) By providing households with low-risk, highly liquid assets, which pay higher returns than competing bank deposits, MMMFs have succeeded in attracting households' transactions balances, despite the absence of government-backed deposit insurance.

The massive shift of liquid household financial assets from banks and other depository institutions to mutual funds has raised a concern about whether that development may be increasing the fragility

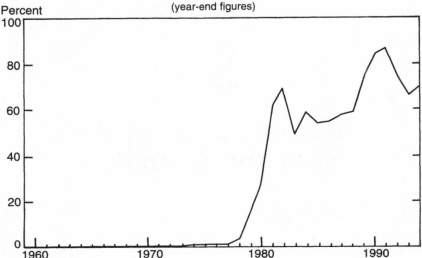

FIGURE 5-1
Ratio of Money Market Mutual Funds to Banks' Checkable Deposits,
1959–1994
(year-end figures)

of the financial system. In particular, if the trend were to continue, and it is difficult to see why it will not, in a short time the majority of transactions balances may be held in MMMFs and other mutual funds. Unlike bank deposits, mutual funds are not insured or backed by a government guarantee. Thus, in the future the bulk of transactions balances may be held in uninsured accounts, which would result in the de facto elimination of (or at least a considerable reduction in) deposit insurance coverage of households' liquid balances. Deposit insurance has long been considered an essential facet of a sound and stable financial system. Thus, the increasing reliance of households on mutual funds as a repository for their liquid assets may arguably make the financial system more vulnerable to "panics" precipitated by banklike runs on mutual funds (Antilla 1993; Eaton 1994; Kaufman 1994; Hale 1994).

A number of recent mutual fund "bailouts" have reinforced those fears. In the past two years more than a dozen MMMFs have experienced portfolio losses of more than $600 million, mostly as a result of using highly leveraged derivatives that lost money when interest rates rose sharply (Calian and Jasen 1994; Calian 1994). With one exception, the Denver-based Community Bankers U.S. Government Money Market Fund, fund managers have kept investors from losing money by making up the losses.[2] Examples of mutual fund bailouts are PaineWebber Group's injection of $268 million to cover derivatives-based losses in some of its Short-Term U.S. Government Income funds; Barnett Bank's purchase of depreciated derivatives from its Emerald Prime Fund at a premium of $100 million; and BankAmerica's $68 million cash infusion into its Pacific Horizon Government and Pacific Horizon Prime Money Market funds. Those bailouts were aimed at reassuring investors of the fundamental safety and liquidity of their mutual fund investments.[3] Concerned observers, however, worry that in the absence of such bailouts a loss of confidence in mutual funds (particularly MMMFs) could precipitate a run on mutual funds. They point to the lack of prudential safeguards of the kind that have been successful in providing stability in the banking industry, such as deposit insurance and risk-based capital requirements, and argue that greater regulation of mutual funds is needed (D'Arista and Schlesinger 1993).[4] Edward J. Markey, the former chairman of the House committee overseeing securities regulation, warned that recent mutual fund losses may only be "the canary in the mine" (Wayne 1994).

Still another concern stemming from the rapid growth of households' holdings of mutual fund shares is the fear that a sharp decline in stock or bond markets may spook fund investors into stampeding out of mutual funds and result in a "Mutual Fund Death Spiral" (Eaton 1994; Antilla 1993). Specifically, there is a fear that mutual fund shareholder redemptions will force fund managers to sell stocks or bonds in large quantity, which will drive prices down and cause more redemptions, which in turn will drive prices down still further and end in a "death spiral" for both the stock and bond markets as well as for mutual funds. That scenario is made even more plausible when households are viewed as unsophisticated investors, easily stampeded by a "mob psychology" into selling in downmarkets and buying in upmarkets. Presumably, if households did not have the option to hold mutual fund shares, they either would not hold stocks and bonds at all or would be subject to higher transactions costs that would discourage them from selling in response to changes in market prices or to mob psychology.

The purpose of this chapter is to evaluate the potential for shareholder runs on mutual funds to destabilize financial markets. The possibility of systemic instability caused by shareholder runs on mutual funds has been cited as a reason for expanding bank-type prudential regulation (such as risk-based capital requirements) to mutual funds. For example, D'Arista and Schlesinger (1993, 14–15) argue that the shift of financial activity from banks to MMMFs and finance companies has increased the fragility of the financial system:

> Given its reliance on the commercial paper market as a source and use of funds, the parallel banking system [by which they mean MMMFs in combination with finance companies] is not inherently stable. Each component of the system shares the banking industry's susceptibility to runs. A failure in any one segment could spread rapidly to other financial and nonfinancial companies that issue or hold commercial paper. The absence of soundness standards and supervision [of MMMFs and finance companies] increases the potential for surprise events that could trigger a breakdown.

They argue that extending bank-type prudential regulations to mutual funds would prevent mutual fund losses from precipitating a run and spilling over into other segments of the financial system.

It is important, therefore, that we determine whether the structure and characteristics of mutual funds make them susceptible to systemic collapse, because of either portfolio losses or widespread shareholder redemptions.

Fear of a Mutual-Fund-Induced Financial Collapse

Concern that the increased role of mutual funds in the financial system has increased systemic risk stems largely from two "doomsday" hypotheticals: that losses incurred by MMMFs will force MMMFs to "break the buck" and thus precipitate a shareholder run on MMMFs, or that a fall in stock or bond prices will cause widespread redemptions of mutual fund shares and thus reinforce and aggravate the fall in stock or bond prices, with the end result being a downward price spiral and a market panic.[5] Either eventuality, it is feared, could cause severe credit disruptions that adversely affect the economy—possibly resulting in a depression or a severe recession. The sections that follow examine both of those "doomsday" scenarios.

Runs on Money Market Mutual Funds Induced by Commercial Paper Defaults. Fear that losses in MMMF portfolios could set off a run by MMMF shareholders centers on the vulnerability of MMMFs to defaults by large commercial paper issuers. Examples of large commercial paper defaults are those by Penn Central in 1970

FIGURE 5-2
Composition of Money Market Mutual Fund Assets, January 1995

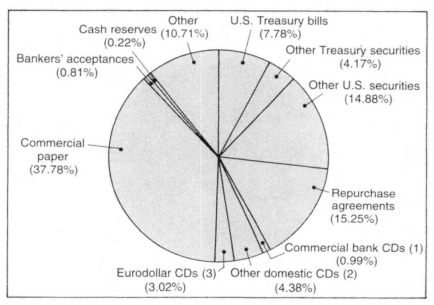

and by Olympia and York Development in 1992. Because MMMFs hold substantial amounts of commercial paper (see figure 5-2 and table 5-1), such defaults could arguably impose substantial losses on some MMMFs that would cause them to have to break par value. That in turn could cause MMMF shareholders in general to fear that additional commercial paper defaults might result in other MMMFs' suffering losses. To avoid future losses, therefore, large numbers of MMMF shareholders might decide to redeem their shares and thus would force MMMFs into a general liquidation of assets, including their commercial paper holdings, that would result in a sharp sell-off and a drying up of liquidity in the commercial paper market. In 1994 MMMFs held almost 45 percent of the total outstanding commercial paper. (See table 5-2.) If a sell-off happened, commercial paper issuers could find it difficult to refinance (or "roll over") their paper. Finally, a general liquidation of assets by MMMFs might cause a substantial decline in the values of secondary market assets generally that would result in additional losses for MMMF shareholders.

That doomsday scenario emphasizes the connection between MMMFs, which are major providers of credit to the commercial

TABLE 5-1
Money Market Funds' Balance Sheet, 1980–1994

	1980	1981	1982	1983	1984	1985	1986	1987	1988	1989	1990	1991	1992	1993	1994
Total financial assets ($ billions)	76	486	249	179	234	244	292	316	338	428	498	540	544	559	605
Time deposits (%)	27.7	23.3	18.8	13.2	9.6	7.0	6.5	10.5	9.9	9.6	6.5	6.1	5.2	4.3	3.3
Security repurchase agreements (%)	7.3	7.8	7.4	7.2	9.8	10.7	11.0	12.4	12.3	12.8	11.8	12.6	12.3	12.1	11.5
Foreign deposits (%)	8.9	10.1	10.9	12.2	9.1	7.8	7.6	6.8	8.8	6.2	5.4	4.0	3.8	1.8	2.6
U.S. government securities (%)	10.7	17.1	24.9	20.2	18.2	17.5	14.8	13.1	8.8	8.4	16.5	22.4	24.8	26.5	24.2
Tax-exempt securities (%)	2.5	2.3	6.0	9.4	10.2	14.9	21.8	19.4	19.4	16.2	16.8	16.7	17.4	18.5	18.3
Open market paper (%)	41.4	37.8	31.6	36.9	42.0	40.6	36.0	35.2	38.2	43.6	41.5	35.6	32.1	29.9	31.8
Other (%)	1.4	1.6	0.8	0.8	1.3	1.5	2.2	2.5	2.5	3.2	1.5	2.6	4.4	6.9	8.3
Total shares outstanding ($ billions)	76	186	219	179	234	244	292	316	338	428	498	540	544	559	605

Source: Flow of Funds Accounts, Federal Reserve Board.

TABLE 5-2
Mutual Fund Holdings as a Percentage of Total Securities Outstanding

	12/31/80	12/31/93	12/31/94
U.S. Treasuries	0.7	8.7	6.7
Mortgage-backed securities	NA	7.1	5.8
Corporate bonds	1.7	7.8	7.2
Corporate equities	2.8	10.8	12.2
Tax-exempt securities	1.7	26.4	26.9
Commercial paper	29.1	39.3	44.7

Sources: Flow of Funds Accounts, Federal Reserve Board; Federal Reserve Bank; Department of Housing and Urban Development; Fannie Mae; Freddie Mac; Ginnie Mae; Inside Mortgage Securities; and Investment Company Institute.

paper market, and the potential fragility of the commercial paper market. Subsequent to the Penn Central default in 1970, and before 1989, defaults in the commercial paper market were rare. In the past few years, however, such defaults have risen dramatically. From 1989 to 1992, twenty-six issuers defaulted on $2.43 billion of rated and unrated commercial paper in publicly offered markets in the United States and Europe (Fons, Carty, and Girault 1993). Of those defaults, nine occurred in U.S. markets and resulted in losses of $960.5 million. But only one issuer with a Prime-1 rating—the highest rating category—has defaulted, and only two defaults in the U.S. market involved paper rated Prime-2 or higher.[6] Nevertheless, in 1992 the largest commercial paper default ever occurred: on May 14, 1992, Olympia and York Development, Ltd., defaulting on $614 million of its commercial paper, filed for bankruptcy protection in the United States and in Canada.

The potential vulnerability of MMMFs to commercial paper defaults became apparent in 1989 and 1990 when defaults by Integrated Resources Inc. and Mortgage & Realty Trust (totaling $442.9 million) resulted in significant losses to two MMMFs: the Value Line Cash and the Liquid Green Trust funds. Neither of the defaulting issuers had been given a commercial paper rating by Moody's (although Integrated Resources' long-term debt carried a speculative-grade rating). Despite suffering losses, neither of the affected MMMFs broke "par value." They avoided having to reduce their share prices to below $1.00 only because the funds' advisors injected funds by purchasing the defaulted paper at par value (rather than at market value). Thus, the owners of the advisory firms, rather than the shareholders of the MMMFs, absorbed the losses incurred by the mutual funds as a result of the commercial paper defaults.[7]

Those defaults, nevertheless, galvanized the Securities and Exchange Comission into action. It amended Rule 2a-7 to tighten the diversification and asset-quality requirements governing MMMFs (*Federal Register*, February 27, 1991, 8113–30).[8] MMMFs now are not permitted to hold the commercial paper of any *single* issuer in an amount greater than 5 percent of their total fund assets, regardless of the credit rating of the issuer. In addition, MMMFs' total holdings of securities with less than the highest credit rating cannot exceed 5 percent of fund assets (*Federal Register*, February 27, 1991, 8113–30), and their total holdings of the securities of any *one* issuer with less than the highest credit rating cannot exceed the lesser of $1 million or 1 percent of fund assets (*Federal Register*, February 27, 1991, 8113–30). Also, the maximum weighted-average maturity of a fund's assets cannot exceed ninety days (*Federal Register*, February 27, 1991, 8113–30). Further, a mutual fund can only use the term *money fund* in its name, prospectus, or advertisements if it satisfies the restrictions of Rule 2a-7.[9] Although those regulatory actions have clearly increased the safety and liquidity of MMMFs, the vulnerability of MMMFs to commercial paper defaults remains an issue.[10]

Market Panics Induced by Redemptions in Stock and Bond Funds. The second fear is that a price break in either the stock or bond market might induce widespread mutual fund redemptions and thus force mutual funds to become massive sellers of equity or bonds. That could precipitate a widespread sell-off in stock and bond markets, with values spiraling downward as panic selling took over.

Either of two presumptions appears to underlie that concern. The first is that holders of mutual fund shares will behave differently from direct holders of stocks and bonds in the event of a market break. In particular, mutual fund shareholders will act more quickly and in greater volume to liquidate their fund holdings than they would if they held stocks and bonds directly. In the absence of that difference in behavior, redemptions by fund holders would simply be a substitute for the selling by direct holders of stocks and bonds that could occur in a market downturn. Thus, for mutual fund redemptions to cause a more severe decline in the prices of stocks and bonds than would otherwise occur, it must be true that mutual fund shareholders would either sell in greater volume or at a faster pace than would direct holders of stocks and bonds.

The second presumption is that, in a general market downturn, mutual funds themselves (unprompted by redemptions) may become massive sellers of securities as part of their general trading strategy. As performance-driven institutional traders, mutual funds might behave differently in a downturn from households (or individual investors). It is well known that institutional investors trade more actively than do individual investors. Mutual funds, therefore, may be more prone to selling early in a downturn in the hopes of being able to buy subsequently at lower prices. Such "positive-feedback" trading also may be reinforced by "herdlike" behavior on the part of mutual funds (Cutler, Poterba, and Summers 1990; Lakonishok, Shleifer, and Vishny 1992). Because no mutual fund can risk being classified as a poor performer, they may all become sellers so that they cannot be distinguished from the herd. As a result, mutual funds as a whole may oversell the market compared with what would have occurred had individual investors been the holders of the stocks or bonds.

I think it is fair to say, however, that concern about systemic instability induced by mutual funds has focused more on the potentially destabilizing effects of shareholders' redemptions (or "runs") than on destabilizing trading by mutual funds. Evidence on the trading behavior of pension funds, for example, suggests that "herdlike, positive-feedback" trading is not common among institutional investors (Lakonishok, Shleifer, and Vishny 1992). Thus, I focus my discussion on the concern that massive redemptions by mutual fund shareholders might precipitate a market collapse.

Those concerns raise the following fundamental issues:

- How likely are shareholder runs on mutual funds? In particular, are defaults by commercial paper issuers likely to trigger a shareholder run on MMMFs similar to a depositor run on banks? Or will a stock or bond market decline trigger widespread shareholder redemptions and massive selling by mutual funds?
- Assuming that a shareholder run on mutual funds were to occur, would the result be a collapse of market liquidity and a sharp decline in asset prices?
- Does the current regulatory system provide an adequate safeguard against a financial crisis induced by runs on mutual funds?

Depositor Runs versus Shareholder Runs

A widely recognized rationale for the prudential safeguards imposed on banks is the vulnerability of banks to panicky depositor runs. Not surprisingly, those who propose extending bank-type prudential regulations (such as risk-based capital requirements) to mutual funds view them as being equally vulnerable to shareholder runs (D'Arista and Schlesinger 1993). This section reviews the basic arguments underlying the bank-run fear and then applies that analytical framework to mutual funds to determine their vulnerability to shareholder runs.

The Susceptibility of Banks to Runs. The banking industry possesses three characteristics that make banks more susceptible to runs than other financial intermediaries. First, banks finance their activities primarily by issuing large quantities of short-dated, demandable debt (deposits). Further, they are either obligated to, or their depositors expect them to, repay those debts at par value—at 100 percent on the dollar. The redemption value of a bank's obligations or liabilities is not tied directly to the value of a bank's assets. If its assets fall in value, the bank must still repay depositors 100 percent on the dollar. There is one circumstance when that will not generally be true: insolvency of the bank. When the value of a bank's assets becomes less than its liabilities (or its net worth becomes negative), depositors (in the absence of deposit insurance) will receive less than a hundred cents on the dollar. They may even get nothing. Thus, faced with the possibility of either getting nothing or having to suffer the delays and costs associated with an insolvency proceeding, depositors who have even the slightest reason to suspect that a bank's real net worth may be negative (or soon will be) can be expected to withdraw their funds from a bank as quickly as possible. It is virtually costless for them to do that, and to delay is to risk personal financial catastrophe. When in doubt, therefore, there is a strong incentive for bank depositors to run on their banks.

Second, a substantial portion of a bank's assets (such as its commercial and real estate loans) are opaque and are not traded in centralized markets. As a consequence, bank assets are often illiquid and difficult to value and cannot be sold quickly to meet depositor withdrawals without substantial loss. A depositor run that forces banks into substantial asset sales, therefore, can bankrupt the bank. That can happen even though the bank's assets may be sound, in the sense that there is a high probability that the bank's counterparties (for example, its borrowers) will repay both the interest and principal they owe in a timely fashion. The nontransparency of the assets, however, creates an information gap (or an "information asymmetry") between banks and the potential buyers of their assets that makes it difficult for buyers to ascertain the true value of the assets.

In particular, buyers in the secondary market do not have the same information that banks have about the creditworthiness of the banks' borrowers. Potential buyers also are likely to be wary about the information and evaluations provided to them by banks anxious to sell their loans. It is time-consuming and costly for buyers to acquire the same information that banks already have. Thus, to compensate for that information asymmetry, buyers can be expected to discount the assets heavily to adjust for the possibility of unanticipated losses. Further, in the event of a run, banks would typically have only a very short time to sell assets, which exacerbates the information gap between potential buyers and the bank. As a result, having to sell assets quickly in the secondary market can be expected to result in substantial losses for banks.[11]

Third, the nontransparency of bank portfolios can cause a shock to one segment of the banking system to spread quickly to the entire banking system. In particular, if a few banks were to suffer substantial losses or become visibly insolvent, depositors in general might panic because they have no way of distinguishing sound from unsound banks. Prudence, therefore, dictates that depositors withdraw their funds as quickly as possible from banks until they can reconfirm the soundness of their own banks.[12] That spillover effect is commonly known as the "contagion" effect.[13]

Much of bank regulation is directed at mitigating or controlling the risks that flow from those characteristics of the banking industry. For example, risk-based capital regulations and portfolio restrictions aim at curbing risk-taking by banks so that they will be able to meet depositor withdrawals without sustaining severe losses. In addition, an objective of deposit insurance is to eliminate the contagion effect by guaranteeing the value of deposits in all banks, thereby making irrelevant the information gap that exists between depositors and their banks and removing the incentive of depositors to run on banks. Finally, the Federal Reserve has been given lender-of-last-resort powers that can be used to aid banks experiencing temporary liquidity problems because of asset opaqueness.

Are Mutual Funds as Susceptible to Runs as Banks? While mutual funds have characteristics that are similar to banks, they differ in important ways. First, no mutual fund, including MMMFs, has a legal obligation to redeem its shares at par value, or at 100 percent of the price paid by shareholders. The value of mutual fund shares is tied directly to the value of the fund's assets, unlike deposits, which banks are obligated to redeem at par value. If a mutual fund experiences losses or gains in its portfolio, those losses or gains are passed through to shareholders, as either a reduction or an increase in the value of their shares. When shareholders redeem shares, they receive their proportionate share of the market value of the fund's total assets. Thus, although mutual funds, just as banks, fund their portfolios with demandable debt (actually equity), they are not obligated to redeem that debt at par value, as are banks. There is, therefore, no discontinuity or "flashpoint" as in banking—no point at which portfolio losses render mutual funds bankrupt or incapable of meeting redemption requests.

Indeed, as far as redemption values go, there is no difference between an investment in mutual fund shares and a direct investment in the same assets as those held by the mutual fund. An owner of a basket of corporate stocks is in virtually the same position as an owner of a mutual fund that holds the same basket of stocks. If the value of those stocks declines (or rises), the value of the mutual fund shares declines (or rises) in lock step. The same is true for investments in bonds or any other asset held by mutual funds.

Those general principles apply to MMMFs as well. Although MMMFs commonly have a stated objective of maintaining a stable net asset value, they are not obligated to redeem their shares at par value. Like other mutual funds, MMMFs have the right to redeem at less than par value. The disclosures that MMMFs are required to make under SEC regulations specifically put shareholders on notice that repayment at par value is not unconditional.[14]

The second important difference between mutual funds and banks is that the assets held by mutual funds are generally more transparent than those held by banks. As a consequence, most assets held by mutual funds are traded in active secondary markets, and market values for those assets are easily attainable.[15] Greater asset transparency, therefore, substantially mitigates the information asymmetry that lies at the heart of banks' vulnerability to runs.

In contrast to bank regulation, a primary goal of SEC regulation is to enhance asset transparency. Mutual funds are allowed to hold only assets that are specifically disclosed and permitted by their prospectuses. They also must mark to market their portfolios daily and provide semiannual reports to shareholders describing their portfolios and the market values of their assets.[16] Thus, compared with the depositors of a bank, mutual fund shareholders have more information about the composition of the portfolios held by their mutual funds and about the values of their assets and are therefore in a better position to evaluate the credit and interest rate risk exposures of the funds. Little is disclosed to depositors about the nature of the assets held by banks and about their market values, so it is difficult for depositors to evaluate the credit and interest rate risks to which banks are exposed. For example, depositors and other bank creditors know little about the characteristics of the bank's borrowers, about the maturity composition of the bank's portfolio, and about its trading activities.[17]

Third, mutual fund assets are generally more liquid than bank assets. Unlike banks, mutual funds do not possess special (or nonmarket) information about the assets they hold, or about the companies that have issued the stocks, bonds, mortgages, commercial paper, and other assets that they hold. Fund managers make their investment decisions on the basis of publicly available information. For example, firms that issue commercial paper held by MMMFs are publicly traded firms, for which a considerable amount of easily obtainable information is publicly available. The obligations of those firms also are "rated" by professional rating companies on the basis of public information (and perhaps additional information known to the rating companies). Thus, there is less of an information gap between mutual fund managers and the potential buyers of mutual fund assets in secondary markets, so that the "lemons discount" for those assets should be considerably less than for bank assets.

Thus, the incentive for shareholders to run on mutual funds is much less than it is for depositors to run on banks. First, the insolvency threat that exists in banking, and which can cause depositors to run on banks to avoid insolvency losses, does not exist for mutual funds because of the absence of an obligation to redeem shares at par value. Second, the informational asymmetry that can cause failures by unsound banks to spread to sound banks is considerably less for mutual funds because of the greater transparency of assets held by mutual funds. Lastly, because mutual funds do not possess unique or specialized information about the assets they hold, their shareholders should not incur a substantial "lemons discount" in the event that a mutual fund finds it necessary to sell assets in secondary markets.

Will Commercial Paper Defaults Cause a Run on MMMFs?

Despite the important differences that exist between mutual funds and banks, some observers continue to believe that MMMFs may still be vulnerable to shareholder runs precipitated by defaults in the commercial paper market and that such runs could result in severe credit disruptions and, in particular, a liquidity crisis in the commercial paper market. They argue that a default by a major commercial paper issuer (such as a Penn Central) could generate widespread concern among MMMF shareholders that other firms will also default on their commercial paper obligations and thus might precipitate massive shareholder redemptions to avoid potential future losses.

A commercial-paper-induced run seems unlikely. First, there is no reason to believe that the failure of one or even a few commercial paper issuers will cause or be coincident with the failure of other issuers. Why should a default by Ford Motor Company on its paper cause, or be coincident with, a default by General Electric or IBM, or even another automotive company for that matter? While systemic economic impacts may affect specific segments of the economy (such as commercial real estate), individual firms also differ in what assets they hold and how they are managed. Second, MMMFs hold diversified portfolios of highly rated commercial paper, as well as other assets. A default by a few commercial paper issuers, therefore, will not significantly reduce the value of a typical MMMF's portfolio. Finally, because almost all firms issuing commercial paper have the backing of a bank guarantee or a line of credit, a liquidity problem in the commercial paper market should not precipitate widespread commercial paper defaults. Firms that are financially sound can draw on bank credit lines to meet their commercial paper obligations. Thus, it seems unlikely that commercial paper defaults will escalate to a run on MMMFs.

A recent study of the commercial paper market by Gorton and Pennacchi (1992b) supports that view. They examine the effect of defaults in the commercial paper market (reported by Moody's from 1972 through 1990) on both the secondary market for commercial paper and the behavior of MMMF shareholders. If defaults by some commercial paper issuers increased the likelihood of default by other commercial paper issuers, we would expect to see a "flight to quality": investors' selling commercial paper and purchasing Treasury bills. Such selling would result in an increase in the spread between the commercial paper and the Treasury bill yields—a reflection of the higher risk (default) premium assigned to commercial paper. Gordon and Pennacchi (1992b) examine that measure of contagion and find that "individual commercial paper defaults have little influence on the yields paid by other commercial paper issuers." They also conclude that "commercial paper investors are able to discriminate between the risks of different issuers, and that the contagion effects from a default are not prevalent."[18] In addition, they find no evidence that MMMF shareholders react to commercial paper defaults by redeeming their shares in MMMFs (Gorton and Pennacchi 1992b).

Concern about the vulnerability of MMMFs to commercial paper defaults probably stems from experience with the Penn Central default in the 1970s. Significant changes have taken place in the commercial paper market since that time, however. First, rating agencies now make more careful evaluations and provide finer distinctions in their ratings of commercial paper issues, so that investors are better informed. Second, almost all commercial paper issuers are backed either by loan commitments or credit guarantees. Loan commitments promise to assist firms in meeting their commercial paper obligations during a general liquidity crisis as long as the borrower remains creditworthy (Calomiris 1989). After evaluating the Penn Central crisis and the changes that have been made in the commercial paper market since that time, Calomiris (1994) concluded that "the use of backup lines of bank credit, backed by access to the discount window, has virtually eliminated risk of another Penn Central crisis in the commercial paper market."

In addition, a number of new SEC regulations have been directed at preventing MMMFs from taking excessive risk. In particular, MMMFs are required to hold a diversified portfolio of highly liquid assets, are permitted to hold only very short maturity paper (no longer than one year), and must have portfolios consisting primarily of highly rated debt instruments—commercial paper, bankers' acceptances, bank certificates of deposits, repurchase agreements, Treasury bills, and so forth (SEC Rule 2a-7).[19] SEC regulations (Rule 2a-7) also prohibit an MMMF from holding commercial paper rated lower than P-2 and require that at least 95 percent of its portfolio be in securities with the highest credit rating. In addition, MMMFs cannot hold securities of a single issuer in excess of 5 percent of the fund's assets and cannot hold the securities of any one issuer having less than the highest credit rating in an amount that exceeds either $1 million or 1 percent of the fund's assets.[20] Thus, holding only highly rated paper with a maximum weighted-average maturity of less than ninety days, MMMF assets are not subject to either significant market risk or credit risk.[21]

Therefore, even a large commercial paper default should not impose destabilizing losses on MMMFs or precipitate a run on MMMFs. The 1992 default by Olympia and York Development supports that conclusion: although the largest commercial paper default ever, it did not trigger a systemic problem for mutual funds.

Will Mutual Fund Redemptions Destabilize Stock and Bond Markets?

Another concern about potential widespread redemptions by mutual fund shareholders is that they will cause a cascading sell-off in the stock or bond market that will result in plummeting asset values. Although stock and bond market sell-offs occur with some frequency, the issue is whether mutual fund redemptions could cause a more severe price break than would otherwise occur.

Mutual fund holdings (as well as other institutional holdings) of stocks and bonds have increased steadily during the past two decades (see table 3-13 and figure 3-5). But mutual funds still hold only about 12 percent of the total outstanding corporate equity. (See table 5-2.) Pension funds hold considerably more stock. (See table 3-13.) Mutual funds also hold only about 7 percent of the corporate bonds outstanding. The largest of the mutual fund holdings are in tax-exempt securities and commercial paper, where they hold, respectively, 26.9 percent and 44.7 percent of the total outstandings. (See table 5-2.)

We can obtain some idea of the potential effects of mutual fund redemptions by looking at past market sell-offs. In particular, mutual fund redemptions during the October 19, 1987, stock market collapse did not appear to be destabilizing. Of the $24 billion of stock transactions that took place on October 19 on the New York Stock Exchange, the American Stock Exchange, and the over-the-counter markets, net sales by mutual funds accounted for only 3.2 percent of those transactions. Also, while the $2.3 billion of mutual fund redemptions on October 19 were clearly substantial, those redemptions constituted only 2 percent of total equity mutual fund assets at the beginning of the day.

Further, to meet the $2.3 billion of redemptions, mutual funds had to sell only *$779 million* of stock.[22] Two-thirds of the redemptions were met by their selling $1.1 billion of (nonequity) liquid assets and by using the proceeds from the *sale* of $365 million of new fund shares on October 19. Thus, had individual owners of stock sold $2.3 billion from their own accounts (as opposed to indirectly through mutual funds), there would have been an additional $1.5 billion of stock sales on October 19. Mutual fund redemptions, therefore, appear to have had a dampening effect on the October 19 sell-off.[23]

It seems clear that investors also did not lose confidence in mutual funds as a whole in October 1987. Eighty percent of the equity mutual fund redemptions that occurred on October 19 were exchanges into other funds, primarily money market funds. Also, during the latter part of 1987, a substantial portion of the funds redeemed moved back into equity mutual funds, as fund sales consistently exceeded redemptions in the ensuing months. Thus, although the October 1987 stock market experience is just one episode, it suggests that mutual fund redemptions have not been a destabilizing factor.

Recent episodes of mutual fund redemptions triggered by actual or threatened shareholder losses also have not had systemic consequences. Although a sharp drop in bond prices caused outflows from domestic bond funds during 1994 and early 1995 that cumulated to 12 percent of average fund net assets at the beginning of 1994, the bond market continued to operate normally (Marcis, West, and Leonard-Chambers 1995). (See figure 5-3.) Those losses and accompanying redemptions were precipitated by Federal Reserve initiatives that raised interest rates in 1994. Nor did widespread derivatives-related losses at MMMFs during 1994 result in a shareholder run. From May to December in 1994, fund sponsors provided capital assistance to twenty-five taxable MMMFs without shareholders' losing confidence. Similarly, the bankruptcy of Orange County, California, on December 6, 1994, did not precipitate a general run on tax-exempt funds, although some shareholders redeemed their holdings in California tax-exempt MMMFs and bond funds. Finally, the sharp devaluation of the Mexican peso on December 20, 1994, resulted in substantial losses in Latin American and Emerging Market mutual funds (30.4 percent over the first quarter of 1995) without causing a panic among fund shareholders (Marcis, West, and Leonard-Chambers 1995). From the devaluation in December to April of 1995, when substantial fund inflows began again, outflows from Latin American equity funds

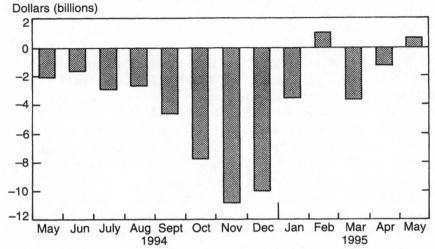

FIGURE 5-3
Bond Mutual Fund Net Redemptions, 1994–1995

Note: Net redemptions are mutual fund sales to new investors, less redemptions by departing shareholders, plus the net result of switches among funds within the same fund group. Reinvested dividends are not included.

cumulated to less than 2 percent of the funds' net assets at the time of the devaluation (Marcis, West, and Leonard-Chambers 1995).

Thus, mutual fund shareholders do not appear to be easily spooked by unanticipated economic reversals. Rather, they appear to behave as investors with long time horizons. Surveys of mutual fund shareholders indicate that the majority of shareholders have long-term investment goals, such as saving for retirement (Investment Company Institute 1994, 3).[24] A survey of shareholder redemption activity in 1991 indicates that the average shareholder redeeming shares had held those shares for about five years, and most of those closing accounts reinvested all of the proceeds in another mutual fund (Investment Company Institute 1993, 6, 8). Further, a survey taken in the spring of 1994 indicates that during the market break in stock and bond prices in March and April of 1994 only 10 percent of mutual fund shareholders either bought or sold shares in reaction to market developments.[25]

Finally, a number of regulatory safeguards and industry practices exist that should act to cushion the effects on asset prices of widespread mutual fund redemptions, should they occur. First, to ensure that mutual funds can meet redemptions in a timely manner, SEC regulations require that the funds hold portfolios that satisfy specific liquidity standards. A mutual fund may not invest more than 15 percent of its assets in "illiquid assets."[26] Second, although mutual funds must honor redemption requests at closing prices on the business days on which such requests are made, they have up to seven calendar days to make payment (Investment Company Act of 1940, sec. 22(e)). That, in effect, provides a cushion of several days during which mutual funds can liquidate assets. Third, mutual funds commonly maintain sizable cash positions to meet redemptions. Fourth, mutual funds can borrow to meet redemptions if secondary markets warrant such action, instead of liquidating assets (Investment Company Act of 1940, sec. 18(f)). Fifth, a final backstop is that mutual funds can redeem "in kind": they can present shareholders with their rightful share of the assets that the mutual funds hold (Investment Company Act of 1940, sec. 2(a)(32)). Shareholders would then have to decide for themselves whether to sell those assets. Finally, the SEC can invoke its "emergency" powers to permit the suspension of redemptions if conditions warrant it (Investment Company Act of 1940, sec. 22(e)). Such conditions include those that prevent a fund from being able to price its shares because either the secondary market for its securities has shut down or the fund itself is experiencing operational problems. More generally, the SEC can order the suspension of redemptions if it believes that such action is necessary to protect mutual fund shareholders (Investment Company Act of 1940, sec. 22(e)(3)). Examples of past incidents when the SEC utilized that power were the assassination of President Kennedy in 1963, the power blackout in New York City in 1977, the municipal bond market break in March of 1986, the closing of the Hong Kong Stock Exchange in November 1987, and the power failure in lower Manhattan in 1990.

Thus, the nature of mutual fund assets together with the characteristics of fund shareholders makes it unlikely that price breaks will result in widespread fund redemptions that destabilize markets. Further, in the event that such redemptions were to occur, various industry practices and regulatory safeguards exist to cushion their effects on asset prices and to prevent a market disruption.

Can the Federal Reserve Still Be Effective as Lender of Last Resort?

A major safeguard against a systemic collapse is the ability of central banks to restore financial stability by acting as a "lender of last resort." A final issue, therefore, is whether the Federal Reserve has the power to be an effective lender of last resort when faced with a possible systemic crisis arising from problems at nonbank financial institutions, such as mutual funds.

Concern that a systemic collapse could be triggered by problems at nonbank financial institutions was a major reason for the recent expansion of the Federal Reserve's lender-of-last-resort authority under the Federal Deposit Insurance Corporation Improvement Act of 1991.[27] Although the Federal Reserve has had authority to lend to nondepository institutions "in unusual and exigent circumstances" since 1932,[28] in 1991 FDICIA revised those "emergency" liquidity provisions to permit nonbank firms (both financial and otherwise) to borrow at the discount window under the *same* collateral terms afforded to banks (Public Law No. 102-242 (December 19, 1991), secs. 131–33, and 141–42).

The Federal Reserve's emergency lending authority can be invoked if at least five of the seven governors of the Federal Reserve Board find that "unusual and exigent circumstances" exist. The phrase *unusual and exigent circumstances* is not defined by statute or regulation, which gives the Federal Reserve considerable latitude to determine when such circumstances exist. In addition, once those emergency lending powers are invoked, the Federal Reserve must make the following determinations before making loans:

- borrowers, although they may be experiencing liquidity problems, must otherwise be solvent;
- borrowers must secure their loans with eligible collateral;
- borrowers must not be able to secure adequate financing from other sources, including sales of assets; and
- the failure of the Federal Reserve to lend would cause harm to the economy.

A major obstacle in the past to nonbank borrowers' using the discount window was their inability to satisfy collateral requirements. The collateral offered by borrowers had to consist of "real bills" and "certain Treasury obligations of the kinds and maturities made eligible for discount for member banks under other provisions of the Federal Reserve Act" (sec. 13(2) of the Federal Reserve Act (12 U.S.C., sec. 343)). In effect, therefore, the only acceptable collateral was highly liquid assets.

FDICIA amended section 13(3) of the Federal Reserve Act to permit emergency advances to nonbanks that are backed by collateral acceptable for depository institutions under section 10B of the Federal Reserve Act (sec. 473 of FDICIA, which amended Public Law No. 72-302, sec. 210, at p. 523). That section permits "advances . . . secured to the satisfaction of . . . [the] Federal Reserve Bank," or by "any satisfactory assets." Thus, the only collateral test remaining under revised section 13(3) is that it be a "satisfactory security," which is the same test applicable to borrowings at the discount window by depository institutions. That change gives the Federal Reserve considerably more authority to aid nondepository firms in emergency situations because it can be flexible about the collateral necessary to support loans to such firms.

The Federal Reserve has seldom found it necessary to use its emergency powers to lend directly to nonbank institutions. Although it has invoked those lending powers on several occasions, in most cases the precipitating factor was a bank failure or at least the threat of one.[29] More commonly, the Federal Reserve has funneled credit to liquidity-constrained nonbanking firms by making credit available through the banking system.

An example is the October 1987 stock market collapse, when there was widespread concern that major securities firms might fail. The Federal Reserve did not use its emergency powers to aid securities firms directly but instead made credit available through banks. On October 20, 1987, the day after the Dow Jones Industrial Average fell 22.6 percent, traders of equity futures and options contracts had to meet massive margin calls. Largely because of timing problems associated with those margin flows, certain large brokerage firms experienced a liquidity squeeze that threatened to send the clearing and settlements system into gridlock. Because it was unclear whether those firms were insolvent or merely liquidity-constrained, banks were understandably reluctant to extend additional credit to them. To prevent a potential systemic collapse, the Federal Reserve announced its "readiness to serve as a source of liquidity to support the economic and financial system" (Miskin 1993, 24). Further, it encouraged money center banks to lend to brokerage firms and made it clear that it would open the discount window to banks making such loans. On October 20 and 21 banks increased their loans to brokers and individuals to support the purchasing or holding of securities by $7.7 billion. Whether for that reason or by chance, a systemic crisis did not occur (Miskin 1993, 24).[30]

Thus, the Federal Reserve has both the legal and economic capacity to deal effectively with potential systemic problems originating in the mutual fund industry or at other nonbank financial institutions. It now has clear legal authority to lend directly to non-banking institutions, such as mutual funds. The Federal Reserve's current policy is to make credit available through banks, however, rather than to lend directly to nonbanking firms. By channeling funds through banks, the Federal Reserve can utilize whatever information and monitoring capabilities banks have and can rely on the incentives that banks have to distinguish between borrowers beset with systemic liquidity problems and those suffering from idiosyncratic credit problems. Further, the Federal Reserve has access to a considerable amount of information about the operations of individual banks, which it can use to evaluate the creditworthiness of bank borrowers. It does not possess such information about nonbanking firms. Finally, in the case of the potential failure of a large nonbank firm, or even the potential collapse of a particular financial market (such as the stock market or the municipal bond market), a policy of direct assistance to nonbank firms may expose the Federal Reserve to substantial political pressure to shore up a particular firm or market regardless of the public policy implications (Wall 1993).

Proposals to Extend Bank Regulation to Mutual Funds: The Parallel Banking System Proposal

Those who believe that the growth of mutual funds has increased financial fragility propose that we extend deposit insurance and bank prudential regulation (capital requirements, prompt corrective action, and least-cost resolution of failing institutions) to all nonbank financial institutions.[31] The logic of that proposal is founded on the belief that the expansion of the nonbank financial sector has simply created a "parallel banking system." In particular, the combination of MMMFs and finance companies is seen as a substitute for the banking system, with short-dated checkable accounts (MMMFs) providing the funding for opaque commercial loans made by finance companies rather than commercial banks. Such a system, therefore, should be regulated just as banks are.

Specifically, the parallel banking system proposal would extend bank prudential regulation to all financial intermediaries that (a) directly accept any funds from the public for investment; (b) make loans to the public or buy securities using funds other than their own equity capital and retained earnings; or (c) sell loans or securities to financial institutions or investors (D'Arista and Schlesinger 1993, 34).[32] Thus, virtually all financial intermediaries—both bank and nonbank—would be subject to prudential regulation.

The proposal recommends establishing a federal chartering agency that would license and regulate all financial institutions. Licensed institutions would have to meet reserve, capital, liquidity, and risk diversification standards comparable to those applied to banks and would be subject to similar systemwide disclosure standards, conflict-of-interest regulations, and anticompetitive laws (D'Arista and Schlesinger 1993, 36). In addition, such institutions would be subject to the Community Reinvestment Act, the Home Mortgage Disclosure Act, the Truth-in-Lending Act, the Equal Credit Opportunity Act, and the Fair Credit Reporting Act. Finally, ownership of licensed financial institutions by nonfinancial firms would be effectively barred.

Proponents of the parallel banking system believe that their proposal would address two concerns. First, they argue that imposing bank prudential regulation on mutual funds would remove the threat of shareholder runs that could cascade into a widespread systemic disruption. Second, they argue that increased Federal Reserve control of nonbanking financial institutions, via the extension of legal reserve requirements to all institutions that either hold the liquid funds of households or businesses or provide credit to households and businesses, is necessary to maintain monetary policy effectiveness (D'Arista and Schlesinger 1993, 33–34).

The analyses of mutual funds in this chapter and of monetary policy effectiveness in the next chapter, however, indicate that neither of those concerns constitutes a valid reason for extending bank regulation to mutual funds. Because they are organized and operated differently from banks, mutual funds are not subject to the kind of disruptive runs that have afflicted banks. The systemic vulnerability of banks fundamentally stems from their funding opaque loans with short-dated deposit liabilities that are payable on demand and at par value. Technological advances have obviated the need to fund loans in that way. MMMFs provide households with liquid balances that are good substitutes for bank deposits and invest those funds in short-dated, liquid, and high-quality assets (such as U.S. Treasury bills), rather than in opaque loans and securities. Finance companies make opaque loans similar to bank loans but fund those loans by issuing both long- and short-dated liabilities (bonds and commercial paper) with maturities that more closely approximate the maturities of the loans they make and that are not payable on demand. Thus, mutual funds and finance companies operate under an institutional structure that is entirely different from that of banks and as a consequence are not subject to the kind of systemic disturbances that have commonly afflicted banks. Further, extending government guarantees and safeguards to mutual funds and other nonbank financial institutions may ultimately *increase* financial fragility by undermining market incentives.[33]

In the next chapter I also show that the proliferation of nonbank substitutes for banks has not undercut the effectiveness of monetary policy. The Federal Reserve can still control the supply of money and credit as well as short-term interest rates, despite its not having the power to impose reserve requirements on nonbank institutions. The evidence, rather, suggests that the effectiveness of monetary policy has not diminished in recent years.

Finally, extending bank prudential regulations and federal guarantees to nonbank institutions would entail substantial costs. First, it would expand the scope of the federal safety net and therefore enlarge the moral hazard problem, thereby increasing the associated costs and resource misallocations. Second, such a move would increase monitoring and supervisory costs enormously, as regulators would be responsible for many more institutions engaged in a wide variety of activities. Third, it would result in new institutional rigidities (such as firewalls) as regulators seek ways to insulate taxpayers from greater potential risks and would thus cause additional capital market distortions. Lastly, and perhaps most important, the expansion of the federal safety net would weaken or eliminate market discipline in the nonbank financial sector and would make the financial system less efficient and probably more risky than the one we now have.

Mutual Funds and Derivatives: Lessons from Recent Events

A few mutual funds have recently begun to use derivatives to alter the risk/return profiles of their portfolios.[34] Derivatives often provide a less costly way to achieve a given level of portfolio risk and return than do alternative investment strategies.

The use of derivatives instruments by mutual funds, however, could raise important public policy issues if this practice were to spread. Most important, the widespread use of derivatives by mutual funds could make it more difficult for fund investors to evaluate the risks associated with particular mutual funds. Many derivatives instruments are relatively new, and some are quite complex, so that it would become more difficult for investors to understand how those instruments alter the risk characteristics of a mutual fund's portfolio. Further, although mutual funds' policies and practices with respect to derivatives instruments are subject to federal disclosure laws, which seek to assure fund investors that mutual fund investments are consistent with investors' reasonable expectations, those disclosures are at present not sufficient to enable investors to evaluate the nature of the derivatives investments being made and their potential risk to the fund's portfolio.[35]

A key element of my earlier conclusion that mutual funds, and in particular MMMFs, are not susceptible to banklike runs is that they hold assets that are generally more transparent than those held by banks. Investments in derivatives reduce the transparency of mutual fund portfolios. That reduction in transparency is particularly troubling with respect to MMMFs, which have as their stated objective the maintenance of constant net asset values. It is important that MMMF shareholders be able to ascertain that an MMMF's use of derivatives is consistent with its stated objectives.[36]

Both the regulatory treatment of mutual funds' investments in derivatives and the required accounting and disclosure principles that govern such investments are currently being reviewed and revised. A primary objective of those revisions should be to maintain the transparency of mutual fund assets. It remains to be seen whether adequate disclosure principles and statements for derivatives can be developed. If not, it may be necessary to consider imposing further restrictions on the use of derivatives by mutual funds, especially MMMFs.

Conclusions and Policy Implications

The massive shift of households' liquid financial assets from banks to mutual funds during the past fifteen years has raised a concern about whether that development will ultimately weaken the financial system by diluting the prudential safeguards that have traditionally protected bank depositors and the banking system in general. A primary concern is whether mutual funds, and particularly MMMFs, are vulnerable to banklike shareholder runs that could adversely affect the entire financial system. To prevent such an occurrence, proposals have been made to extend banklike prudential safeguards, such as deposit insurance and capital requirements, to mutual funds.

This chapter examines two theories of financial instability induced by mutual funds. The first is that MMMFs may be vulnerable to shareholder runs precipitated by losses resulting from high-profile commercial paper defaults, such as the notorious collapse of Penn Central in the early 1970s. Because MMMFs hold a substantial portion of the outstanding commercial paper, defaults by commercial paper issuers could impose substantial losses on fund shareholders. The second is that a price break in the stock or bond market could precipitate widespread redemptions by fund shareholders, which would result in a massive selling by mutual funds that could send stock or bond prices into a descending "death spiral."

The analyses in this chapter conclude that neither of those theories is especially plausible. The characteristics of mutual funds are quite different from those of banks, and those differences make a systemic collapse of the mutual fund industry unlikely. In particular, the greater transparency of mutual fund assets together with the absence of a requirement to redeem at par value makes mutual funds less susceptible to runs and less likely to experience a contagion effect. In addition, changes in the commercial paper market since the Penn Central default and in the regulation of MMMFs since the late 1980s substantially lessen the vulnerability of MMMFs to commercial paper defaults. Also, the nature of both mutual fund assets and fund shareholders makes it unlikely that fund redemptions will trigger a widespread market sell-off. That view is supported by recent experiences with redemptions in stock and bond mutual funds precipitated by losses in mutual fund portfolios: such redemptions have not been a destabilizing factor in markets.

Finally, were systemic problems to occur in the mutual fund industry because of an unlikely event, the Federal Reserve as lender of last resort has the power to prevent a financial meltdown. Specifically, the Federal Reserve possesses both the legal authority and the economic capacity to make loans to nonbank financial institutions (such as mutual funds) to prevent a market disruption from cascading into a financial panic.

The chief conclusion of this chapter, therefore, is that there is no need to extend banklike prudential safeguards to mutual funds. Such safeguards and regulations are not necessary to maintain the stability of either the mutual fund industry or the financial system as a whole. Extending those safeguards to nonbank financial institutions would also expand the moral hazard problem and ultimately result in greater costs' being imposed on society.

✦ 6 ✦

The Changing Structure of Financial Intermediation and the Effectiveness of Monetary Policy

There is increasing concern that the declining role of depository institutions in financial intermediation may be undercutting the effectiveness of monetary policy. That concern stems primarily from two sources. First, financial innovation and the rapid growth of non-bank "money substitutes" (such as money market mutual funds) have blurred the distinction among financial assets to the point where the concept of "money" has become virtually indefinable. In particular, critics argue that there no longer exists an identifiable monetary aggregate that has a stable relationship to either nominal or real GNP (or to price inflation). If that is correct, the Federal Reserve will no longer be able to target a particular monetary aggregate (such as M2) as a strategy for determining either GNP growth or the rate of inflation. That fear also has been fueled by recent statistical studies documenting the breakdown of what were previously believed to be reasonably dependable and predictable relationships between economic activity and certain monetary aggregates (Friedman 1993).

Second, there is concern that, even if a stable relationship were still to exist between *some* monetary aggregate and economic activity, the Federal Reserve might no longer be able to control the relevant monetary aggregate, which would render monetary policy ineffective in any case. Specifically, with the proliferation of nonbank money substitutes such as checkable mutual fund shares, it seems likely that in the future the crucial monetary aggregate will include a substantial quantity of nonbank liabilities, over which the Federal Reserve will have no jurisdictional or regulatory authority. Thus, critics argue that without the power to impose legal reserve requirements on the institutions supplying those rapidly growing money substitutes, the Federal Reserve's ability to control the money supply will be compromised. As a consequence, proposals have been made to give the Federal Reserve the power to impose legal reserve requirements on all institutions supplying money or money substitutes (Feldstein 1992).

The poor performance of the American economy during the early 1990s, together with the failure of the Federal Reserve to achieve its targeted growth rates for M2 during the early 1990s, has lent creditability to those concerns. Critics point to our experience in 1991 and 1992, when the actual annual growth rate of M2 (about 2 percent) fell far short of the Federal Reserve's announced target range for M2 of 4.5 percent, despite the Federal Reserve's engineering a rapid growth in the monetary base.

Does a Stable Relationship Still Exist between Money and Economic Activity?

The debate about whether past empirical relationships between money and economic activity have broken down has sharply divided academics. Some argue that there no longer exists a stable relationship between *any* monetary aggregate and economic activity (Friedman 1993).

An element of that debate is how money should be defined. While there is general agreement that currency and demand deposits—the two most widely used instruments for effecting transactions in the United States—should be included in any definition of money, innovations in recent years have blurred the difference between those assets and many other financial assets that are now used for transaction purposes. In particular, NOW accounts (negotiable orders of withdrawal), money market deposit accounts (MMDAs), money market mutual funds (MMMFs), and checkable assets (or shares) at mutual funds other than MMMFs all have money characteristics. An indication of the relative "moneyness" of those different transaction assets is the frequency with which they are used for transaction purposes, which can be measured by an asset's turnover ratio.[1] Table 6-1 shows annual turnover ratios for the different assets currently included in M2.[2] Of particular note is that the turnover of all non-demand-deposit bank and nonbank liabilities is very small compared with that of bank demand deposits. Also, the turnover of general purpose MMMFs is typically about half that of bank MMDAs. Thus, while the proliferation of nonbank money substitutes has blurred the definition of money, those substitute assets do not all appear to have the same transactions characteristics as bank deposits. It remains difficult, however, to determine where to draw the line in defining money.

In the absence of a general theory to guide us in determining which assets should be included and which should be excluded from money, both scholars and monetary authorities have come to rely primarily on past empirical relationships between alternative monetary

TABLE 6-1
Turnover Rates on Bank Deposits and Taxable Money Market Mutual Funds, 1980–1994

Year	Demand Deposits	Saving Deposits (including MMDA)	General Purpose	MMMFs Broker Dealer	Institutional
1980	202.5	3.6	2.3	3.2	4.5
1981	286.1	4.1	1.7	2.6	4.0
1982	342.4	4.5	1.8	2.8	4.6
1983	385.8	3.2	1.8	2.9	4.3
1984	441.1	3.3	1.7	2.9	4.1
1985	499.9	3.8	1.9	3.5	5.3
1986	556.7	4.1	1.8	3.1	4.6
1987	607.5	4.5	1.9	3.8	5.0
1988	620.0	5.1	1.6	3.5	5.0
1989	733.4	6.0	1.7	3.6	4.8
1990	798.3	6.0	1.6	3.3	4.4
1991	803.6	5.2	2.1	3.3	5.2
1992	826.1	4.7	2.4	3.6	7.3
1993	785.4	4.6	3.0	3.9	7.6
1994	813.8	4.9	2.7	3.9	7.1

Note: Turnover rates are, respectively, the ratio of total annual debits-to-deposits to average annual bank deposits, and the ratio of total annual redemptions to average annual money market mutual fund assets.
Sources: Federal Reserve Board; Investment Company Institute.

aggregates (or money) and economic activity to identify the key monetary aggregates. In particular, central banks customarily target monetary aggregates with a close empirical relationship to aggregate economic activity. Unfortunately, studies have reached different conclusions regarding those relationships—often because they have used alternative methodologies. Thus, the matter is in dispute.

There is, however, a consensus that during the 1980s the relationship of M1 to either nominal GDP (gross domestic product) or the inflation rate did become erratic and unpredictable. Previously, from 1960 through 1980, the GDP-to-M1 ratio (or the income velocity of money) showed a predictable trend, increasing at roughly 3 percent per annum with only small fluctuations around that trend. (See figure 6-1.) In the 1980s that changed: the ratio reversed course, began to fall, and became considerably more variable (Friedman 1988; Roberds and Whiteman 1992; Hetzel and Mehra 1989). Thus, M1 has become an unreliable policy target because of its erratic relationship to aggregate economic activity (Friedman 1988; Bosworth 1989; Blinder 1989).

Institutional changes in financial markets during the 1980s probably account for the growing instability of the M1-GDP relationship. In particular, the composition of M1 has changed signifi-

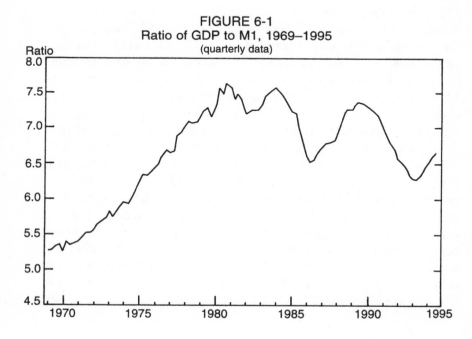

FIGURE 6-1
Ratio of GDP to M1, 1969–1995
(quarterly data)

cantly. In addition, the substitutability between M1 and the non-M1 components of M2, such as savings and time deposits, MMDAs, and MMMF shares, has increased. NOW accounts are a good example of that. Those accounts, which are checkable deposits at banks and thrifts that pay interest similar to savings accounts, grew from $79 billion in 1981 (when they were introduced) to over $400 billion in 1994. In 1994 they constituted almost 35 percent of M1 and surpassed demand deposits as the largest component of M1. (Demand deposits fell from 64.4 to 34.2 percent of M1 from 1980 to 1994. See table 6-2.) In addition, MMMFs have grown sharply relative to M1. (See figure 6-2.) Thus, increased substitutability between M1 and other monetary aggregates has made the M1-GDP relationship less predictable than in the past.

Not surprisingly, the Federal Reserve in the early 1980s began instead to emphasize the targeting of the more inclusive M2 definition of money, and by 1987 it completely gave up targeting M1 ranges (Board of Governors of the Federal Reserve System 1982, 747–53; 1987, 286–89). That decision was supported by research studies showing that, unlike the demand for M1, the demand for M2 remained reasonably stable during the 1980s, so that M2 outperformed M1 (as well as other measures of the money supply) in predicting economic activity (or nominal GDP) (Feinman and Porter 1992; Hallman, Porter, and Small 1989; Hetzel and Mehra 1989; Rasche and Johannes 1987; Feldstein and Stock 1993; Ramey 1993). Further, shifts in the components of M2, such as between small time deposits and bank savings deposits, as opposed to changes in aggregate M2, did not appear to affect economic activity (Hetzel and Mehra 1989). The most variable components of M2 have been bank components, such as savings deposits, small time deposits, overnight repurchase agreements, and Eurodollars, rather than MMMF shares.

Not everyone agrees with the assessment that a stable M2-GDP relationship still exists. After examining the recent business cycle (1987 to 1992), Benjamin Friedman (1993, 25) concludes that the recent behavior of M2 and nominal GDP is "anything but reassuring." Friedman (1993, figure 6) finds that the demand for M2 has become quite unpredictable in recent years.[3] He examines the statistical relationship between the various monetary aggregates and both nominal income (nominal GDP) and prices (the GDP price deflator) over two long periods—1960 to 1979 and 1979 to 1992—and finds that although stable statistical relationships did exist in the earlier

TABLE 6-2
Components of Money Supply, 1950–1994

	1950	1960	1970	1980	1981	1982	1983	1984	1985	1986	1987	1988	1989	1990	1991	1992	1993	1994
M1 ($ billions)	119	144	220	420	447	486	533	565	633	740	766	803	811	843	917	1,047	1,154	1,174
Currency (%)	21	20.3	22.5	28.0	27.9	27.7	27.9	28.1	26.9	24.7	26.0	26.7	27.8	29.6	29.4	28.2	28.2	30.5
Travelers checks (%)	NA	0.2	0.4	0.9	0.9	0.8	0.8	0.8	0.8	0.8	0.8	0.8	38.0	0.9	0.8	0.7	0.7	0.7
Demand deposits (%)	79.0	79.5	77.1	64.4	53.6	49.9	46.4	44.8	43.7	42.4	39.0	37.1	35.9	34.3	33.1	33.9	34.9	34.2
Other checkable deposits (%)	NA	NA	0	6.7	17.7	21.5	24.9	26.3	28.6	32.1	34.2	35.3	35.5	35.2	36.7	37.2	36.3	34.6
M2 ($ billions)	NA	315	629	1,636	1,800	1,961	2,197	2,388	2,587	2,833	2,935	3,096	3,255	3,369	3,470	3,528	3,591	3,624
M1 (%)	NA	45.8	35.0	25.6	24.8	24.8	24.3	23.6	24.5	26.1	26.1	26.0	24.9	25.0	26.4	29.7	32.1	32.4
Overnight repurchase agreements and Euro-dollars (%)	NA	0	0	1.8	2.1	2.1	2.6	2.6	2.9	3.0	3.0	2.7	2.5	2.3	2.3	2.3	2.6	3.2
MMMF balance[a] (%)	NA	0	0	3.8	8.4	9.5	6.3	7.0	6.9	7.4	7.6	7.9	9.9	10.6	10.6	9.9	9.7	10.3
Savings deposits (%)	NA	50.3	41.2	24.3	19.0	20.3	31.1	29.4	31.4	33.1	31.9	29.9	27.4	27.3	29.9	33.5	33.8	31.6
Small time deposits (%)	NA	3.9	23.6	44.5	45.7	43.4	35.7	37.3	34.3	30.3	31.4	33.5	35.4	34.8	30.7	24.6	21.8	22.5

a. Excludes institutional funds.
Source: Federal Reserve Board, *Federal Reserve Bulletin* (various issues).

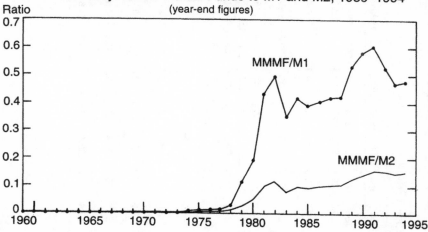

FIGURE 6-2
Ratios of Money Market Mutual Funds to M1 and M2, 1959–1994
(year-end figures)

period, those relationships all but disappeared in the later period
(Friedman 1993, tables 1–3).

The unusual behavior of the velocity of money (M2) can be seen
in figure 6-3, which shows the ratio of aggregate income (gross dis-
posable income) to the money supply (M2) over a twenty-seven year

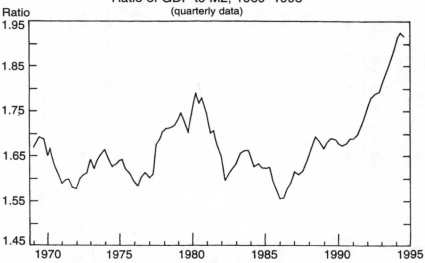

FIGURE 6-3
Ratio of GDP to M2, 1969–1995
(quarterly data)

Source: Federal Reserve Bank.

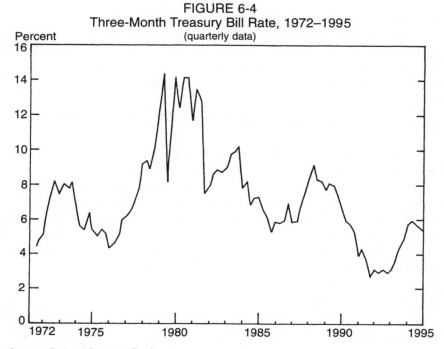

FIGURE 6-4
Three-Month Treasury Bill Rate, 1972–1995
(quarterly data)

Source: Federal Reserve Bank.

period beginning in 1969, using quarterly data. From the mid-1980s to the present, the velocity of money rose steadily, from 1.55 to about 1.92, an increase of almost 24 percent. Further, that increase in velocity was a sharp reversal in the downward trend that occurred from the first quarter of 1981 through the fourth quarter of 1986.

Nevertheless, despite the apparent instability in the velocity of money, scholars remain divided over whether a structural shift has occurred in the M2-GDP since the mid-1980s. Other macroeconomic factors may account for the sharp reversal in velocity. In particular, rising interest rates could cause a rise in the velocity of money by providing an incentive for households and business firms to economize on their holdings of monetary assets, on which they customarily receive a lower return than on other financial assets. Since the mid-1980s, however, short-term interest rates have *fallen* substantially, which should have caused velocity to fall rather than rise. (See figure 6-4.) Lower interest rates should increase the willingness of households and firms to hold larger money balances for a given level of GDP, which would cause the velocity of money to fall. Thus, there is no obvious explanation for the sharp rise in velocity that has occurred since the mid-1980s other than structural changes in financial markets.[4] It is impossible to predict, of course, whether a stable income velocity of money may again emerge once the transition to a new equilibrium financial structure is completed.[5]

Can the Federal Reserve Still Control the Supply of Money?

The failure of the Federal Reserve in recent years to achieve its growth targets for monetary aggregates has intensified concern about whether it can still control the money supply. More specifically, there is concern that the normal relationships between the monetary base (MB)—the Federal Reserve's primary policy tool—and the various monetary aggregates have broken down (Feldstein 1992). Figures 6-5 and 6-6 show the historical relationships between both M1 and M2 and the monetary base. It is obvious that those relationships have changed significantly since the mid-1980s. In particular, the critical M2 money multiplier (the ratio of M2 to MB) has declined sharply since the mid-1980s; it fell by nearly a third from 1985 to 1995.

Part of that decline in the money multiplier can undoubtedly be explained by the substantial fall in short-term interest rates that

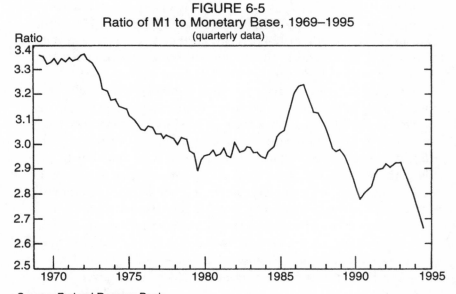

FIGURE 6-5
Ratio of M1 to Monetary Base, 1969–1995
(quarterly data)

Source: Federal Reserve Bank.

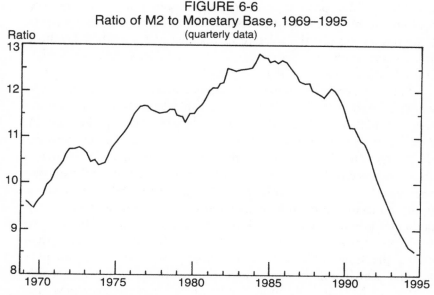

FIGURE 6-6
Ratio of M2 to Monetary Base, 1969–1995
(quarterly data)

Source: Federal Reserve Bank.

occurred during the same period. (See figure 6-4.) Lower interest rates cause households to hold larger cash balances and thus reduce the money multiplier. But statistical tests reveal that the decline in interest rates alone cannot explain the extent of the fall in the money multiplier. Estimates of first-difference regressions of M2 on a distributed lag of both the monetary base and short-term interest rates confirm that there in fact has been a structural shift in the MB-M2 relationship since the mid-1980s.[6] That shift is probably due to the institutional changes that have occurred in financial markets. Thus, without a stable and predictable relationship between M2 and the monetary base, it may have become more difficult for the Federal Reserve to achieve its monetary aggregate (or M2) targets.

A possible explanation for the decline in the M2 money multiplier is the changing composition of M2 since the early 1980s. In search of higher yields, households and business firms appear to have begun in the early 1980s to shift their saving accounts from banks to mutual funds. Total savings deposits in banks and thrifts fell from 68.8 percent of M2 in 1980 to 54.1 percent of M2 in 1994. (See table 6-2.) That shift in turn resulted in a relative increase in the M1 components of M2: as a percentage of M2, M1 grew from 25.6 percent in 1980 to 32.4 percent in 1994. (See table 6-2.) Since reserve requirements are higher on M1 components than on M2 components of the money supply, the relative increase in M1 absorbed much of the increase in the reserves created by the Federal Reserve, which resulted in a decrease in the money multiplier.

Thus, structural changes in financial markets that have made nonbank assets more substitutable for bank deposits appear to have made the MB-M2 relationship less predictable than in the past. A critical question is whether a new and stable MB-M2 relationship will emerge after the transition to the new equilibrium financial structure is completed. In particular, in a less regulated financial environment, stable and predictable price (or interest rate) relationships among bank and nonbank financial assets may emerge and restore stable and predictable relationships among the different components of M2 as well as between those and other financial assets. If that occurs, the flows of funds among those assets will be more predictable, which will in turn make the relationship between bank reserves (or MB) and M2 more predictable. Alternatively, a new and more inclusive monetary aggregate target might be adopted that will have a stable and predictable relationship to the monetary base.

Proposals to Expand the Coverage of Legal Reserve Requirements

The growing instability in the money multiplier has caused some economists to propose that legal reserve requirements be extended to all components of M2 to enhance the Federal Reserve's ability to control M2 (Feldstein 1992). That would require reversing recent actions by the Federal Reserve that eliminated legal reserve requirements on bank time and savings deposits and extending legal reserve requirements for the first time to nonbank components of M2, or to MMMF shares. Because the Federal Reserve pays no interest on bank reserves, legal reserve requirements are in effect a tax on bank deposits (or on the assets on which they are imposed). As such, they constitute a disadvantage for an institution on which they are levied and a competitive distortion in markets. As a general principle, therefore, legal reserve requirements should be imposed only when such action is necessary to achieve an important social objective.

As a general principle, legal reserve requirements are not necessary for the Federal Reserve to be able to control the money supply.[7]

Regardless of whether legal reserve requirements exist, all banks need to hold some reserves in the form of vault cash and other clearing balances for business purposes. In addition, the amount of such reserves that banks choose to hold will be sensitive to the opportunity cost of holding those reserves, or to the level of interest rates generally. Thus, even in the absence of legal reserve requirements, banks would still hold "reserves," and as long as they hold at least some reserves the money multiplier (or the ratio of money to reserves) will have a finite value. The Federal Reserve, therefore, would still be able to alter the supply of money by changing the volume of reserves that banks choose to hold, which it can do through open market operations and by influencing interest rates.

The only issue is whether the money-supply multiplier will be more or less stable (or predictable) under a legal-reserve-requirement regime than under a regime of no legal reserve requirements. There is no evidence to suggest that the multiplier will be less predictable in the absence of legal reserve requirements. Indeed, in the past, differential legal reserve requirements may have resulted in less stability in the money multiplier. Further, if the objective is to enhance the Federal Reserve's power to control the money supply by increasing its power to control the amount of bank reserves held by banks, a far better way to achieve that is to allow the Federal Reserve to pay interest on the reserve balances that banks hold. By altering the interest rate it pays on such balances, the Federal Reserve can encourage banks to hold more or less reserves and thereby can enhance its power to increase or decrease the supply of money (and the availability of bank credit).

Thus, extending the scope of legal reserve requirements is unnecessary and will result in competitive distortions that exacerbate the structural problems that already exist. There are also better ways to enhance the Federal Reserve's ability to control the money supply—specifically, by allowing the Federal Reserve to pay interest on reserve balances held by banks.

Alternative Views of the Monetary Transmission Mechanism

Assessing the effectiveness of monetary policy is complicated by the lack of unanimity among scholars about how monetary policy works—or about the exact nature of the "monetary transmission mechanism."[8] Through which mechanisms does monetary policy affect aggregate demand, inflation rates, and the level of real income? The concerns discussed above implicitly assume that monetary policy works primarily through the ability of the Federal Reserve to achieve certain money supply growth targets, which in turn permit it to achieve certain policy targets, such as a targeted rate of change in prices. There is, however, considerable uncertainty and disagreement among both scholars and practitioners about the precise channels through which monetary policy works. This section reviews two prominent views of the monetary policy transmission mechanism and their implications for the effectiveness of monetary policy in the current financial environment.

The Money View. According to the money view of monetary policy, the Federal Reserve affects aggregate economic activity (or aggregate spending) by altering the supply of money—or the medium of exchange—relative to its demand. Business firms and households are assumed to hold a certain amount of money for a given level of aggregate spending (or the demand for money is assumed to be stable). By changing the amount of money in existence, therefore, the Federal Reserve provides an impetus for aggregate spending to change.

In that view the Federal Reserve, by increasing or decreasing bank reserves or changing legal reserve requirements, increases or decreases the money supply. For example, to contract aggregate spending the Federal Reserve engages in open market sales, a measure that decreases bank reserves and reduces the money supply (or its rate of growth). With less money available, but with the demand for money unchanged, short-term interest rates rise and set in motion asset-arbitrage and expectational effects that result in a general increase in the cost of funds. Finally, a higher cost of funds, relative to the return on capital expenditures of all types, results in a reduction of aggregate capital spending and, ultimately, in aggregate demand generally.

Thus, in the money view, controlling the supply of money plays a central role in monetary policy. Money is the only asset for which there do not exist perfect or near-perfect substitutes, and it is the only asset that provides transaction (or liquidity) services.[9] By reducing or increasing the supply of money, therefore, the Federal Reserve can increase or decrease interest rates and thus cause changes in aggregate spending and in the rate of change in prices. As such, the effectiveness of monetary policy depends critically on the Federal Reserve's being able to define and measure money accurately and on its being able to increase or decrease the money supply as needed.

The Credit View. The credit view of monetary policy places greater importance on the availability of credit generally rather than on controlling some monetary aggregate representing money. While continuing to recognize the importance of the interest-rate transmission mechanism central to the money view, it adds another monetary transmission channel: the availability of credit.

There are several versions of the credit view. A *narrow* version focuses only on *bank credit*. Banks are seen as possessing a special informational advantage that makes them more efficient lenders and monitors of borrowers. In particular, it has been argued that because banks provide deposit services to their borrowers, they are better able to monitor their borrowers (Diamond 1984). As a consequence, they can provide credit to those borrowers (particularly small businesses) at lower cost than other financial institutions, and their borrowers cannot easily substitute other forms of credit for low-cost bank credit.[10] Thus, when bank credit becomes either more difficult to obtain or more costly, firms that customarily borrow from banks will find it more costly to obtain funds and will thus reduce their overall spending and economic activity (Bernanke and Blinder 1988; Fuerst 1992).[11]

Suppose, for example, that the Federal Reserve attempts to reduce aggregate spending by open market sales, which drains bank reserves from the system and reduces the money supply. As reserves fall, there is a contraction in bank liabilities, and a concomitant contraction in bank credit that reduces the availability of bank credit. The unavailability of bank credit in turn forces some firms either to forgo credit entirely or to use a more expensive form of credit, causing those firms to curtail their spending independent of any interest rate effects.

The crucial assumption that underlies that credit view is that bank loans are a distinct financial asset, different from money, bonds, or any other financial asset: they are imperfectly substitutable with those assets. Consequently, by controlling total bank credit, or banks' portfolios, the Federal Reserve can affect aggregate spending, independent of whatever effects it can achieve through altering the supply of money and changing interest rate levels.

A *broader* credit view emphasizes the relationship between monetary policy and the cost differential between external and internal funds. Such a cost differential arguably exists because of imperfections in financial markets: the cost of external funds may be greater than the cost of internal funds because of informational asymmetries (Bernanke and Gertler 1989). That cost differential, which may increase or decrease as a consequence of disturbances in the economy, can also be affected by monetary policy. Monetary policy, therefore, can affect different borrowers in different ways, depending on how it affects the differential cost between internal and external funds. For example, small businesses that borrow primarily from banks will be more affected by a monetary policy that curtails bank credit because they will be forced to seek out higher-cost external funds. Thus, in the broad credit view, monetary policy effectiveness depends, in addition to the usual interest rate transmission mechanism, on the Federal Reserve's ability to affect the cost differential between internal and external funds by controlling the supply of bank credit and credit generally.[12]

In summary, alternative views of the monetary transmission mechanism, while emphasizing different policy targets and different policy effects, all recognize the critical link between Federal Reserve actions and the availability of money and credit. In the money view, the Federal Reserve, by changing the supply of money, affects general interest rate levels. In the credit view, by altering the availability of either bank credit or total credit, the Federal Reserve affects the cost of funds for firms.

Implications of Recent Structural Changes. In both the money and credit views of monetary policy, the effectiveness of monetary policy depends on market imperfections. In particular, in the money view imperfections at the household level enable changes in the money supply to affect general interest rate levels because money is not perfectly substitutable with other financial assets. In the credit view imperfections at the firm level (such as those due to asymmetric information) enable changes in credit availability to affect the cost of funds to firms. Thus, financial innovations and structural changes that work to reduce current imperfections in financial markets should reduce the effectiveness of monetary policy.

It seems clear that recent changes in financial markets have reduced market imperfections at the household level. In particular, better substitutes for money (or for bank deposits), such as MMMFs, are continually being developed. That trend should reduce the uniqueness of money and increase the substitutability between money and other financial assets. In the future we can also expect innovations to further reduce the distinction between money and other financial assets by permitting all financial assets to be used to make payments. If that occurs, monetary policy will be less able to influence the general level of interest rates by altering the supply of money.

Similarly, it seems probable that innovations have reduced market imperfections at the firm level as well, which reduces the effectiveness of the credit channel of monetary policy. First, more firms than ever before can efficiently access capital markets directly. Second, more firms can now obtain credit through nonbank intermediaries, such as MMMFs, finance companies, and pension funds. Finally, bank credit is losing its uniqueness. As the financial structure changes, there is no reason to believe that banks will retain a particular advantage in monitoring borrowers. Thus, firms have available a wider array of substitute sources of credit than ever before, and that availability can be expected to grow in the future. As a result, we can expect the credit channel of monetary policy to become less effective than in the past.

Despite the reduction of market imperfections in financial markets, some imperfections still remain, so that it is unclear whether the effectiveness of monetary policy has been impaired. As long as some imperfections continue to exist, achieving the same monetary policy goal as before may simply require a larger change in money or credit availability. Thus, although from a theoretical perspective recent changes in financial markets point in the direction of making monetary policy less effective, there is no theoretical basis for concluding that market imperfections have been reduced to the extent that monetary policy is no longer effective. We are, therefore, left with the task of determining on an empirical basis the question of whether monetary policy effectiveness has diminished in recent years.

Assessing Monetary Policy Effectiveness in the 1990s

It seems clear that the Federal Reserve does in fact have the power to influence short-term interest rates via the federal funds rate and open market operations. The federal funds rate responds immediately to open market purchases and sales. In addition, recent experience indicates that the Federal Reserve also has the power to control other short-term interest rates. For example, although unable to achieve its targeted monetary aggregate growth rates during the 1990s, the Federal Reserve appears to have been able to bring down short-term

FIGURE 6-7
Short-Term and Long-Term Daily Interest Rates,
January 2, 1990–April 13, 1995

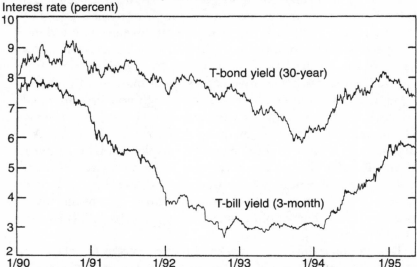

Interest rate (percent)

Notes: Daily Treasury bill yields are annualized discount yields. Daily Treasury bond
yields are annualized bond-equivalent yields.
Source: Knight-Ridder.

interest rates to their lowest levels in nearly thirty years.[13] From 1990
to 1993 both the federal funds rate and the three-month Treasury bill
rate fell from around 8 percent to about 3 percent. (See figure 6-7.)

There is, however, some question about whether the Federal
Reserve can control long-term *real* interest rates. Investment spending
and economic activity depend more on the level of long-term *real*
interest rates than on short-term *nomimal* rates. In the early 1990s, for
example, under pressure from the Federal Reserve, six-month commercial paper rates fell from 7.49 to 4.49 percent between December
1990 and December 1991, while high-grade corporate bond rates fell
by only seventy-four basis points, from 9.05 to 8.31 percent. (See figure 6-7.) Further, a reduction in the CPI inflation rate during that period suggests that the expected rate of inflation may also have fallen,
which implies that a lesser decline may have occurred in long-term real
interest rates than in long-term nominal interest rates.

Thus, whether the Federal Reserve's ability to control short-term
interest rates is sufficient for it to be able to influence aggregate eco-

nomic activity via long-term real interest rates is less clear. Recent Federal Reserve policy, as well as comments made by Federal Reserve Chairman Alan Greenspan, indicate, however, that the Federal Reserve has in fact pursued an "inflation/interest rate" policy. That policy appears to have succeeded in keeping inflation in check while facilitating economic growth (Bradsher 1994; Nugent 1994).

In specific, the Federal Reserve appears to be using commodity prices and other price indexes as a guide to inflationary forces and responding to those signals by altering the federal funds rate. If those factors indicate that prices are likely to remain stable, the Federal Reserve pursues a policy of keeping interest rates low to facilitate economic growth. If they signal that prices will soon begin rising faster than is acceptable, the Federal Reserve attempts to raise interest rates until price stability is restored. For example, during most of 1991 and 1992 the commodity spot price index remained either below or near the lower end (an index level of 120) of what appears to have been the Federal Reserve's policy inflation band (or range) at that time. During that period the Federal Reserve substantially lowered the federal funds rate, from a high of 7 percent in early 1991 to a low of 3 percent in December 1992. In 1993, however, the commodity spot index began to move up, and by early 1994 had moved above the upper end (an index level of 130) of the Federal Reserve's inflation band. The Federal Reserve responded to the increasing price pressures in 1993 by stabilizing the federal funds rate at about 3 percent. In February 1994, after the commodity spot price index had risen to a level above the upper boundary of the inflation-policy band, the Federal Reserve promptly announced a further increase in its targeted federal funds rate.

The policy of targeting short-term interest rates to achieve economic growth and a stable inflationary environment has been successful. During the latter part of 1993, the economy, fueled by strong growth in interest-sensitive sectors such as housing and auto parts, grew rapidly. In addition, the implicit price deflator rose by only 1.3 percent on an annual basis. Thus, notwithstanding the structural changes that have occurred in financial markets, and the inability of the Federal Reserve to achieve its monetary aggregate targets during the 1990s, the Federal Reserve's interest-rate policy appears to have succeeded in achieving its ultimate policy objectives. Whether that policy will continue to be effective as the financial system evolves remains to be seen.

Evidence from Large-Scale Econometric Models

The findings of large-scale econometric models provide additional evidence that structural changes in financial intermediation have not undercut the effectiveness of monetary policy. For example, a study of monetary policy effectiveness using the Federal Reserve's multi-equation, macroeconomic, econometric model of the United States (Mauskopf 1990, 1004) concludes:

> The sensitivity of aggregate output to changes in monetary policy [changes in M2 and the federal funds rate] is about the same now as it was in the 1960s and 1970s, until about the third or fourth year after a change.

In addition, the study finds that

- monetary policy affects consumption spending and investment in producers' durable equipment much the same as before;
- [although] both residential and nonresidential construction are less sensitive to interest rates . . . the reduction in sensitivity reflects the absence of disintermediation-induced episodes of credit rationing [and] does not reflect any reduction in the direct effect of interest rates on the demand for housing; and
- long-term interest rates appear to have responded more quickly in the 1980s than they did before to changes in short-term rates (Mauskopf 1990, 986).

Thus, the study concludes that structural changes during the 1980s appear to have made long-term interest rates more rather than less responsive to changes in short-term interest rates, so that as long as monetary authorities can directly influence short-term interest rates, monetary policy can be effective.

Another study by the New York Federal Reserve Bank, using several large-scale macroeconomic models, examines the effectiveness of monetary policy during the 1980s and concludes that

> the bulk of the evidence presented here suggests that the real economy is at least as sensitive to monetary policy today as it was ten to fifteen years ago. In fact, some exercises show that policy has substantially larger effects on output currently. The lags in policy effects, however, are probably longer (Mosser 1992, 48).

Evidence from large-scale econometric models, therefore, supports the view that structural changes in financial intermediation have not diminished the effectiveness of monetary policy.

Conclusions and Policy Implications

The main conclusion of this chapter is that structural changes in financial markets do not appear to have reduced the effectiveness of monetary policy. Although there is disagreement about whether a stable relationship still exists between monetary aggregates and general economic activity, there is substantial evidence that the Federal Reserve continues to have the power to influence economic activity through its ability to control short-term interest rates. Both recent experience and the findings of large-scale econometric models support the view that the effectiveness of monetary policy has not diminished in recent years.

The chapter also concludes that there is no need to expand the coverage of legal reserve requirements or to extend those requirements to nonbank financial intermediaries. Legal reserve requirements are not necessary for the Federal Reserve to be able to control either money or credit. If, however, we wish to enhance the Federal Reserve's power to control those monetary aggregates, a preferable way to accomplish that is to permit it to pay interest on bank reserves (or bank balances held with the Federal Reserve).

✦ 7 ✦

OTC Derivatives Markets and Financial Fragility

In the past few years losses suffered by users of off-exchange (or OTC) derivatives instruments totaling more than $12 billion have created widespread concern that a major default in the OTC derivatives market could set off a chain reaction of defaults that would culminate in a systemic collapse of the entire financial system.[1] A prime example is the near bankruptcy of Metallgesellschaft A.G. (MG), Germany's fourteenth largest industrial corporation, which lost nearly $2 billion on an ill-fated hedging strategy using both exchange-traded energy futures and OTC energy swaps (Eckhardt and Knipp 1994; Protzman 1994). If not for a massive $1.9 billion rescue operation by 150 German and international banks led by Deutsche Bank (Germany's largest bank and a major stockholder in MG), MG would almost certainly have had to declare bankruptcy. Had that happened, MG might have defaulted on its futures and swap obligations and imposed substantial losses on a major futures exchange (the New York Mercantile Exchange) as well as on its swap counterparties, some of which were major international banks and investment firms.[2] We can only speculate about what the ultimate ramifications of such defaults might have been for both derivatives markets and financial markets generally.

MG is not alone. The sizable losses that other large firms and investment funds using derivatives have incurred in recent years sug-

120

gest that those instruments are intrinsically dangerous and that many users either do not understand or do not appreciate the risks involved. Examples of such losses are those incurred by Orange County, California ($1.5 billion), Showa Shell Sekiyu ($1.5 billion), Kashima Oil ($1.4 billion), Pacific Horizon Funds of Bank of America ($167.9 million), Procter & Gamble ($157 million), Air Products and Chemicals ($113 million), and Gibson Greetings ($19.7 million), to name just a few ("Fill That Gap!" 1994, 29). And even more recently, an out-of-control futures trader caused the illustrious British bank, Barings PLC, to lose some $1.4 billion, a loss that bankrupted the bank. Those incidents leave the clear impression that even financially sophisticated users do not understand and appreciate the potential risks associated with derivatives and that derivatives-related losses can be so large that they can impair the solvency of even sizable industrial firms and financial institutions.

Concern about the potential systemic effects of defaults by large counterparties in OTC derivatives transactions such as swaps has spawned nearly a dozen studies of the OTC derivatives market. Prominent among them are those by the Bank for International Settlements (the Promisel Report), the Bank of England, the Group of Thirty, the Office of the U.S. Comptroller of the Currency, the Commodity Futures Trading Commission, and the U.S. General Accounting Office. The GAO report, the most recent study, notes that because all the major OTC dealers are large financial institutions, the bankruptcy of an OTC derivatives dealer could result in spillover effects that "close down" all OTC derivatives markets, with potentially serious systemic ramifications for the entire financial system. (Table 7-1 lists the largest fifteen U.S. OTC dealers.)[3] To keep that from happening, the GAO report (1994) recommends that additional government regulation be imposed on participants in OTC derivatives markets.

The GAO report makes a number of recommendations aimed at strengthening the regulation and supervision of OTC derivatives markets. Most important, it recommends bringing "unregulated" OTC dealers, such as those affiliated with securities and insurance firms, under federal supervision and imposing on those dealers "safety and soundness" regulations similar to those imposed on banks (such as capital requirements). In addition, the report recommends that the Securities and Exchange Commission be given enlarged powers to oversee the use of derivatives by major end-users and calls for

TABLE 7-1
Fifteen Major U.S. OTC Derivatives Dealers and Their Notional/Contract Derivatives Amounts, 1992 and 1994
($ millions)

Dealers	1992	1994
Banks		
Chemical Banking Corporation	1,620,819	3,177,600
Citicorp	1,521,400	2,664,600
J. P. Morgan & Co., Inc.	1,251,700	2,472,500
Bankers Trust New York Corporation	1,165,872	2,025,736
BankAmerica Corporation	886,300	1,400,707
Chase Manhattan Corporation	787,891	1,360,000
First Chicago Corporation	391,400	622,100
Securities firms		
Salomon, Inc.	752,041	1,509,000
Merrill Lynch & Co., Inc.	729,000	1,326,000
Lehman Brothers, Inc.	724,000	1,143,091
Goldman Sachs Group, L. P.	424,937	995,275
Morgan Stanley Group, Inc.	337,007	843,000
Insurance companies		
American International Group, Inc.	198,200	376,869
General Re Corporation	121,515	306,159
Prudential Insurance Co. of America	82,729	102,102
Total	10,994,811	20,324,739

Sources: Annual reports from Shearson Lehman for 1992; General Accounting Office (1994, 188); annual reports for 1994.

improved accounting and disclosure principles for both dealers and end-users. The report also proposes that market-value accounting be implemented for all financial instruments but stops short of spelling out exactly how such a system would work.

The objective of this chapter is to evaluate the concern that OTC derivatives markets pose a systemic risk to financial markets. Because the GAO report has significantly heightened that concern, much of the discussion in this chapter is directed at evaluating the arguments and evidence that the report presents. While it goes without saying that the possibility of a systemic crisis's occurring can never be completely ruled out, I conclude that OTC derivatives markets are working well and do not pose an unacceptable risk to the financial system. Further, although there is room for improvement in the accounting and disclosure principles applicable to derivatives users, much of the additional SEC regulation of OTC derivatives markets that the GAO calls for would raise costs for market participants without having an appreciable effect on the likelihood of a systemic crisis.

How Would a Derivatives-Induced Systemic Crisis Occur?

An obfuscating aspect of the debate about OTC derivatives markets is that no one ever clearly articulates the sequence of events that could trigger such a systemic collapse. Frequently, critics simply allege that OTC derivatives trading has increased "systemic risk" and, if not reined in by additional regulation, could cause a "systemic crisis." The precise sequence of events that they envision causing such a crisis is left to the imagination.

The Bank for International Settlements (1992), in its Promisel Report, defined a *systemic crisis* as

> a disturbance that severely impairs the working of the financial system and, at the extreme, causes a complete breakdown in it. Systemic risks are those risks that have the potential to cause such a crisis. Systemic crises can originate in a variety of ways, but ultimately they will impair at least one of these key functions of the financial system: credit allocation, payments, and pricing of financial assets.

Why should we expect a disturbance in OTC derivatives markets to spread to other firms and cause a complete breakdown in the financial system? It is difficult to evaluate that concern without some understanding of the sequence of events that might trigger a systemic crisis.

The GAO report (1994, 39) identifies several factors which it argues make OTC derivatives markets vulnerable to a systemic collapse:

> Concerned regulators and market participants said that the size and concentration of derivatives activity, combined with derivatives-related linkages, could cause any financial disruption to spread faster and be harder to contain. Because the same relatively few major OTC derivatives dealers accounted for a large portion of trading in a number of markets, regulators and market participants feared that the abrupt failure or withdrawal from trading of one of these dealers could undermine stability in several markets simultaneously. This could lead to a chain of market withdrawals, or possibly firm failures, and a systemic crisis.

Thus, both the GAO and some regulators appear to have in mind a sequence of events along the lines that follow.

An Initial Disturbance Due to the Failure of a Large End-User. Perhaps because of mismanagement or an operations control failure, a large derivatives end-user fails to meet its counterparty obligations to one or more derivatives dealers. Metallgesellschaft, for example, could have defaulted on its swap obligations to banks. The failure of such a firm could result from the misuse of derivatives by the end-user or could be due to factors totally unrelated to derivatives, such as general business problems.

The Failure of a Large Derivatives Dealer. As a result, derivatives dealers that are the counterparties of the failed firm incur substantial losses, resulting in the insolvency of one or more of those dealers, some of which are major financial institutions.

Counterparty Spillover Effects. Spillover effects occur when the defaulting dealers fail to meet their own counterparty obligations to other derivatives dealers and to end-users, and possibly even to the clearing associations of major futures exchanges.[4] As a chain reaction of counterparty defaults spreads throughout the system, other dealers and financial institutions experience losses and have difficulty meeting their own counterparty obligations. Finally, since some of those dealers are sure to be financial institutions, confidence in the solvency of financial institutions in general is undermined.

Price Effects in Other Derivatives Markets. Because of the customized nature of OTC derivatives and their general opaqueness, actual and potential dealer defaults result in considerable uncertainty, which causes dealers to refuse to trade with each other or with other end-users until the risk of further counterparty defaults diminishes. Thus, there is a general lack of liquidity—or a "freeze-up" of OTC derivatives markets—that forces dealers and end-users to turn to the more liquid exchange-traded futures and options markets to hedge or "liquidate" their positions, which puts those markets under intense pressure as well. The result is a "price break" on both exchange-traded and OTC derivatives markets.

Market Linkages Spread the "Price Break." Extensive links between derivatives markets and most other financial markets cause the "price break" to spread quickly to other markets and create widespread uncertainty about asset values in general. That in turn sets off a general wave of panic selling, which sends asset prices plummeting in financial markets throughout the world.

Credit Disruptions and Real Economic Effects. Finally, sharply falling asset prices, heightened uncertainty, and a disruption of normal credit relationships make it difficult for firms to obtain credit and thus result in a general disruption of business and economic activity.

Sources of Risk

The vulnerability of the OTC derivatives market to that kind of systemic meltdown allegedly stems from four characteristics of the market: the enormous size of the dealer counterparty risk that exists, the concentration of derivatives activity among a few large dealers, the extensive market linkages among those dealers and financial markets generally, and the "regulatory gap" that exists because nonbank OTC derivatives dealers are relatively unregulated (GAO 1994). Further, because most of the large derivatives dealers are banks, defaults on OTC derivatives could undermine the solvency of major banks, with potentially serious consequences for the banking system.

Dealer Risk Exposure. OTC dealers are exposed primarily to two kinds of risk: market risk and credit (or counterparty) risk.[5] Market risk refers to the potential for changes in market conditions, and especially prices, to cause changes in the value of a derivatives contract that impose losses on one of the parties to the contract. Just as bonds change in value when market interest rates change, derivatives change in value when price changes occur in the underlying instrument. The sensitivity of a particular derivative's value to a price change depends on the characteristics of the derivatives instrument: some (like leveraged swaps) are more sensitive than others. Market risk, obviously, is not unique to derivatives—almost all financial instruments expose holders to greater or lesser market risk.

Credit risk arises because of the possibility that a party to a derivatives contract could renege on his contractual obligations. Credit *exposure* on a derivatives contract, however, exists only for parties holding "in-the-money" contracts. For example, suppose that A enters into a forward contract with B to buy Mexican pesos from B in one month at a peso-dollar exchange rate of ten. If the exchange rate were to remain constant for the indefinite future, neither party would have a credit exposure to the other because nonperformance by either party would not impose costs on the other party. Alternatively stated, in the event of nonperformance, the nondefaulting party could replace the forward contract at the same peso-dollar exchange rate of ten. Under those assumptions, therefore, there is no "replacement cost" associated with nonperformance.

Assume, however, that the peso-dollar exchange rate falls to five before nonperformance. In that case the value of the forward contract is said to be "in-the-money" for B and "out-of-the-money" for A: it has value to B but not to A. If A were now to renege on his obligation to purchase pesos from B at a peso-dollar exchange rate of ten, B would suffer a loss—B would have a credit exposure. That exposure would be equal to B's replacement cost for the contract—what it would cost B to replace the forward peso-dollar contract with another forward contract with the same favorable terms as the original contract.[6]

Thus, derivatives pose a counterparty credit exposure only to parties holding in-the-money contracts. Losing counterparties—those holding out-of-the-money derivatives—do not have a credit exposure. The credit exposure of a party holding an in-the-money derivatives instrument, therefore, is similar to that of a party who has loaned a sum of money equivalent to the amount that the derivatives contract is in-the-money. As such, managing derivatives-related credit risk is similar to managing credit risk generally.

The predominant concern about systemic risk in OTC derivatives markets appears to center on the possibility that major counterparty defaults could trigger a "domino effect" among OTC dealers that would result in a market meltdown. Two critical issues, therefore, are whether dealers' counterparty credit exposures are so large that they represent a substantial threat to the system and whether dealers are managing their credit exposures prudently. In addition, it is important to recognize that OTC dealers would still have a credit risk even if they completely and correctly hedged their entire derivatives portfolio against *all* market risks (or changes in prices) by, for example, taking offsetting positions in exchange-traded futures contracts or with other derivatives dealers.

How Large Are Current Dealer Counterparty Credit Exposures?

Driving the concern about dealer credit risk is the enormous notional size of OTC derivatives markets. Outstanding contractual (or notional) amounts in OTC derivatives are in the trillions of dollars. Estimates for 1993 put the total notional outstandings for OTC financial forwards, options, and swaps at around $17 trillion (see table 3-15), and current estimates put the notional value of swaps alone at about $10 trillion (Swaps Monitor Publications, various issues).[7] Interest rate swaps constitute the bulk of that amount, with currency swaps making up the remainder.[8] (See table 3-15.) Further, because the bulk of those contracts is held by a small number of dealers (see table 7-1 and figure 7-1), dealers are viewed as having an enormous potential credit exposure.[9] That view of credit exposures in OTC derivatives markets, however, stems from a misunderstanding of derivatives instruments generally and, in particular, from a misunderstanding of the role of notional amounts in derivatives contracts.

Focusing on the notional size of OTC derivatives contracts provides a misleading picture of potential counterparty credit exposure. Derivatives transactions do not involve an exchange of principal (or notional) amounts. Notional amounts are used solely to determine the magnitude of the periodic cash payments made by the parties to a contract. A default by a party to a swap contract, for example, puts his counterparty at risk only for the cash payments owed now or in the future. Neither party risks losing the notional amount of the contract, unlike a loan or a bond, where counterparties are at risk for the principal amount as well. Thus, counterparty credit exposures on OTC derivatives contracts are much less than those suggested by the enormous notional values associated with those contracts.

A survey of fourteen major OTC derivatives dealers by the GAO

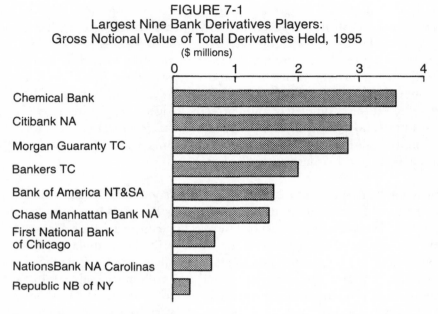

FIGURE 7-1
Largest Nine Bank Derivatives Players:
Gross Notional Value of Total Derivatives Held, 1995
($ millions)

Sources: Company annual reports.

(1994) indicates that, as of year-end 1992, the *gross* credit exposure of those dealers was only 1.8 percent of the $6.5 trillion of their notional outstandings (or $114 billion).[10] Even that figure, however, does not take into account the various risk-management devices that dealers commonly use to reduce counterparty credit exposures. In particular, bilateral contractual netting provisions allow dealers to offset losses on some contracts with gains on other contracts outstanding with a defaulting party or its corporate affiliates. In addition, when swaps are undertaken with lower-quality parties, such counterparties are often required to post collateral on a marked-to-market basis. After taking those risk-reducing mechanisms into account, the GAO reported that the *net* credit exposure of the fourteen dealers was less than 1 percent of the notional value of their outstanding derivatives contracts—about $68 billion.

OTC dealers also manage their credit exposures in a variety of ways that further limit those exposures. In particular, internal credit limits are used to diversify credit risk and to restrict the size of exposures to individual counterparties, industries, and countries. Most counterparties in swap transactions also are required to have investment grade ratings (GAO 1994, 59, table 3.1), and credit "triggers"

FIGURE 7-2

Credit Exposures from Derivatives and Loans of Seven Largest U.S. Banks as a Percentage of Equity, 1994

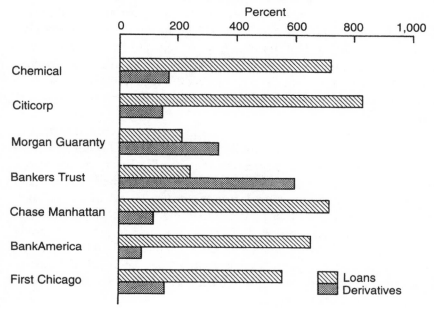

frequently require the automatic termination of a swap agreement if the credit rating of either party falls below a prespecified threshold, such as a single-A rating, with losing counterparties required to make immediate payments.

We can obtain a perspective on the magnitude of credit exposures in OTC derivatives markets by comparing exposures in the swap market with those in other credit markets. In 1992 gross credit exposures in the bond market were estimated to be about $14.4 trillion (Group of Thirty 1993, 58, table 6). In comparison, at fiscal-year-end 1992 the notional value of swaps outstanding was $4.7 trillion, so that we can estimate gross credit exposures in the swap market to be about $84 billion—or 1.8 percent of the notional amount—which is less than 1 percent of the exposure in bond markets.

Alternatively, we can compare the gross derivatives exposures of the largest seven bank-derivatives dealers with the gross credit exposures that the same banks have in their loan portfolios (GAO 1994, 54–55). As a percentage of equity, the derivatives exposures of those banks are only about a fourth of their loan exposures. (See figure 7-

2.) Only Bankers Trust New York Corporation and Morgan Guaranty TC have gross derivatives credit exposures greater than their loan exposures. Further, although it is true that the gross derivatives credit exposures exceed 100 percent of the equity for almost all those banks, a bank's capital would be wiped out by derivatives losses only if *all* counterparties were to default, no offsetting netting agreements or other risk-reduction mechanisms were in force, and actual counterparty losses were identical to total credit exposures. Such assumptions are extreme for loan defaults as well as for derivatives-related exposures.[11]

Thus, while derivatives-related credit exposures are not insignificant, the oft-cited notional amount of outstanding OTC derivatives instruments greatly exaggerates the magnitude of that credit exposure. Properly measured, credit exposures are a small fraction of reported notional amounts and do not seem to be out of proportion to credit exposures in other financial markets. Finally, there is no evidence that derivatives dealers do not manage their derivatives-related exposures as well as their other credit exposures. The GAO (1994, 55) reports that actual losses incurred by derivatives dealers as a result of counterparty defaults have been less than .2 percent of their combined gross credit exposures.

Dealer Concentration. High concentration among OTC derivatives has been cited as an important source of systemic risk. The GAO report emphasizes the high level of dealer concentration that exists and the potential spillover effects that could flow from a default by one of the dealers. The Group of Thirty study reports that the largest eight U.S. or foreign bank OTC derivatives dealers account for 56 percent of the total worldwide notional outstandings of interest rate and currency swaps (GAO 1994, 36).[12] There are only five U.S. securities-affiliate dealers of any size. (See table 7-1.)

The GAO's own data, however, suggest a lower level of dealer concentration than the 56 percent reported by the Group of Thirty study. Using the GAO's list of the fifteen largest U.S. OTC dealers in 1992, the top eight U.S. dealers (seven banks and one securities firm dealer) together held outstanding derivatives contracts totaling $8.7 trillion.[13] The GAO report (1994, table IV.1) also notes that in 1992 the largest fifty dealers held $25.9 billion of derivatives.[14] Thus, the largest eight U.S. dealers appear to account for only about 33 percent of the worldwide notional amounts held by those dealers. Further, the largest U.S. derivatives dealer holds 6 percent of the total. Those estimates may overstate dealer concentration because they do not take into account all of the reported 150 OTC derivatives dealers that exist worldwide, but they may also understate dealer concentration by failing to account for a foreign dealer large enough to rank among the top eight dealers worldwide.[15]

Whatever the true level of dealer concentration, it is by no means obvious that high dealer concentration increases systemic risk. On the contrary, large dealers and the resultant dealer concentration may be a source of financial stability. Dealer concentration in OTC derivatives markets, as in many OTC markets, arises out of a need for large dealers. There are economies of scale associated with managing risk, raising capital, and developing and maintaining in-house expertise and operational systems. Large dealers also are better able to diversify risk than are small dealers. For those reasons dealer concentration in derivatives and other OTC financial markets—such as U.S. government bonds—is generally high. It is doubtful that an OTC derivatives market populated by many small financial institutions acting as dealers would be less susceptible to a systemic crisis. Large financial institutions should be less susceptible to bankruptcy than small institutions.

Linkages among Dealers and Financial Markets. The GAO report argues that the growth of derivatives markets has increased systemic risk because derivatives have expanded linkages among markets and financial institutions. Those increased linkages, it is feared, could cause a liquidity problem in a derivatives market to spread quickly to other financial markets (GAO 1994, 37).

While it is true that derivatives have increased linkages among financial markets, it is not obvious that such linkages have increased the likelihood of a systemic crisis. As markets become more interlinked, market participation widens, which should result in greater overall market liquidity. The more substitution there is among assets, the more elastic the demand for those assets, so that a demand or supply shock should result in smaller (not greater) price changes. Thus, rather than exacerbate market disturbances, increased market linkages should cushion financial disturbances by spreading price shocks over many markets. If we have learned anything in recent years, it is that firms are better able to manage financial risks when markets are not segmented. The collapse of the thrift industry in the

United States is testimony to the financial instability that can result from problems in segmented financial markets—in that case government-mandated market segmentation.

Concern about the potential impact of expanded market linkages appears to stem from our experience with the October 1987 stock market crash, where price declines in the U.S. stock market were ostensibly transmitted to equity markets around the world. But there is another side to that story. In October 1987 we experienced one of the most severe collapses in equity prices ever, *without* that price break's precipitating a systemic crisis. Whether that outcome was due to the increased market linkages that acted to diffuse the financial shocks, timely central bank intervention, or just plain good luck, we have no way of knowing. Evidence from a more recent market collapse—the September 1992 European Monetary System's currency crisis—suggests, however, that in that incident links between the underlying currency markets and related derivatives markets helped to diffuse price shocks and prevented a systemic crisis from developing (Board of Governors of the Federal Reserve System et al. 1993). Thus, rather than being a weakness, greater market linkages may be a source of systemic strength.

Unregulated Derivatives Dealers. Critics contend that the relatively unregulated nonbank OTC derivatives dealers create a dangerous gap in regulatory coverage because regulators would not have the authority to intervene if those dealers were to get into trouble (GAO 1994, 8, 11–12, 85–91). Although most major derivatives dealers are banks, five large U.S. securities firms and three U.S. insurance companies have affiliates dealing in derivatives. Together, those nonbank dealers account for about 30 percent of total U.S. OTC derivatives dealers' outstandings. (See table 7-1.) Nonbank dealers are subject to SEC or state reporting requirements, but unlike bank derivatives dealers, they are not subject to federally imposed prudential standards or to examination by federal regulators. (Table 7-2 provides a summary of the current federal regulatory oversight of the different kinds of OTC derivatives dealers.) In addition, unlike banks, nonbank financial institutions and their derivatives affiliates are not backed by government deposit insurance and the associated implicit government guarantees.

There is, however, no evidence that nonbank dealers take more risks or are more vulnerable to counterparty defaults than are bank dealers. Indeed, there is evidence that nonbank derivatives dealers are

TABLE 7-2
U.S. Federal Regulatory Oversight of OTC Derivatives Activities of Financial Institutions and Financial Institution Affiliates as of April 1994

Type of Institution	Examination Requirements	Capital Requirements	Reporting Requirements
Banks	Banks are subject to annual examinations. Those major OTC derivatives dealers regulated by the Office of the Comptroller of the Currency are subject to continuous on-site examinations.	For credit risk, banks are to hold capital against their derivatives positions equal to 8 percent of the adjusted value of their positions. The adjustments serve to reduce required capital, depending on the type of counterparty and the maturity of the contract. Since March 1994, those firms also must hold at least 3 percent of the unadjusted replacement cost of certain contracts.	Banks are to report quarterly their total derivatives notional amounts by product type. They also are to report the total gross replacement cost of those positions. Reporting on individual counterparty credit exposures is not required, but the exposures may be reviewed by regulatory staff during periodic examinations.

(Table continues)

TABLE 7-2 (continued)

Type of Institution	Examination Requirements	Capital Requirements	Reporting Requirements
Securities firm affiliates	None.	None.	Since October 1992, securities firm affiliates have been required to report quarterly their total derivatives notional amounts by product type. They also are to report the total gross replacement cost of those positions. Information on individual counterparty credit exposures is to be reported only when exposures are above a certain threshold.
Insurance firm affiliates	None.	None.	Insurance firm affiliates' financial information is consolidated with parent company reports.

Source: GAO.

subject to substantial market discipline. Dealers report that rating agencies and counterparties insist that they set aside substantial capital, based on calculations of their risk exposures (GAO 1994, 89). Nonbank derivatives dealers generally had relatively large amounts of capital compared with banks.[16] Also, GAO interviews with five securities firms concluded that those dealers were both well managed and well capitalized (GAO 1994, 11). Thus, pressures from rating agencies and self-preservation incentives appear to provide strong market discipline for nonbank derivatives dealers.

Finally, with respect to the feared "domino effect" among dealers, the primary regulatory objective should be to maintain the stability of the banking system. That can be accomplished by regulating banks; it is not necessary to regulate institutions that deal with banks. A key regulatory issue, therefore, is whether current regulation of bank derivatives dealers is sufficient to ensure the soundness of banks as well as the stability of the banking system as a whole.

Banks

Banks have increased their participation in derivatives markets dramatically in the past few years. In 1995 U.S. banks held derivatives contracts totaling more than $17 trillion in notional value. (See table 7-3.) The nine largest bank dealers also held over 90 percent of all derivatives contracts held by banks. (See figure 7-3.) The bulk of

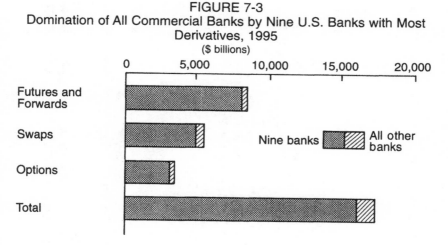

FIGURE 7-3
Domination of All Commercial Banks by Nine U.S. Banks with Most Derivatives, 1995
($ billions)

Note: 1995 first-quarter data are preliminary.

TABLE 7-3

Notional Amount of Off-Balance-Sheet Derivatives Contracts of the Twenty-five Commercial Banks and Trust Companies with the Most Off-Balance-Sheet Derivatives Contracts, March 31, 1995

($ millions)

Rank	Bank Name	State	Total Assets	Total Derivatives	Total Futures (Exch. Tr.q)	Options (Exch. Tr.)	Total Forwards (OTC)	Total Swaps (OTC)	Options (OTC)	Spot FX
1	Chemical Bank	NY	149,034	3,633,994	494,498	93,479	1,377,950	1,439,228	228,839	127,840
2	Citibank NA	NY	228,437	2,872,943	296,845	110,850	1,656,793	471,503	336,952	163,984
3	Morgan Guaranty TC	NY	143,348	2,833,956	177,093	338,868	619,207	1,191,684	507,104	67,555
4	Bankers TC	NY	82,119	2,082,579	287,452	265,470	611,424	654,955	263,267	84,905
5	Bank of America NT&SA	CA	159,010	1,603,803	110,059	22,457	893,963	440,360	136,964	55,372
6	Chase Manhattan Bank NA	NY	99,349	1,547,905	78,764	23,282	811,525	388,662	245,672	70,950
7	First National Bank of Chicago	IL	47,679	677,786	27,459	21,806	337,441	174,873	116,206	40,741
8	NationsBank NA Carolinas	NC	51,144	627,018	160,925	141,867	72,537	101,609	150,081	10,352
9	Republic National Bank of NY	NY	33,461	284,236	29,657	23,308	75,536	89,253	66,483	16,316
10	First National Bank of Boston	MA	36,872	88,831	28,072	2,585	33,019	14,272	10,884	2,552
11	Bank of NY	NY	41,703	77,673	6,548	10,410	44,135	13,626	2,954	5,204
12	Natwest Bank NA	NJ	29,131	73,148	12,232	40,838	6,738	13,016	324	1,377
13	First Union NB NC	NC	24,190	54,951	7,936	18,623	8,508	14,102	5,783	0
14	State Street Bank &TC	MA	22,778	52,164	858	920	48,135	2,144	107	5,409

#	Bank	State								
15	Bank of Amer IL	IL	16,902	44,331	7,097	130	839	28,986	7,279	0
16	Mellon Bank NA	PA	33,399	39,275	1,398	840	11,714	19,207	6,115	1,052
17	Seattle-First National Bank	WA	15,775	33,876	14,762	0	4,252	14,671	191	25
18	PNC Bank NA	PA	43,817	31,513	3,369	300	63	18,434	9,347	82
19	Wells Fargo Bank NA	CA	51,175	29,125	6,017	3	716	3,434	18,956	165
20	Bank One Columbus NA	OH	6,467	27,476	0	0	113	21,739	5,624	24
21	Boston Safe Deposit & TC	MA	6,188	20,688	0	0	18,636	1,950	103	0
22	Harris T&SB	IL	11,690	19,186	476	1,050	12,102	1,484	4,074	1,958
23	Marine Midland Bank	NY	18,558	18,680	670	0	3,839	13,709	463	5
24	National City Bank	OH	9,628	16,947	933	1,600	368	9,639	4,406	122
25	CoreStates Bank NA	PA	21,067	16,191	1,068	30	1,611	11,274	2,209	176
	Top 25 commercial banks and trust companies with derivatives		1,382,923	16,808,276	1,754,188	1,118,715	6,651,162	5,153,825	2,130,386	656,165
	Other 596 commercial banks and trust companies with derivatives		1,727,718	515,211	43,835	20,975	51,758	291,301	107,343	11,866
	Total for all banks and trust companies with derivatives		3,110,640	17,323,486	1,798,023	1,139,690	6,702,919	5,445,125	2,237,729	668,031

Notes: Data are preliminary. In previous quarters, total derivatives included spot foreign exchange. The first quarter 1995 reports spot foreign exchange separately.

Source: Office of the Comptroller of the Currency, *Call Report*, schedule RC-L.

those were OTC forwards, swaps, and options. (See figure 7-3.) The attraction of derivatives to those banks has clearly been their profitability. Of the derivatives held by banks, more than 90 percent are held for trading purposes. (See table 7-4.) Further, for the largest banks derivatives trading in 1994 accounted for between 15 and 65 percent of total trading income. (See table 7-5.)

The participation of banks in OTC derivatives markets is a concern because OTC derivatives are highly leveraged, opaque transactions that can quickly result in substantial losses to one of the parties (Edwards 1995). In the past few years, for example, many banks sustained substantial losses on interest rate derivatives when interest rates rose unexpectedly. Further, poor operational controls can quickly result in losses so large that they bankrupt the bank.[17] Those experiences, together with the complexity of many derivatives transactions, have created a fear that many banks may not have adequate risk-control systems in place to measure and track potential exposures and that regulators are not in a position to monitor banks' derivatives activities adequately.

Such concerns are reflected in the remarks of Representative Henry Gonzalez (1993, H 3322), the former chairman of the Banking Committee of the House of Representatives:

> I have long believed that growing bank involvement in derivative products is, as I say and repeat, like a tinderbox waiting to explode. In the case of many market innovations, regulation lags behind until the crisis comes, as it has happened in our case with S&L's and banks. . . .
>
>   We must work to avoid a crisis related to derivative products before, once again, . . . the taxpayer is left holding the bag.

How Risky Really Are Banks' OTC Derivatives Activities? As dealers in OTC derivatives, banks may have substantial potential exposure to both market and counterparty credit risk. Gorton and Rosen (1995) find that banks have large net swap positions, the values of which are highly sensitive to changes in interest rates. But they also find that banks typically hedge those exposures with other assets or positions that they hold. Gorton and Rosen conclude, therefore, that at present banks' derivatives positions do not expose them to substantial market risk.

Table 7-6 shows the credit exposures that the largest twenty-five banks had on their derivatives positions in March 1995. On average,

TABLE 7-4

Notional Amount of Off-Balance-Sheet Derivatives Contracts Held for Trading by the Nine Commercial Banks and Trust Companies with the Most Off-Balance-Sheet Derivatives Contracts, March 31, 1995

($ millions)

Rank	Bank Name	State	Total Assets	Total Derivatives	Total Held for Trading and Mark to Market	% Held for Trading and Mark to Market
1	Chemical Bank	NY	149,034	3,633,994	3,510,758	96.6
2	Citibank NA	NY	228,437	2,872,943	2,742,873	95.5
3	Morgan Guaranty TC	NY	143,348	2,833,956	2,528,343	89.2
4	Bankers TC	NY	82,119	2,082,579	2,046,815	98.3
5	Bank of America NT&SA	CA	159,010	1,603,803	1,538,812	95.9
6	Chase Manhattan Bank NA	NY	99,349	1,547,905	1,485,071	95.9
7	First National Bank of Chicago	IL	47,679	677,786	671,539	99.1
8	NationsBank NA Carolinas	NC	51,144	627,018	600,673	95.8
9	Republic NB of NY	NY	33,461	284,236	276,523	97.3
	Top 9 commercial banks and trust companies with derivatives		993,581	16,164,221	15,401,407	95.3
	Other 612 commercial banks and trust companies with derivatives		2,117,059	1,159,265	485,831	41.9
	Total for all banks and trust companies with derivatives		3,110,640	17,323,486	15,887,238	91.7

Notes: In previous quarters, total derivatives included spot foreign exchange. The first quarter 1995 reports spot foreign exchange separately.
Source: Office of the Comptroller of the Currency, *Call Report*, schedule RC-L.

TABLE 7-5
Derivatives Trading: Contribution to Total Trading Income, 1993 and 1994
($ millions)

	1993	Percent	1994	Percent
Chase	201	28	108	15
Chemical	453	42	391	61
Citicorp	800	27	400	29
J. P. Morgan	797	39	663	65
Total/Average	2,251	34	1,562	42

Sources: Company annual reports.

the net credit exposure on those positions was about 1.56 percent of their notional outstandings of the derivatives. In addition, the banks' net derivatives credit exposure constituted on average 141 percent of their capital, which was much less than the credit exposures they had on their more traditional assets, such as one-to-four family residence mortgages.[18]

Thus, contrary to the impression left by critics who point to the huge notional values associated with the OTC derivatives positions held by banks, the actual market and credit risks on those positions appear to be small in comparison with many other activities in which banks engage.

The Regulation of Banks' Derivatives Activities. An important question is whether the derivatives activities of banks can be effectively regulated. OTC derivatives have three characteristics that make them difficult to regulate. First, they are often opaque transactions, which can make it difficult to measure and monitor the risk exposures associated with a bank's derivatives positions. Derivatives positions can and often do interact in complex ways with other positions held by the bank, which makes it difficult to determine the net effect of the derivatives positions on the bank's overall risk exposure. Second, valuing OTC derivatives positions can be problematic because there does not exist a liquid secondary market for them. Consequently, it is often necessary to value them with a pricing model, which requires making critical assumptions that may seem sensible *ex ante* but that appear foolishly optimistic from an *ex post* perspective.

Third, derivatives are highly leveraged instruments that can be used to change a bank's overall risk exposure both quickly and substantially. That makes it difficult for regulators to monitor risk exposures in a timely fashion. To monitor effectively banks' derivatives positions, regulators would need to conduct virtually on-line surveillance.

Thus, an argument can be made that, under the current system of bank regulation (which emphasizes capital requirements as a deterrent to risk-taking), banks should not be permitted to engage in derivatives activities. Because derivatives are difficult for regulators to value and to monitor, it would be hard for regulators to establish and monitor effective bank capital requirements for derivatives activities. Alternatively, it has been suggested that banks be permitted to engage in derivatives activities indirectly through separately capitalized and separately managed nonbank subsidiaries or affiliates, such as bank holding company subsidiaries. The plausibility of that proposal depends critically on one's faith in the effectiveness of regulatory firewalls in protecting the bank itself.

The counterarguments are, first, that derivatives are no different from many other bank activities and therefore can be regulated just as effectively as those activities. Many other bank assets—business and commercial real estate loans, for example—are also opaque, illiquid, and difficult to value, so that it is just as difficult for regulators to monitor the value of those assets and to determine appropriate capital requirements. Nevertheless, very few have argued that banks should not be permitted to engage in those activities, and regulators apparently feel comfortable setting capital requirements for those assets and monitoring the risk exposures associated with them. Why should derivatives be treated any differently?

Second, prohibiting banks from engaging in derivatives activities would eliminate the synergies that exist between those activities and other banking activities. Derivatives have become an important component of firms' risk-management and capital-raising strategies. If banks were unable to provide those services to firms, they would undoubtedly lose customers to nonbank financial institutions that are able to provide a complete array of risk-management and capital-raising services. Further, even requiring banks to conduct their derivatives trading activities in separately capitalized and separately managed subsidiaries would eliminate important synergies. In particular, banks now use trading positions in derivatives as a hedge against

TABLE 7-6
Credit Exposures of the Twenty-five Commercial Banks and Trust Companies with the Most Off-Balance-Sheet Derivatives Contracts, March 31, 1995
($ millions)

Rank	Bank Name	State	Total Assets	Total Derivatives[a]	Bilaterally Netted Current Exposure[b]	Future Exposure[c]	Credit Exposure from All Contracts[c]	Credit Exposure to Capital Ratio (%)[e]
1	Chemical Bank	NY	149,034	3,633,994	30,100	14,455	44,555	375
2	Citibank NA	NY	228,437	2,872,943	33,838	16,030	49,868	223
3	Morgan Guaranty TC	NY	143,348	2,833,956	37,096	16,484	53,580	571
4	Bankers TC	NY	82,119	2,082,579	20,287	11,994	32,281	589
5	Bank of America NT&SA	CA	159,010	1,603,803	13,479	9,442	22,921	152
6	Chase Manhattan Bank NA	NY	99,349	1,547,905	13,859	9,484	23,343	230
7	First NB of Chicago	IL	47,679	677,786	8,808	4,041	12,849	295
8	NationsBank NA Carolinas	NC	51,144	627,018	3,813	1,565	5,378	175
9	Republic NB of NY	NY	33,461	284,236	4,509	1,684	6,193	196
10	First NB of Boston	MA	36,872	88,831	771	229	1,000	27
11	Bank of NY	NY	41,703	77,673	1,697	488	2,185	47
12	Natwest Bank NA	NJ	29,131	73,148	183	92	275	11
13	First Union NB NC	NC	24,190	54,951	145	120	265	13
14	State Street B&TC	MA	22,778	52,164	1,306	516	1,821	136
15	Bank of America IL	IL	16,902	44,331	840	128	968	35
16	Mellon Bank NA	PA	33,399	39,275	487	167	654	18
17	Seattle-First NB	WA	15,775	33,876	87	53	140	8
18	PNC Bank NA	PA	43,817	31,513	94	102	196	6

19	Wells Fargo Bank NA	CA	51,175	29,125	122	101	224	5
20	Bank One Columbus NA	OH	6,467	27,476	264	59	323	39
21	Boston Safe Deposit & TC	MA	6,188	20,688	451	105	556	107
22	Harris T&SB	IL	11,690	19,186	2,337	15	2,352	214
23	Marine Midland Bank	NY	18,558	18,680	136	43	179	9
24	National City Bank	OH	9,628	16,947	218	68	286	33
25	CoreStates Bank NA	PA	21,067	16,191	106	51	158	8
	Top 25 commercial banks and trust companies with derivatives		1,382,923	16,808,276	175,034	87,516	262,550	Average 141
	Other 596 commercial banks and trust companies with derivatives		1,727,718	515,211	4,231	1,647	5,878	NA
	Total amounts for all banks and trust companies with derivatives		3,110,640	17,323,486	179,265	89,163	268,428	9

a. In previous quarters, total derivatives included spot foreign exchange. The first quarter 1995 reports spot foreign exchange separately.

b. The bilaterally netted current credit exposure is the current credit exposure across all off-balance-sheet derivatives contracts, after considering bilateral netting arrangements.

c. Future exposure is calculated in the following manner: .01 [notional amounts of short term (less than one-year) contracts from foreign exchange, gold, other precious metals, other commodity, and equity derivative contracts] + .05 [notional amounts of long term (one year through five years) of the above contract] + .005 [notional amount of long-term interest rate contracts]. Short-term interest rate contracts get a zero risk weight and therefore do not factor into the summation.

d. Credit exposure from all contracts is the sum of the bilaterally netted current credit exposure and future exposure.

e. Credit exposure to capital ratio is calculated by using risk-based capital (tier 1 plus tier 2 capital).

Source: Office of the Comptroller of the Currency, Call Report, Schedule RC-R.

their other positions and activities. That provides a low-cost, effective means for them to manage their risks. Forcing them to segregate derivatives trading activities into separate nonbank affiliates would eliminate those benefits.

Derivatives, therefore, raise anew the debate about the effectiveness of bank regulation in general, and about whether regulators can effectively monitor what are essentially opaque and potentially very risky activities. Further, derivatives trading is just one example of the direction in which banks are heading. In the future we can expect banks to continue to diversify into many new activities, some of which will be increasingly opaque and difficult to monitor. The current regulatory regime lacks logical and coherent criteria for determining which should be permissible activities for banks. Further, because regulators will continue to be under pressure to liberalize bank activities to shore up the declining competitive position of banks, the result may be regulatory compromises that are not in our best long-run interests. The problems with the current regulatory system in banking are examined more fully in the next chapter, where a number of proposals are made for changing the system to make it more compatible with today's financial realities.

Conclusions and Recommendations

Belief that the growth of OTC derivatives markets has increased financial fragility stems largely from a misunderstanding of how those markets work. In particular, the view that the risk exposures of OTC derivatives dealers are exceptionally high is simply not true. Critics commonly cite the huge notional outstandings of dealers' OTC derivatives positions as evidence of the enormous risk that dealers are taking. That view, however, misrepresents risk exposures of dealers by confusing notional values with risk exposures. While there is a significant amount of potential market risk associated with dealers' positions, dealers customarily hedge that risk with other assets or positions. In addition, the credit risk on dealers' derivatives positions is in reality only a fraction of the notional outstandings—probably less than 1 percent. Further, that risk is considerably less than are the exposures that bank derivatives dealers (the largest OTC dealers) have on many of their other (more traditional) banking activities.

Critics also contend that the high level of concentration among OTC derivatives dealers makes OTC derivatives markets particularly vulnerable because the insolvency of a single dealer could precipitate a systemic crisis. Neither theory nor fact supports that view, however. Because of superior diversification, large dealers should be less vulnerable than small dealers to insolvency.

Finally, the expanded market linkages brought about by derivatives trading should be viewed as a stabilizing rather than a destabilizing factor. Derivatives provide an effective mechanism for sharing risk and for distributing losses among a greater number of market participants. Thus, derivatives should broaden market participation by cushioning rather than accentuating financial shocks.

Bank derivatives dealers, which are by far the largest OTC derivatives dealers, are already highly regulated. Their activities are subject to the same kinds of regulatory requirements and supervision as are bank activities generally. Although derivatives activities often pose difficult measurement and supervisory problems for regulators, those problems are not unlike the ones that regulators already confront with respect to some other bank activities. Nevertheless, banks' derivatives activities, as well as some recent experiences that banks have had with derivatives, have highlighted what in my view are fundamental weaknesses in the current bank regulatory system. In the next chapter I discuss those deficiencies and propose changes in the regulatory system that I believe will enhance the stability of both banking and the entire financial system.

Additional prudential regulation of nonbank derivatives dealers, however, is neither necessary nor desirable. Attempting to protect nonbank financial institutions is not necessary for financial stability and can inadvertently exacerbate market stresses by creating regulatory rigidities. It is instructive to remember that the worst U.S. financial crisis since the Great Depression occurred in a highly regulated industry—the thrift industry. Restrictive regulations and inept regulatory management were primary culprits in that incident. Similarly, the genesis of the Eurocurrency crisis in October 1992 was not destabilizing speculation but rather the Bank of England's attempting to peg the exchange rate at an unrealistic level—giving speculators a "heads-you-win/tails-I-lose" opportunity they could hardly be expected to pass up.

The best preventive against instability in any financial market is to foster an environment in which all participants have both an incentive to manage risks prudently and the ability to respond quickly and innovatively to changing market conditions. To a large extent, those conditions already exist in OTC derivatives markets. An area where improvement can be made, however, is with respect to accounting and disclosure practices for derivatives dealers and users. Better public disclosure of the risks incurred by both derivatives dealers and end-users would improve market transparency and enhance market discipline and market efficiency. Improved transparency would enable investors and creditors to better "price" the risks that firms take and to monitor risk-taking more effectively so that they can penalize firms when they take excessive risks. The result would be that firms would have better risk management incentives.

A concerted effort is now underway to improve accounting and disclosure practices for derivatives users. The Financial Accounting Standards Board (1994, 1995) recently issued an exposure draft addressing such issues as disclosure of fair values for derivatives transactions, the value of derivatives over an entire reporting period, and the purpose for which derivatives transactions are entered. In addition, in September 1994 the Bank for International Settlements and the Central Banks of the Group of Ten Countries (1994) released a discussion paper entitled "Public Disclosure of Market and Credit Risks by Financial Intermediaries." The paper proposes that quantitative public disclosures be made about the market and counterparty risks to which financial institutions are exposed when using derivatives, and about how effective institutions have been in the past in managing those risks.

At present there is no consensus on how derivatives risk should be measured and disclosed. Nevertheless, two external reporting requirements would seem to be a necessary minimum. First, all financial assets and liabilities should be recorded at fair value, or should be marked to market, except for derivatives positions used to hedge cash flows associated with nonfinancial assets or future expenditures. With respect to hedges, it is often difficult and costly to establish market values because of the absence of liquid secondary markets for the assets or positions being hedged. Adopting market-value accounting may entail the use of models to estimate or infer fair values because prices may not be directly observable.

Second, hedges of nonfinancial assets or future expenditures should be reported in accordance with the matching principle: gains or losses on the hedging instruments are recognized in the same period that the specified event or the hedged item is taken into income or expense. If the hedging instrument is not liquidated when the hedged item is brought into income, it converts to an instrument that is marked to market. Also, gains on hedging instruments realized before the accounting recognition of the specified event should be deferred until they can be matched against the income or expense associated with the hedged item. Further, realized or measured losses on hedging instruments should be deferred only to the extent that they do not exceed the unrecorded gains to date associated with the hedged items. Finally, at the end of each accounting period, material unrealized and deferred gains and losses on hedging instruments along with (offsetting) unrealized losses or gains on the hedged items should be disclosed in a footnote.[19]

Adoption of even those minimal accounting and disclosure principles will greatly improve information available about how firms are using derivatives. As such, they will enhance market discipline and reduce the potential for a financial disturbance to precipitate a financial crisis.

✦ 8 ✦

Financial Regulation for the 21st Century: Proposals for Reforming Bank Regulation

Ineffectual and out-of-date bank regulation currently poses the greatest threat to financial stability. Contrary to what many would have us believe, the threat to financial stability today does not come from the rapid expansion of mutual funds and derivatives markets but from the fragility of banks and banking systems. Government guarantees coupled with ineffectual regulation and an intensified competitive environment have created an intrinsically unstable banking system. Bank failures continue to pose a threat to financial stability because of the possibility that they will set off a depositor run that will destabilize the entire financial system.[1]

Present-day Japan is only the latest example of many episodes of bank-induced financial fragility. The envy of the world only a few years ago, the Japanese banking and financial systems are in turmoil, with bank failures and miniruns on financial institutions threatening to escalate into a full-blown financial panic. The Japanese situation today is hardly unique. From the mid-1970s to the present, some sixty countries have experienced major episodes of bank failures, including most of the industrialized countries (such as the United States, Japan, and Great Britain). Table 8-1 lists the dates of those episodes and where they occurred. Bank fragility is a pervasive and persistent characteristic of

148

economic systems, rather than an exception to otherwise well-functioning financial systems, and financial history suggests that there is a fatal flaw in how banking is traditionally conducted. There is, in particular, something intrinsically destabilizing either about the way that the business of banking has been conducted or about the regulatory systems that have customarily governed the business of banking.

In many countries, including the United States, bank regulation is outdated and needs to be changed. U.S. regulation remains hopelessly out of step with technological and market changes, despite recent legislative efforts to improve the essentially bankrupted and discredited regulatory system that emerged from the ashes of the thrift debacle at the conclusion of the 1980s. If left unchanged, the current regulatory system will not be able to maintain the soundness of the U.S. banking system and will almost certainly result in a banking system that will be unable to compete in global financial markets. Driven largely by political rather than economic considerations, the current regulatory system imposes artificial and unnecessary restrictions on banks, and, if allowed to continue on its present political evolutionary course, will lead to a financial system burdened by an enormous regulatory and bureaucratic edifice that will cost taxpayers far more than it is worth.

This chapter begins by describing the regulatory system applicable to U.S. banks and depository institutions and the rationale that underlies that system. Next, I discuss the shortcomings of that system and examine various proposals to remedy those deficiencies. That discussion concludes with a list of regulatory reforms that need to be instituted to make the current system function effectively in maintaining financial soundness and in fostering competitive and efficient financial markets. Finally, I discuss an alternative approach to regulatory and financial reform that deserves serious consideration: replacing the current banking system with a system of "collateralized banks." Such a system would permit us to reduce the scope of regulatory restrictions and enlarge the role of market forces in the financial system, while still protecting both small depositors and the payments system. A major conclusion of this chapter is that in the future we shall have to rely more on the discipline of private markets to curb excessive risk-taking than on government regulation and oversight. A collateralized banking system will provide more scope for market mechanisms to control institutional risk-taking and will substantially reduce the need for costly and invasive regulatory oversight and monitoring.

TABLE 8-1
Major Episodes of Bank Insolvencies, 1974–1995

Industrial Countries	Period of Crisis
Australia	1989–1990
Great Britain	1974–1976
France	1994–1995
Finland	1991
Germany	Late 1970s, 1989
Japan	1990s
New Zealand	1987–1990
Norway	1987–1989
Spain	1977–1985, 1994
Sweden	1991
United States	1981–1991

Latin America	Period of Crisis
Argentina	1980–1982, 1989, 1995
Bolivia	1986–1987
Brazil	1990, 1995
Chile	1976, 1981–1983
Colombia	1982–1987
Costa Rica	Several instances
Ecuador	Early 1980s
Mexico	1981–1982 (perhaps until reprivatized 1990–1991), 1995
Uruguay	1981–1984
Venezuela	1980, 1994

Asia	Period of Crisis
Bangladesh	Late 1980s–present
Hong Kong	1982–1983, 1983–1986
India	1994–1995
Indonesia	1994
Malaysia	1985–1988
Nepal	1988
Philippines	1981–1987
Singapore	1982
Taiwan	1983–1984
Thailand	1983–1987
Turkey	1982–1985, 1994

Africa	Period of Crisis
Benin	1988–1990
Cameroon	1987
Central African Republic	1980s, 1994
Chad	1980s, 1990s
Congo	1980s, 1991
Egypt	Early 1980s, 1990–1991
Eritrea	1993
Ghana	1982–1989, 1995
Guinea	1985, 1994–1995
Ivory Coast	1988–1991
Kenya	1985–1989, 1993–1995
Madagascar	1988
Mauritania	1984, 1988, 1993
Morocco	Early 1980s
Mozambique	1987–present
Nigeria	1990s
Senegal	1988–1991
Tanzania	1987, 1995
Togo	1993
Uganda	1994

Middle Eastern Country	Period of Crisis
Kuwait	1980s

Transitional Socialist Economies	Period of Crisis
Estonia	1992
Hungary	1991–1994, 1995
Latvia	1995
Romania	1990s

Source: Gerard Caprio and Daniela Klingebiel, "Dealing with Bank Insolvencies: Cross-Country Experiences," World Bank Working Paper, October 1995.

The Current Regulatory Structure: Rationale and Deficiencies

The current regulatory system for safeguarding the banking system in the United States has five key components: deposit insurance, minimum capital requirements, activity restrictions, supervisory monitoring and intervention to prevent losses from disrupting the financial system, and the Federal Reserve's lender-of-last-resort capability. In this section I discuss those and other aspects of the current regulatory system. I argue that unless a number of reforms are made to that system, it is unlikely to work effectively in the future.

Deposit Insurance. Deposit insurance is the linchpin of our system of prudential regulation of banks. All bank deposit accounts up to a limit of $100,000 are de jure insured by the Federal Deposit Insurance Corporation. In addition, in the past most deposits in excess of the $100,000 limits have been de facto insured by the FDIC because regulators have adopted a "too-big-to-fail" policy with respect to large banks. Thus, except for a small number of depositors who were unlucky enough to have held deposits in excess of $100,000 in smaller banks (or thrifts), bank deposits in the United States have been backed by a federal government guarantee. That is true as well, either explicitly or implicitly, in all countries with highly developed financial markets.

Deposit insurance is seen as the primary safeguard against bank runs. With a government guarantee of deposits there is no reason for depositors to panic and run on banks in the event of a real or imagined financial disruption. Even if a problem were to arise with respect to the solvency of a particular bank or banks, deposit insurance should keep that problem from spreading to other banks and to other segments of the financial system and should thus prevent a meltdown of the financial system.

That "safety net" does not come without costs. The collapse of the thrift industry in the 1980s and the massive $200 billion government—or taxpayer—bailout of thrift depositors are vivid reminders of what those costs can be if the deposit insurance safety net is mismanaged. The costs associated with deposit insurance arise from two sources: those associated with having to maintain a substantial regulatory bureaucracy to manage the system and to monitor and supervise insured banks, and those associated with the distortion of depositors' incentives, which among other things encourages banks to take excessive risks. The ultimate costs to society include the misallocation of investments and the unintended redistribution of income and wealth that results from such a system.

Perverse Effects of Deposit Insurance. The existence of de jure and de facto deposit insurance changes the incentives of depositors and encourages excessive risk-taking by banks. Because depositors will be made whole no matter what happens to the bank, they have no incentive to assess the risks that the bank is taking or to monitor its performance. Normally, creditors of firms care deeply about the creditworthiness of borrowers; they demand a higher interest rate or return from higher-risk borrowers. That is not true for bank depositors. Deposit insurance makes them indifferent to the riskiness of their particular banks. They neither seek nor demand information from the bank about its activities; they are content to receive the same yield on their deposits irrespective of the particular characteristics of the bank. As a consequence, the typical creditor discipline present in other debt markets is largely absent in banking.

Theoretically, government (or whoever the insurer might be) could set risk-based deposit insurance premiums that would mirror—or substitute for—the risk premiums that depositors could be expected to demand in the absence of a federal guarantee. In the property and casualty insurance industry, for example, premiums reflect the value at risk. That is not true for the banking industry. In practice, it has proven difficult to devise a satisfactory risk-based premium structure for deposit insurance. For most of our history with deposit insurance, we have relied instead on a "flat" premium structure: a premium schedule that is independent of the risks that particular banks are taking. Thus, banks taking greater risks pay the same insurance premiums—or have the same cost of funds—as those taking less risk. There is, consequently, an incentive for banks to take greater risks, or to take excessive risk in comparison with the insurance premium they are being charged. By taking greater risks banks can increase their profits at the expense of taxpayers because their cost of funds does not rise commensurately with the risks they take. The result is an implicit government—or taxpayer—subsidy extended to banks.

Risk-Based Deposit Insurance Premiums. Recent legislation, the Federal Deposit Insurance Corporation Improvement Act of 1991 (FDICIA), has directed the Federal Deposit Insurance Corporation to institute a system of risk-based deposit insurance premiums. A logical question is why we waited more than sixty years to institute a system of risk-based insurance premiums. For such a system to work, two conditions must be present. First, the FDIC must be able to measure accurately the values of the bank's assets and liabilities—or the bank's net worth—and must be able assess the risk exposure of the bank—how much the bank's net worth will change under different potential scenarios. Second, the FDIC must be able to constrain the ability of a bank to alter its risk exposure or to change the volatility of its net worth. If an insured bank can unilaterally change the variability of its net worth *ex post*—or subsequent to the insurance premium's being set—established risk premiums will no longer reflect the bank's risk exposure. The ability of banks to change *ex* *post* their risk exposures creates a moral hazard that is common to all insurance schemes.

Both those conditions—measuring the values of banks' assets and liabilities and controlling banks' risk-taking—are difficult to achieve. First, many bank assets, such as corporate and commercial real-estate loans, are "opaque." Valuing such assets requires extensive information about borrowers and about underlying loan collateral, information that is neither readily obtainable nor easily evaluated. Second, for various reasons, regulators have been reluctant to institute a system of market-value accounting for banks. As a consequence, the information necessary to set accurate risk-based deposit insurance premiums is usually not available and is in any case costly to obtain.

The moral-hazard problem implicit in setting risk-based insurance premiums is even more difficult to surmount. A satisfactory *ex post* "settling-up" procedure for adjusting insurance premiums to discourage *ex post* unilateral changes in risk exposure has not yet been developed. Thus, while instituting a crude risk-based deposit insurance premium system, such as the FDIC has recently done, may have some benefits, it will neither provide adequate protection for the FDIC and taxpayers nor eliminate the distortions caused by deposit insurance.

A World without FDIC Insurance: Implications. Given the problems associated with a government-backed, risk-based premium, deposit insurance system, it is of some interest to speculate about how private markets would operate in the absence of government deposit insurance. In such an environment private creditors and depositors, in lending to banks, would have to determine the appropriate risk premiums to charge banks and would confront the same obstacles faced by regulators—asset opaqueness and risk of moral hazard.

How would creditors and depositors respond? First, they would almost certainly demand to have more and better information about what banks do, about the current values of banks' assets and liabilities, and about the risks that banks are taking. Second, they would undoubtedly impose on banks restrictive contractual covenants aimed at restraining a bank's ability to alter its risk exposure *ex post*. As a consequence, banks would in turn have a greater incentive to disclose more and better information to creditors and depositors and voluntarily to restrict their activities to be able to borrow at lower rates. Realistically, however, there is only so much that depositors, especially small depositors, can be expected to do to protect themselves. A less costly course of action for many of them might be simply to reduce their holdings of bank deposits in favor of holding the liabilities of more transparent institutions, such as MMMFs, where the asset opaqueness and moral hazard problems are less severe. Thus, we would expect a decline in the demand for bank deposits and a shrinking of the banking industry.

Alternatively, in the absence of government deposit insurance, banks may seek other, private, guarantors. Private insurance companies, for example, may come to provide some deposit insurance coverage and to perform various monitoring functions. But such insurance would be limited by the fact that private guarantors would confront the same opaqueness and moral hazard obstacles faced by regulators and would be exposed to an uninsurable systemic risk in the event of a severe macroeconomic disturbance that affected many banks simultaneously. Further, from a public policy perspective, a deposit insurance system based on private guarantors would not be satisfactory unless the solvency of the guarantors themselves could be assured. Such a system in effect shifts the regulatory problem from that of guaranteeing banks to that of guaranteeing private insurers.[2]

In any case, the reality is that Congress is unlikely to eliminate government-backed deposit insurance at any time in the future. Government-backed deposit insurance is considered fundamental to a sound financial system and can also be defended as a useful device for reducing transactions costs associated with use of the payments system. Thus, any plausible proposal for regulatory reform must deal with the asset opaqueness and moral hazard problems inherent in the current system of government-backed deposit insurance.

The current bank regulatory system employs a combination of three devices to cope with those problems: capital requirements, activity restrictions to control banks' risk-taking, and supervisory monitoring coupled with early corrective action by regulators to resolve failing institutions before they impose losses on the FDIC and taxpayers. I discuss those and other aspects of the current regulatory system in the sections that follow.

Capital Requirements. Requiring banks to have a minimum amount of net capital serves two purposes.[3] First, capital is a form of collateral—or "deductible"—that can be used to absorb losses before they result in losses to the FDIC's insurance fund. As long as a bank's losses are kept to amounts smaller than the capital held by the bank, the FDIC and taxpayers will not incur losses. Second, to the extent the banks are required to hold capital based on the amount of risk that they are taking, banks will be deterred from taking excessive risk. Owners and shareholders of a bank taking a lot of risk will suffer substantial losses if the bank fails.

The preconditions for risk-based capital requirements to provide adequate protection for taxpayers are very similar to those that underpin a successful risk-based-premium deposit insurance system. Regulators must be able to value a bank's assets and liabilities, measure the bank's potential risk exposure, and constrain the bank from altering its portfolio or changing its risk exposure subsequent to the establishment of the capital requirements. In setting minimum capital standards, regulators confront the same asset opaqueness and moral hazard problems as when they attempt to determine risk-based insurance premiums. Thus, the current risk-based capital requirement system has been supplemented with severe "activity restrictions" aimed at controlling risk-taking and at constraining the ability of banks to alter their risk exposures. In addition, that system has been subjected to extensive regulatory monitoring and supervision, and regulators have been given the power to take early corrective action to resolve failing institutions with minimum losses to the insurance fund and to taxpayers.

Activity Restrictions, Nonbank Affiliates and Subsidiaries, and Firewalls. Activity restrictions and prohibitions can be viewed as a supplement to capital requirements and regulatory monitoring: they constrain the ability of banks to increase their risk exposures by engaging in activities perceived to be either excessively risky or overly opaque. If it were easy to monitor banks' activities and to impose the appropriate capital requirements on those activities, activity restrictions would be unnecessary.

Activity restrictions take two forms: outright or partial prohibitions of certain activities, and requirements that banks undertake certain activities only through separately incorporated and separately capitalized affiliates or subsidiaries. An example of the first kind of restriction is regulation that prohibits banks from underwriting or selling insurance, either directly (in-house) or through affiliated institutions. An example of the second is that banks can conduct securities activities only through separately incorporated and capitalized securities affiliates.[4] The rationale for the latter requirements is that they insulate banks from losses associated with the activities carried on in their separately incorporated and separately capitalized affiliates. In particular, "firewalls" can be used to insulate banks from the activities of affiliates and subsidiaries. Such firewalls typically take the form of legal and operational restrictions aimed at walling off the bank from the risks taken by their affiliates. An example is the restrictions imposed on the shifting of assets or funds between banks and their affiliates or subsidiaries.[5] Those restrictions are enforced by regulation, and violations can result in stiff penalties for offending institutions.

Two general bank organizational forms utilize separately incorporated and separately capitalized affiliates: the bank-subsidiary structure and the bank (or financial service) holding company structure. Under the former, banks are permitted to own separately incorporated and capitalized subsidiaries directly and are required to conduct nonbanking activities through those subsidiaries. A number of major countries, such as the United Kingdom and Canada, have adopted that model. Under the holding company structure, a holding company is permitted to own both banks and various separately incorporated and capitalized nonbank subsidiaries. The United States is the only major country to have adopted a bank holding company institutional structure. In contrast, "universal banking," as adopted by Germany, permits banks to conduct both banking and nonbanking activities within a single corporate entity with a bank charter, and there are no regulatory firewalls within the banks to separate banking and nonbanking activities.

The requirement that "nonbanking" activities be conducted only through separately incorporated and capitalized entities represents a regulatory compromise: activities considered inappropriate for banks to do directly (because of their perceived riskiness or opaqueness) are nevertheless permitted via a bank affiliate or subsidiary on the rationale that corporate separateness insulates the bank's capital from losses flowing from such activities. Even if losses were to bankrupt a bank's nonbank affiliates, neither the bank's capital nor the FDIC's insurance fund would be impaired. The precondition for this to be true is that there must be effective barriers or firewalls between banks and their affiliates that prevent resources from flowing from banks to their affiliates and subsidiaries when those entities are under stress.

There are two criticisms of the use of firewalls to insulate banks. First, they may not work when they are most needed: when nonbank affiliates or subsidiaries suffer life-threatening losses. For understandable reasons, banks are often reluctant to allow their nonbank affiliates and subsidiaries to fail, and on some occasions banks have shifted funds to troubled affiliates in times of acute stress (the most recent being the failure of Barings PLC).[6] If that occurs, firewalls will not be effective in insulating the bank's capital from losses incurred by nonbanking affiliates. A second criticism is that firewalls may eliminate or substantially reduce the synergies or efficiencies associated with a bank's providing nonbanking services. Firewall restrictions prevent the full integration of activities and thus keep banks from capturing the associated economies of scale and scope. If true, the public policy case for allowing banks to extend their activities via nonbank affiliates is considerably weakened. Why expose taxpayers and the insurance fund to additional potential risks if there are few economic (or social) benefits to be gained?

With respect to maintaining the financial strength of banks, the use of wholly owned bank subsidiaries seems superior to that of a bank holding company affiliate structure. The earnings of a bank subsidiary are free to flow directly to the bank, so that subsidiaries would provide banks with a more diversified earnings structure than would the holding company model (where subsidiary earnings flow to the parent rather than to the bank affiliate of the holding company). In addition, it is more costly to operate as a holding company than to form subsidiaries. Finally, there is no reason to believe that firewalls will be any less effective when applied to bank subsidiaries than to holding company affiliates. Thus, of the two approaches to implementing activity restrictions, conducting nonbank activities through bank subsidiaries seems the preferable institutional structure.[7]

Regulatory Monitoring and Early Corrective Action. Effective regulatory monitoring and supervision are key elements in a system of risk-based capital requirements. Regulators must be willing and able to take early corrective action to prevent losses from escalating to levels greater than the capital held by the bank. Among other things, effective monitoring requires that the net worth of a bank be frequently (if not continually) reassessed and that a bank's activities be monitored to ensure that the bank does not take inappropriate risks. In addition, at some point regulators must have the power to quickly seize the bank and liquidate its assets to pay off the bank's guaranteed deposits. Besides protecting the deposit insurance fund, requiring early corrective action to recapitalize a bank that has suffered an erosion in its capital provides predictability for banks and bank shareholders. A precondition for successful monitoring is that regulators be able to measure accurately both a bank's capital and its potential risk exposure. It is the liquidation value of the bank that ultimately protects the FDIC fund and taxpayers. Thus, the use of market-value accounting and market-valuation measures of risk are essential to effective monitoring.

The costs of implementing a monitoring system that satisfies those conditions are high. First, while the concept of market-value accounting (or mark-to-market valuation) is straightforward, implementing such a system for commercial banks will be politically difficult and potentially quite costly. Many bank assets are opaque and difficult to value because they are not traded in secondary markets (for example, commercial loans). Thus, estimates of their market values are costly to obtain and are subject to considerable error. In addition, the valuation process itself is unclear and leaves considerable discretion to the party doing the valuation (whether it be management or regulators). That creates opportunities to manipulate values to mislead both regulators and creditors. Nevertheless, continuing to rely on simple *book-value* measures of bank capital to trigger supervisory action is clearly inadequate. Similarly, without adequate market-valuation measures of banks' risk exposures, regulatory supervision cannot be effective.

Second, in today's financial environment effective supervision requires shorter monitoring intervals than in the past, which substantially increases supervisory costs. For example, derivatives (futures, forwards, options, and swaps) can be useful in reducing a bank's risk but can also be used to increase risk exposure quickly and dramatically. A bank can change its risk exposure substantially within minutes by simply altering its trading positions in derivatives. Thus, we are moving toward a financial system where effective monitoring will require regulators to reassess the market value of a bank's capital as well as the bank's risk exposure on a continuous basis. Even setting capital requirements at what may, before the fact, seem to be sufficiently high levels may not be able to compensate for less frequent monitoring intervals. Mistakes in the highly leveraged world of derivatives trading (even when hedging) can be difficult to detect and can quickly result in huge losses that dwarf a firm's capital.[8]

Another precondition for effective supervision is that regulators not only must have the power to intervene in a timely fashion but

must have the incentive to do so and must actually do so in a predictable and timely fashion. That has not always been the case. "Regulatory forbearance"—the failure of regulators to take action when
necessary—was a common occurrence during the thrift debacle of the
late 1980s. In the past regulators have delayed taking action to evade
responsibility or have deluded themselves into thinking that things
would get better if only they waited it out. While FDICIA addressed
that problem in 1991 by directing regulators to take prompt corrective action based on clearly articulated criteria to resolve a troubled
or failing insured institution before the bank's net worth becomes
negative, regulators continue to have considerable discretion in
designing and implementing early intervention and closure policies.[9]

Further, regulatory effectiveness and efficiency require that taxpayers or their representatives be able to monitor and evaluate the
actions of regulators. Regulatory systems, therefore, need to be
transparent so that inappropriate behavior by regulators does not
undercut well-meaning monitoring and supervisory standards.[10]

Public Disclosure Requirements. Requiring banks to make public
disclosures about their operations and financial performance could in
principle reinforce regulators as monitors of banks. By making relevant information available to the public, banks could be made subject to depositor and creditor discipline that would backstop government regulation. If banks were to take excessive risks, for example,
depositors and creditors could demand higher risk premiums or leave
the bank entirely and thereby provide an incentive for banks to operate more prudently.

In the present regulatory environment, the prospect of public
disclosure's controlling bank risk-taking is unrealistic. First, deposit
insurance and an implicit "too-big-to-fail" policy effectively remove
the incentive for depositors to monitor banks closely. Second, current
accounting and disclosure conventions are inadequate in that they do
not now and probably will never provide sufficient information for
depositors and creditors to make accurate assessments of a bank's
risk exposure. It is impossible, for example, for depositors to evaluate the credit risks associated with either a bank's loan portfolio or
its derivatives trading book, or to assess a bank's overall interest rate
exposure (or the "duration" of the bank's portfolio). In contrast, regulators have access to extensive nonpublic information about a
bank's operations—information that is not available to a bank's

depositors, stockholders, creditors, and rating agencies. It is fool-hardy to believe that bank depositors and creditors are in a position to second-guess regulators about the condition of the bank. More logically, they will look to regulators for protection. Thus, in the current regulatory environment the notion that through greater public disclosure depositor and creditor discipline could be a substitute for prudential bank regulation is fundamentally illogical.[11]

Public disclosure, of course, may serve other purposes. It may permit stockholders to assess *ex post* the performance of bank managers and thus reduce the associated agency costs. It may increase market efficiency by keeping consumers better informed about the prices of bank services and about the returns on various bank products. That is the goal underlying disclosure laws such as the Truth in Lending Act of 1968, the Fair Credit and Charge Card Disclosure Act of 1988, and the Truth in Savings Act of 1991. Under the present system, however, public disclosure is not a substitute for prudential bank regulation and supervision.

Alternative Supervisory Frameworks. Under the current regulatory framework, U.S. banks engaging in significant nonbanking activities must do so under the umbrella organization of a bank holding company, which becomes the owner (or parent) of the nonbanking affiliates. The Federal Reserve is responsible for regulating the bank holding company. It sets capital requirements on a consolidated basis for the bank holding company as a whole, has the authority to supervise all parts of the company, determines the permissible activities of the nonbanking affiliates and subsidiaries, monitors compliance with firewall provisions, and approves all holding company mergers and acquisitions. That consolidated supervision and regulation is in addition to other regulations to which holding company affiliates may be subject. For example, a securities affiliate of a bank holding company is subject to both SEC and Federal Reserve regulation, and a national bank subsidiary of a bank holding company is regulated by the Office of the Comptroller of the Currency and by the Federal Deposit Insurance Corporation, as well as by the Federal Reserve.

The need for consolidated supervision can be viewed as a vote of no confidence in firewalls. If firewalls were capable of protecting the parent affiliated bank, and therefore the FDIC insurance fund, there would be no need for consolidated supervision. It is the fear that firewalls will fail to prevent the risks taken by nonbank affiliates from ultimately undermining the soundness of the insured bank that underpins the logic of consolidated capital requirements and consolidated supervision. Consolidated regulation, therefore, adds still another layer of supervisory costs to an already heavily regulated banking and financial system.

Further, because the current system of regulating the activities of bank holding companies is based primarily on regulation of the *firm* or *institution* (bank, securities firm, insurance company, and so forth), rather than on the nature of the activities or functions performed by those firms, it is likely to result in unequal and competitively destructive regulation. In particular, two different financial institutions (say banks and securities firms) engaged in the identical financial activity are likely to be subject to different regulations. An alternative framework is "functional regulation," where regulatory responsibilities are divided up among regulators according to the activities or functions performed by firms. For example, SEC regulations would apply to all firms engaged in securities activities, regardless of the type of firm (whether a broker-dealer, a bank, or an insurance company). Under that system each activity would be regulated by a common regulator, with common rules and procedures.[12] Although either system—regulation by *institution* or by *function*—could be supplemented by the kind of consolidated supervision and regulation that we now have, the case for consolidated supervision is far from obvious.

The complexity of today's financial markets and the supervisory process makes clear two facts. First, in permitting banks to engage in a wide variety of nontraditional activities, we are greatly complicating the regulatory and supervisory process. We shall have complex firm organizational structures, separately incorporated and capitalized affiliates, extensive firewalls and the need to monitor and enforce such provisions, octopus-like consolidated federal regulation and supervision, and inconsistent and overlapping regulation of the same activity carried out by different types of firms. Second, there will have to be an expansion of the regulatory bureaucracy, which will undoubtedly increase costs significantly. The president of the Federal Reserve Bank of Cleveland, Jerry Jordan (1993), estimated that out-of-pocket costs of the present system of bank regulation ranged from 25 to 50 percent of the banking industry's total profits in 1992. We can expect those costs to rise appreciably in the future.

The Central Bank's Lender-of-Last-Resort Function. An important component of any system for safeguarding the banking system and maintaining financial stability is the Federal Reserve's capacity to intervene as "lender of last resort" in the event of a systemic problem. The Federal Reserve has the power to make credit available both generally and to individual banks and financial institutions to keep a potentially destabilizing disturbance from spreading to other institutions and other segments of the financial system.

In contrast to the regulatory provisions discussed above, which are aimed primarily at maintaining individual bank solvency, the lender-of-last-resort facility is intended to prevent a temporary liquidity crisis or a payments system disruption from escalating into a full-blown financial crisis. If banks and other financial institutions become insolvent through imprudent risk-taking, there is little central banks can do to restore their solvency. Central banks can, however, prevent a liquidity disruption involving solvent institutions from mushrooming into a situation that results in the inability of even solvent institutions to meet their obligations. Thus, central banks must stand ready to prevent a financial disturbance from creating a liquidity problem that undermines the ability of even solvent institutions to meet short-term liquidity needs.[13]

Improving the Current System of Bank Regulation

The current bank regulatory system of risk-based capital requirements, despite recent reforms enacted by FDICIA, still does not provide adequate protection against excessive risk-taking. Further, the system is already very costly and will become more costly in the future as regulators struggle to keep pace with an increasingly complex and difficult-to-monitor financial system.

First, current capital requirements do not provide adequate deterrence to excessive risk-taking. Although capital requirements arguably do provide some deterrence to risk-taking because they are a form of "deductible" against bank owners in the event of insolvency, that deterrent alone is unlikely to keep banks from taking excessive risk. To begin with, the "deductible" is levied against bank owners, but the interests of bank owners and bank managers are often not the same, especially in large banks where there is a clear separation of ownership and control. Control often rests in the hands of bank managers, not owners. Further, in a declining industry like banking, which is under intense competitive pressure, entrenched managers may not wish to see the banks under their control shrink in size. They may, instead, prefer to undertake risky projects in the hope of maintaining the size and profitability of their banks. In addition, risk-based capital requirements can be expected to lag a bank's actual risk exposure, so there is a benefit to both owners and managers in taking on additional risk, a temptation that will surely be tested when banks come under increased competitive stress.

Second, as banks move into new activities that are more complex and less transparent, such as derivatives activities, it will become progressively more difficult for regulators to monitor and to control risk-taking. At a minimum, monitoring will have to occur much more frequently and will require that more regulatory resources be devoted to the monitoring and supervision process. The result will be less effective supervision, or less accurate capital requirements, and increasing regulatory costs.

Third, reliance on firewalls as effective risk insulators may be unwise. When an important nonbank affiliate is threatened with bankruptcy, banks will have a strong incentive to come to its rescue, which potentially puts the bank in jeopardy. Further, the trend toward extending the range of permissible bank activities via the use of "walled-off" nonbank affiliates reduces the very efficiencies that are the raison d'être for permitting banks to extend the range of their activities. Extensive use of affiliates and firewalls also will create a costly system of regulatory barriers and monitoring that can be expected to result in the establishment of a pervasive and invasive consolidated regulator (such as the Federal Reserve).

Finally, no system of risk-based capital requirements coupled with regulatory monitoring can be expected to be effective so long as we continue to refuse to employ market-value-based measures of bank capital and risk. Further, critics are correct when they assert that regulators are unlikely to move quickly to institute a market-value-based system.

Those criticisms point to important deficiencies in the current regulatory system, and suggest a number of steps that need to be taken to make the existing system more effective:

- Effective risk-based capital standards and regulatory monitoring require that the assets and liabilities of banks be measured reasonably accurately on a *market-value* (or liquidation) basis and that regulators be able to reassess a bank's net worth and its potential risk exposure at frequent intervals and at reasonable cost. At a minimum, therefore, banks should be required to adopt market-value accounting and disclosure principles.

- Capital standards should be revised to reflect *all* risks taken by banks—credit, market, operational, and legal. Regulators are currently working toward that goal, but it is unlikely to be achieved until market valuation of both banks' assets and liabilities and banks' risk exposure is implemented.

- Banks should make available to the public market-value-based risk-disclosure statements that provide a reasonably accurate picture of the risks to which they are exposed. Such disclosures will enhance economic efficiency and may help to deter excessive risk-taking by providing better information to regulators, customers, creditors, and stockholders.

- Although it is widely recognized that effective supervision requires prompt corrective action by regulators to protect the deposit insurance fund and taxpayers (Benston and Kaufman 1988), it is questionable whether at present we have clearly articulated and effective early intervention and closure policies.[14] Despite the improvements made by FDICIA in 1991, there remains substantial scope for supervisory forbearance. Better and more concrete early intervention criteria need to be developed, and regulatory actions need to be made more transparent so that such actions can be more easily evaluated.[15]

- For capital requirements to be an effective deterrent to excessive risk-taking by banks, the interests of bank owners and bank managers must be more closely aligned. Requiring banks to disclose information based on market-value-driven estimates of risk and of assets and liabilities will help to do that. But more needs to be done. A further alignment of the interests of bank managers with those of bank shareholders can be achieved by removing obstacles to effective corporate governance and to bank "takeovers" so that poorly performing bank managers can be removed more easily. Repeal of the Bank Holding Company Act would help to accomplish that.

- "Banking" needs to be redefined. We need to articulate more clearly the activities that banks that accept insured deposits—which I refer to as "core" banks—can engage in *directly* and the logic that underlies that determination. The logic of the current regulatory system implies that as long as capital requirements and supervisory monitoring are sufficient to control banks' risk-taking, there need be no limits on the kinds of activities in which banks can *directly* engage. Alternatively, if, as my analysis suggests, those prudential controls are unlikely to be effective when a bank's activities are either opaque or can be used to change a bank's risk exposure quickly, "core" banks should not be permitted to engage in such activities. To do otherwise would create an unacceptable moral hazard problem for taxpayers.[16]

Acceptance of even that principle still leaves Congress and regulators with the imponderable task of having to determine which activities are either too opaque or too difficult to monitor. Failure to come to grips with that fundamental principle, however, has resulted in inconsistent and indefensible regulatory decisions and legislative rules. In particular, legislators and regulators have permitted core banks to engage directly in opaque activities (such as making commercial real estate loans) and in activities that are exceedingly difficult to monitor in a timely fashion (such as derivatives trading). At the same time legislators and regulators have not permitted activities that are both more transparent and easier to monitor (such as selling and underwriting life insurance). It is clear that fundamental economic principles have not guided those determinations and that we need to return to such principles if we are to have a logically coherent regulatory system.

- Once the scope of "core" banking is defined, we need to determine the permissible activities for bank-related entities, or to determine the activities that banks can engage in *indirectly* via bank subsidiaries or holding company affiliates. That definition will depend upon one's belief (or faith) in the effectiveness of firewalls. If one assumes that firewalls are effective, even activities that are deemed unsuitable for banks to engage in directly should nevertheless be permitted through either bank subsidiaries or bank-affiliated enterprises, since there would be no risk to the "core" bank. Further, there would be no need to put restrictions on bank subsidiaries or affiliates or to have consolidated federal regulation and supervision.[17] If one assumes that firewalls *cannot* be relied on to insulate banks, activities deemed unsuitable for banks to engage in directly should also not be permitted via subsidiaries or affiliates.

- The Federal Reserve should reduce risk to the payments system by eliminating subsidies extended to clearing banks as a result of its current policy of permitting large intraday overdrafts on its Fedwire system. It can do that by providing real-time clearing against only collected funds or by charging an intraday overdraft fee equivalent to the market interest rate (such as the average federal funds rate).[18]

Finally, even if reforms consistent with the foregoing principles were implemented (which seems highly unlikely), it would still be exceedingly costly to make the current system work effectively. In particular, as banks expand into increasingly complex and opaque activities, it will become more and more difficult for regulators to determine appropriate capital standards and to monitor and police the activities of banks. Partly for that reason, some critics of the present regulatory system argue for narrowing the scope of government guarantees and regulation to only that which is absolutely necessary—protection of the payments system—and for relying more on the discipline of private markets to monitor and police both the payments system and the activities of financial institutions generally.

Collateralized Banking

A number of proposals to narrow the scope of government guarantees have been advanced (Burnham 1991; Kareken 1986; Litan 1987; Pierce 1991; Pollack 1992; Tobin 1987; Merton and Bodie 1993). Those proposals can be generically labeled as collateralized banking proposals, although there are substantial differences among them. In general, they would limit the provision of liquidity services or payments services to newly formed institutions called collateralized banks. Those banks would be the only institutions permitted to provide demand deposits (or transactions balances payable on demand at par value), and would be required to invest (or to "collateralize") all depositor funds in short-dated, low-risk assets.[19] Under some proposals collateralized banks would be permitted to hold only U.S. Treasury bills; under others they could hold additional high-quality, short-maturity assets, such as highly rated commercial paper (assets similar to those that MMMFs are now permitted to hold). Thus, collateralized banks would have very little exposure to market risk and very little or virtually no credit risk, and therefore could be relied on to meet all deposit withdrawals at par. Finally, all fund transfers, whether by check or electronic transfer, would be required to flow through collateralized banks, which would effectively guarantee the soundness of the payments system by collateralizing all payments.[20]

The specific collateralization mechanics would work much like the successful margin and clearing systems used by futures exchanges. In particular, a bank would be required to post collateral assets equal to or greater than the value of its deposit liabilities, and those assets would be marked to market daily with daily variation margin payments required.[21] In addition, those assets would be held by independent custodians.[22] Such an arrangement would ensure that the market value of the bank's collateral assets would never fall below the redemption value of its deposit liabilities. Further, in the event that it was deemed necessary to allow banks to collateralize with low-risk but not entirely default-free short-dated assets, such as highly rated commercial paper, collateralization requirements could be appropriately adjusted to reflect that risk.

A collateralized-bank institutional structure would eliminate the need for government-backed deposit insurance since all of the liabilities of collateralized banks would be fully secured through collateralization. Depositor losses could occur only in the event of fraud or gross mismanagement. Thus, the only role for deposit insurance would be to signal to depositors that their deposits were safe. Further, the need for regulatory monitoring and supervision would be greatly reduced, since collateralized banks would hold only low-risk, transparent assets that would eliminate moral hazard risk. Regulators need only verify that the correct assets were being held, which in the absence of opaque assets becomes a relatively simple supervisory task. Collateralized banks would still be subject to other types of regulation, such as SEC disclosure requirements and antitrust laws.

While proposals for reforming bank regulation differ on whether banks should be permitted to be part of, or be affiliated with, non-bank financial institutions and commercial enterprises, a strength of collateralized banking is that it does not require such separation to ensure the integrity of deposits. Collateralized banks can be safely operated "within house" even by financial institutions or firms with unrestricted powers (such as universal banks). Collateralized banks can function simply as "departments" within diversified financial service firms. There would be no need for corporate separateness and firewalls. As long as all liabilities effectively payable on demand at par value were appropriately collateralized and custodialized, there would be no risk to depositors or to the insurance fund by affiliation with nonbanking firms. The only role for regulation would be to ensure that the appropriate collateralizing assets were being held and to monitor compliance with the collateralization requirements. Requiring collateralized banks to operate as separate affiliates walled off by elaborate firewalls would unnecessarily raise costs and reduce efficiencies.

Thus, other than collateralization requirements, full-service banks or financial service firms would be free to engage in whatever activities they wished to and could raise whatever funds they needed to support those activities. They could issue stocks and various kinds of subordinated debt instruments—bonds, commercial paper, and possibly even longer-dated, uninsured, deposits—and could use those funds to support whatever risky investments they chose to make—commercial loans, consumer loans, or real estate loans—or to engage in activities such as securities underwriting and derivatives trading. Debt holders of full-service banks, unlike insured depositors, would as general creditors be subject to losses if the bank were to become insolvent. Thus, except for collateralization requirements, all activities of a bank or financial services firm would be free of banklike prudential regulation.[23]

Adoption of a collateralized-bank system promises five major advantages. First, it would eliminate most government restrictions on the activities of banks and other financial services firms, which would increase competition and improve the allocation of financial resources. Second, the system would increase efficiencies by allowing full-service banks and financial services firms to capture economies of scope by permitting them to provide a wide array of diversified products. Third, the system would reduce supervision costs by simplifying the regulatory structure so as to reduce substantially the need for and scope of regulatory monitoring. Fourth, by limiting government guarantees, the system would increase the use of market discipline to control excessive risk-taking by financial institutions in general. Finally, the collateralized-bank system would increase transparency in the regulatory process, which would permit taxpayers to monitor regulators more effectively. In addition, because the liabilities of financial service firms would no longer be guaranteed by the government, investors would demand that those firms issue market-value-driven financial statements as well as market-valuation assessments of their risk exposures. That would improve public disclosure and enhance market discipline. The distorting effects of the moral hazard risk implicit in deposit insurance, as well as the perverse effects that flow from efforts to evade regulatory restrictions, also would be largely eliminated.

Critics of a collateralized banking system have raised six objections. First, there would not be a sufficient volume of low-risk, short-dated assets available for collateralized banks to hold. Second, collateralized banks would not be competitive and therefore would not be economically viable. Third, when the system changed, there would be less credit available or there would be a disruptive reallocation of credit, or both. Fourth, the synergies between the deposit-taking and the lending functions of banks would be lost. Fifth, the financial system would be more rather than less vulnerable to systemic problems because a greater volume of liquid financial assets would be held in relatively less regulated financial institutions, such as mutual funds. Finally, monetary policy would be less effective than at present.

Of those concerns, I believe only the latter two raise fundamental issues. Ironically, those two fears are the same ones that motivated the "parallel banking system" proposal discussed earlier in chapter 5, which would substantially expand the scope of government guarantees and bank prudential regulation to nonbank financial institutions. The first four concerns are less important. MMMFs, which are similar in concept to collateralized banks, have found assets to hold and have grown rapidly. That suggests that collateralized banks are both feasible and practicable and can find a competitive niche alongside other financial institutions.[24]

With respect to credit availability, there is no reason to believe that ample credit will not continue to be provided by banks and nonbank financial institutions, such as finance companies and pension funds. In recent years nonbank lenders have substantially increased their credit-granting abilities because of increased asset securitization and the growth of the commercial paper market and other debt markets. Further, to the extent that there is an unfilled demand for credit services, new lenders can be expected to fill that gap quickly since formidable entry barriers for new lenders will not exist. While the allocation of credit may change somewhat to reflect the removal of bank subsidies presently associated with deposit insurance, there is no reason to expect that collateralized banking will result in a general credit shortage or in a serious credit disruption.[25] Finally, to the extent that synergies still exist between the deposit-taking and the lending functions of traditional banks, banks will continue to capture those synergies because collateralized banks will be permitted to operate within diversified, full-service banks. In any case, recent changes in financial markets have substantially reduced the importance of such synergies.[26]

The more serious concerns about financial stability and the effectiveness of monetary policy arise because collateralized banking can be expected to shrink the role of traditional (insured) bank deposits in the financial system. Collateralized banks will presumably pay lower yields on their insured deposits than investors can obtain elsewhere, so that households may shift additional assets to higher yielding but higher risk assets.[27] Households may, for example, shift assets formerly held at banks to various types of mutual funds (some of which would be managed by banks) or choose to hold longer-dated, uninsured, bank liabilities. Thus, critics argue that collateralized banking will shift the problem of maintaining financial stability from that of guaranteeing banks and bank deposits to that of guaranteeing the uninsured liabilities provided by less regulated financial institutions, such as mutual funds and uninsured banks. Critics contend that the result will be a more fragile financial system than we now have (Ely 1991). Further, they argue that, in the event of a run on uninsured financial institutions, or of widespread bankruptcies among uninsured institutions, regulators and the central bank will still have to intervene to prevent a financial panic, just as they now do when banks are threatened, but that the Federal Reserve will be less effective as a lender of last resort because it will lack regulatory jurisdiction. Thus, critics assert that collateralized banking will simply shift the regulatory problem to that of maintaining the stability of unregulated and uninsured financial institutions.

After examining mutual funds in chapter 5, I concluded that they are not subject to the same kind of systemic vulnerability as are banks. The characteristics of mutual funds are quite different from those of banks: there is no requirement that they redeem their liabilities at par value; they hold mostly transparent assets; they adhere to market-value accounting and disclosure principles, and they mark their assets to market every day. For those reasons I argue that if households were to hold in mutual funds the financial assets that they chose not to hold in collateralized banks, there would be no risk to the financial system. One could easily envision a financial system in which households and businesses would place their funds in a variety of mutual funds, one of which would be a collateralized bank similar to an MMMF.

This leaves the question of whether uninsured, noncollateralized banks should be permitted to exist. Some critics contend that the mere use of the terms *bank* and *deposit* will mislead the public, so that all banks would by necessity have to be backed by a federal guarantee, once again necessitating banklike prudential regulation.[28] If that is accurate (which I doubt), the solution is to restrict the use of the terms *bank* and *deposit* to only collateralized banks and not to prohibit collateralized banks. Uninsured financial institutions would have to use a different name (such as finance companies), and their uninsured liabilities could not be called *deposits* but would have to be called something like *participating certificates, shares*, or simply *debt obligations*. Alternatively, the critics may be wrong: the public may be able to grasp quickly the difference between insured and uninsured deposits if their interests depend on their ability to do so.

Finally, there is a question about whether government should make available to the public a small-denominated, par-value, long-dated, riskless (at least nominally) savings vehicle. Currently, long-dated, insured bank time and savings deposits serve that function. Under a collateralized-bank system such insured deposits may disappear. To the extent that households wish to hold such assets under a collateralized-bank system, however, there is reason to believe that the private market will find a way to supply them. For example, uninsured institutions would be free to offer fixed-term liabilities, payable at par value, that were collateralized by riskless assets of equal maturity. Or they could obtain a third-party guarantee of their liabilities (from an insurance company, for example).[29] In short, in today's financial markets there are more logical and more direct ways of providing a fixed-term, risk-free savings vehicle than the current system of banks' issuing government-insured deposit liabilities backed by long-dated, opaque assets.[30]

Conclusions and Implications for Regulatory Reform

In the next decade advances in telecommunications and computing technology will transform the infrastructure through which firms provide financial services. Innovations have already reduced the costs of providing most financial services, lowered entry barriers into financial markets, and made it possible for nonbank financial firms to compete head-to-head with banks. The result has been enhanced competition, which has eroded the franchise value of banks and increased pressure on banks to maintain profitability by expanding into more complex, less transparent, and more risky activities. That in turn has made it more difficult for regulators to monitor and to control risk-taking by banks.

Rapid innovation also has made it difficult for regulators to draft rules to control specific activities and institutions. In today's dynamic markets, regulatory conventions quickly become obsolete. The new finance does not fit easily into the old regulatory boxes. Regulators are relegated to a "catch-up" role, in which they continually impose new restrictions to close new and unforeseen gaps in regulation and constantly seek new powers to keep pace with their increased monitoring and supervisory responsibilities. The result is an increasingly costly and less effective regulatory system, together with an ever-expanding regulatory bureaucracy.

In the future financial institutions will be asked to provide products with returns that match the risk tolerances of investors. Just as the mutual fund industry has grown dramatically in response to investor demand for investment products with different risks and returns, financial institutions will have to provide a wide array of new products and services to suit investors' needs.[31] Financial institutions can be expected to find more efficient ways to provide liquidity and transactions services, to fund long-term investment projects, to provide risk-sharing and risk-pooling mechanisms, and to provide savings vehicles for small investors. Some of those will undoubtedly be low-risk instruments that provide savers with a guaranteed floor on their returns.

In addition, institutions will be able to construct an investment product with a given risk and return profile in many different ways; we can expect them to choose the least costly alternative. The institutions that survive will be those that can provide the products at the lowest cost. Although many of today's financial institutions will survive, their structure and the way in which they provide their products and services will change dramatically as innovations open up new ways of doing things.

In the past, regulation has concentrated on preserving particular financial institutions, such as banks and thrifts, often by impeding the growth of more efficient products and competitors. Sometimes, as in the case of the ill-fated thrift industry, that policy has had disastrous results, even for the protected institutions. In the future, financial functions must be allowed to determine the institutional structure, rather than institutions' and regulators' determining which financial functions will exist. An important goal of regulation should be to facilitate the provision of financial services in the most efficient way by permitting institutional flexibility. Financial institutions must be free to adapt quickly to changing technologies and market innovations. Regulatory restrictions must be reduced, the regulatory structure simplified, and greater use made of market mechanisms to control institutional risk-taking. In addition, the activities of both financial institutions and regulators must be made more transparent.

Adoption of a collateralized-banking approach to regulating financial institutions will accomplish those objectives. That approach provides a simpler and more transparent regulatory structure that will substantially lower regulatory costs without sacrificing financial stability. It provides a way to protect the payments system while not imposing an elaborate and costly regulatory structure on all financial institutions and activities. Once banks and other financial service firms have satisfied the applicable collateralization requirements, their other activities can be left largely unregulated. Also, there will no longer be a need for the elaborate system of separately incorporated and separately capitalized affiliates, firewalls, and regulatory monitoring and supervision that now threaten to swamp the system in regulatory costs.[32] By removing regulatory restrictions, competition in financial markets will be enhanced and the allocation of resources improved. Financial institutions will have to meet the test of the marketplace, and their decisions will be subject to the discipline of investors.

The major objections to collateralized banking are, first, that it will result in greater financial instability because uninsured banks (or noncollateralized banks) and competing nonbank financial institutions will be less regulated and, second, that it will undermine the effectiveness of monetary policy because the Federal Reserve will no longer be able to control the money supply. Neither of those concerns, I believe, provides a convincing objection to collateralized banking. The analyses in chapters 5 and 6 suggest that less regulated nonbank financial institutions, such as mutual funds, do not pose a threat to systemic stability and that the effectiveness of monetary policy does not depend either on the Federal Reserve's having the power to impose reserve requirements on institutions providing "money substitutes" or on the Federal Reserve's power to regulate nonbank financial institutions. In particular, mutual funds generally and MMMFs in particular are not subject to the kind of systemic vulnerability that has historically plagued banking, and their provision of "money substitutes" has not undercut the effectiveness of monetary policy.

The politics of regulatory reform does not favor collateralized banking. Banks may not want to institute collateralized banking because they will have to give up the remaining deposit insurance subsidy. To the extent that banks now use low-cost, government-backed deposits to fund risky activities, they receive a government subsidy that they may not want to relinquish. Mutual fund companies also may resist collateralized banking because they will fear that it will lead to more regulation for them. If, for example, MMMFs were to become collateralized banks, they would be subject to bank regulation as well as SEC regulation, and there is no certainty that in the future bank regulators can be kept from expanding their powers over MMMFs as well as other mutual funds. Other nonbank financial firms, such as insurance companies and broker-dealers, will not like collateralized banking because it will increase competition. Banks will be set free to enter all areas of the financial services market on the same terms as firms already operating in those areas. Thus, whatever its economic merits, converting to a collateralized banking system may not at present be politically feasible.

A plausible public policy alternative is to do both: adopt collateralized banking while at the same time keeping the current regulatory system for full-service banks in place. In particular, investment companies could be permitted to operate collateralized banks as part of their mutual fund families. For example, MMMFs could, if they wished to, provide shareholders with unlimited payment services similar to those now provided by banks so long as they fully collateralized their liabilities with acceptable assets. The liabilities of such MMMFs, in principle, could also be insured by the government, although that would not be essential. Current experience makes it clear that households will hold MMMF shares even in the absence of government backing. Finally, while not essential to that proposal, appropriately collateralized MMMFs could be given access to Fedwire facilities for payments clearance. There are no significant obstacles to doing that. Collateralized MMMFs would not pose an insolvency risk to the Federal Reserve.[33]

At the same time, the present system of banking and bank regulation can be retained. Full-service (noncollateralized) banks and financial service firms can continue to operate as they do now, so long as they satisfy all the current regulatory requirements. Alternatively, those institutions can be permitted to operate collateralized banks as part of their institutional and corporate structure. All such institutions can then be permitted to compete directly with one another and with mutual funds operating collateralized banks, and the public can decide where to hold its funds.[34]

Under that proposal, full-service banks will not be required to give up their implicit deposit insurance subsidy, and banks, MMMFs, and other financial service firms will be free to choose whether or not to operate collateralized banks. Institutions can decide for themselves which is the best competitive alternative, and households and businesses can decide where is the best place to put their funds. If one alternative is clearly superior to the other, the market will tell us. It is important that we break the political stalemate that is locking us into an inefficient financial structure and a progressively more costly and ineffective regulatory system. Adopting a collateralized bank approach to regulation is one way to provide financial institutions with the flexibility to adapt quickly to changing market conditions without sacrificing financial stability.

✦ 9 ✦

Conclusion

Dramatic changes in information and telecommunication technologies have transformed U.S. financial markets in the 1980s and 1990s. Traditional financial intermediaries, like banks, have had to change what they do and how they do it in response to a steady stream of new financial products and instruments that have crumpled the competitive barriers that have historically separated financial intermediaries in the United States. This book examines the changes that have taken place in financial markets and explores the implications of those changes for financial intermediaries and public policy. One of the book's central conclusions is that the current system of bank regulation is out of step with today's financial realities and needs to be substantially changed. The challenge is to change regulation in a way that increases the freedom of financial institutions to compete while at the same time making the financial system less vulnerable to excessive risk-taking by individual financial institutions. My analysis leads me to conclude that the best way to achieve such seemingly incompatible goals is to adopt a system of collateralized banking. The book discusses how adopting such a system will result in a more stable financial system, both by reducing our reliance on government to maintain financial soundness and by enhancing the effectiveness of private markets in controlling institutional risk-taking.

The dramatic changes that have occurred in financial markets have affected banks (or depository institutions) more than any other financial intermediary. Traditional commercial banking—making long-dated loans with funds raised by issuing short-dated deposits—is in rapid decline. Traditional bank borrowers are increasingly bypassing banks in favor of going directly to capital markets, and households are shifting funds from bank deposits to competing nonbank intermediaries, like mutual funds. In an effort to maintain profitability, banks have increased their risk-taking and have sought to expand into new and often more risky, nontraditional financial activities, either by circumventing existing regulations or by getting those regulations changed. Banking also is undergoing a massive consolidation, as banks seek either to exit the market or to bolster their competitive position though mergers with other banks. In the future the face of banking in the United States will be far different from what it was in the past.

Some simple statistics make evident the dramatic transformation that has occurred in U.S. financial markets. In 1970 depository institutions (commercial banks and thrifts) held more than 61 percent of the assets of all financial intermediaries; in 1994 they held less than 38 percent of those assets—a twenty-three percentage point decline in market share. But even that figure understates the rapidity of the changes that are taking place. Almost all the decline in the market share of depository institutions has occurred in the past fifteen years: from 1980 to 1994 those institutions' share of financial intermediary assets fell from over 58 percent to under 38 percent. During that period more than 4,000 banking organizations also disappeared.

The declining fortunes of banks also have been mirrored by the stupendous growth of nonbank financial intermediaries. The growth of pension funds and investment (or mutual) funds has been nothing short of phenomenal. The share of intermediary assets held by those two nonbank intermediaries grew from 20 percent in 1980 to almost 40 percent in 1994, and that growth shows no sign of abating. Further, from 1982 to 1994 pension and mutual funds accounted for 67 percent of the net growth of households' total financial assets, compared with only 19.3 percent for depository institutions. Clearly, pension funds and mutual funds are providing a more attractive way for households and businesses to hold financial assets than are banks. Through those institutions households and businesses now hold participations in huge diversified portfolios of stocks, bonds, real estate, and even commodities.

More important, the dramatic growth of mutual funds shows the increased willingness of households to hold liquid assets whose values change on a daily basis, depending on the performance of the assets backing their investments. Investments in mutual funds are collateralized investments: investors' funds are collateralized by portfolios of prespecified types of financial assets (as designated in a fund's prospectus), about which investors have preconceived views as to their likely riskiness and future returns. For example, a high-growth equity mutual fund holds a portfolio of high-growth stocks. Those collateral assets are marked to the market on a daily basis, so that the value of investors' participation changes in accordance with the performance of the underlying assets. Mutual fund investors can choose to have their investments collateralized with assets ranging from virtually riskless—in MMMFs—to high-risk equity and bond instruments, such as long-dated, mortgage-backed, bond funds.

Those collateralized investments stand in sharp contrast to bank deposits, which carry the bank's promise to repay at par value. Depositors depend primarily on the creditworthiness of the bank, and on explicit and implicit government guarantees, rather than on the value of the assets that the bank holds. The value of deposits is not marked to market on a daily basis commensurate with the performance of the bank's assets. Rather, most depositors rely solely on the bank's promise to repay their funds at par value and are largely indifferent about what happens to the bank's assets. Further, notwithstanding some constraining regulations, banks can invest their deposit funds in assets of virtually any riskiness, and that process is for all practical purposes nontransparent to bank depositors. Only regulators and government guarantees stand between depositors and financial catastrophe. Despite government assurances and guarantees, however, in recent years households have steadily reduced their holdings of government-insured bank deposits in favor of competing collateralized investments such as mutual funds that provide higher yields. In 1982 deposits constituted 51 percent of households' liquid assets, whereas in 1994 deposits constituted only 30 percent of their liquid assets.

In response to those developments, banks have sought to change what they do and how they operate. Since 1980 they have more than doubled the amount of their funding obtained from nondeposit sources—to 40 percent of their total liabilities. Banks have also increased their holdings of risky loans such as commercial real estate and have substantially expanded their reliance on off-balance-sheet activities—doubling the share of their income generated by such activities since 1978, from 17 percent to 34 percent. Competitive pressures also have quickly become political pressures, as banks have pushed for legislation that would liberalize their powers and enable them to expand rapidly into nontraditional financial activities, such as securities and insurance activities. Only our archaic laws and regulations have kept them from fully expanding such activities. Thus, whether or not the importance of banks as financial intermediaries has diminished, it is clear that both banks and financial markets have changed in important ways and that those changes have important implications for how financial markets and institutions should be regulated in the future.

A critical problem for banks is that they are severely constrained in what they are allowed to do by regulations written more than a half-century ago, when financial technologies and the competitive environment were entirely different from what they are today. It should surprise no one, therefore, that an important goal of bankers is to find ways either to circumvent or to eliminate entirely the regulatory obstacles that constrain them. Bank regulators, as well, are struggling to find ways to free banks to compete that do not jeopardize either their ability to make good on explicit and implicit government guarantees or their ability to maintain the soundness and stability of financial markets. But while the need to modernize financial regulation to make it compatible with today's financial realities is obvious to all who care to look, there is no consensus on how to do so. Reform proposals typically founder on the shoals of unending controversy and political maneuverings driven by self-interest.

Neither the U.S. Congress nor regulators anticipated or planned for the changes that have occurred. Charged with the responsibility of maintaining the stability and integrity of financial markets, U.S. banking regulators are saddled with an outdated regulatory structure forged mainly during the 1930s in response to stresses on the financial system created by the Great Depression. But the current regulatory system is not only inefficient because it is out of step with today's technologies and market realities; it is also dangerous, because it is deceptive. It lulls us into believing that it is adequate to cope with the financial risks that now exist, while in reality it is not.

An important motivation for my writing this book is to bring what is happening in financial markets to a wider audience, and to inform and stimulate critical discussion of how to modernize the financial system. To make progress, discussion must be informed enough to cut through the political rhetoric and posturing that now prevent serious financial reform. In addition, past criticism of the changes that are taking place in financial markets have all too often focused on the wrong issues.

In particular, there are those who believe that the ascendancy of nonbank financial intermediaries such as mutual funds and the concomitant decline of traditional banking have in effect "deinsurancized" the financial system and thus increased its susceptibility to a systemic meltdown. They fear that mutual fund shareholders, unlike government-insured bank depositors, can be stampeded into running on mutual funds, an event that could precipitate a financial meltdown. Others fear that the proliferation and growth of unregulated financial instruments and markets, such as derivatives and off-exchange derivatives markets, have become the Achilles heel of financial markets. They argue that unless those markets are reined in by additional government regulation, they will eventually collapse—with dire consequences for the entire financial system. Still others believe that the structural changes that have occurred in financial intermediation have undercut the ability of the Federal Reserve both to identify key monetary aggregates and to control those aggregates and thus have diminished the effectiveness of monetary policy.

This book analyzes and evaluates those concerns. After examining them, however, I conclude that they do not constitute major threats to the financial system, and most probably spring from a misunderstanding of the changes that have occurred. The primary threat to financial stability in the future, I believe, will come from the banking industry, where we continue to rely on an outdated regulatory system to monitor and control institutional risk-taking. The current regulatory system is inappropriate for today's financial system and the one that will exist in the twenty-first century and will have to be substantially restructured if we are to avoid an escalation of the kind of institutional risk-taking that caused the U.S. thrift debacle in the 1980s and the Japanese banking crisis of the 1990s. We must find a way to enhance the role of private markets as a mechanism for controlling institutional risk-taking and for increasing market efficiency, and we must reduce our reliance on government guarantees and government regulators to maintain financial stability. Government regulators are no longer in a position to effectively monitor and control institutional risk-taking, however much we may want them to be. Further, all financial history, in this country and in other countries, points to the unstable and potentially explosive compound that results from the mixing of government guarantees and politics.

This book sets out a plan for restructuring the regulatory system that will enhance the stability of financial markets while reducing our reliance on government regulators. Further, it will expand the freedom of all financial institutions to compete and to better serve their customers. The key to this system is protecting the payments system by collateralizing or backing it with private assets sufficient to ensure that participating institutions will always be able to meet their payment obligations. In particular, financial institutions that choose to provide liquid transaction balances or deposits, and the associated payment and clearing services, would be required to collateralize those liabilities with low-risk, liquid assets—much as member organizations in futures clearing associations now collateralize their obligations to other clearing members. By collateralizing and custodializing the payments system, we can reduce the need for government regulators to monitor and control institutional risk-taking and can free banks and other financial firms to compete more effectively with each other and with foreign banks. Alternatively viewed, collateralization of the payments system is a way of privatizing the clearing and payments system that eliminates the need for government guarantees and subsidies that in turn require the government to monitor and police institutional risk-taking.

Whether the recommendations contained in this book are adopted, however, is of secondary importance to the book's overriding objective of stimulating informed debate about the public policy implications of the revolution that is overtaking financial markets. We have been far too complacent about the changes sweeping over financial markets and about the inadequacies of the current regulatory system. Those who read this book, I believe, will come away with a better understanding of what is happening in financial markets and why it is necessary to change how we regulate our financial industries.

Notes

CHAPTER 3: THE DECLINE OF TRADITIONAL BANKING

1. Wheelock finds that most of that decline occurred in the group comprising the smallest banks, which declined from 11,658 institutions in 1990 to only 7,661 by 1993. See also table 4-1 in chapter 4 for the total number of banking institutions.
2. All of those studies have deficiencies, however. In particular, in attempting to measure the decline of banking, they make adjustments to banks' balance sheets in an effort to incorporate off-balance-sheet activities but do not make similar adjustments to the balance sheets of nonbank financial intermediaries. Thus, it is impossible to determine whether the relative position of banks as providers of financial services generally has increased or decreased. In any case, studies that look only at earnings or profitability completely miss the transformation that is taking place. A simple mind experiment makes that obvious. Suppose that banks totally ceased taking deposits and making loans, and, instead, simply traded derivatives to maintain their earnings and profitability. Studies of bank profitability would show no change in the position of banks as financial intermediaries. That would clearly misrepresent the changes that are occurring in both banking and financial intermediation.
3. Specifically, banking is a highly regulated, government-backed industry. If banks substantially change what they do, as is happening, that has implications for how (or whether) they should be regulated and what the government's role as guarantor should be.

4. That measure of bank profitability is consistent with the performance of bank stocks during the 1980s. During the 1980s the S&P 500 index rose by 38 percent more than the Salomon Brothers index of bank stocks.

5. U.S. banks have an incentive to take additional risk because of federal deposit insurance. Insured depositors have little incentive to monitor banks and to penalize them for taking excessive risk. That moral hazard problem is compounded by our de facto "too-big-to-fail" policy for large banks. Empirical support for the view that banks have taken greater risk is presented by Kane and Unal (1990), who find that bank stocks became riskier investments during the 1980s. See also Furlong (1988).

   Although the 1991 FDICIA legislation contains a "least-cost resolution" provision that makes it more difficult for regulators to bail out large depositors and therefore large banks, it does not rule out a "too-big-to-fail" policy. If a two-thirds majority of both the Board of Governors of the Federal Reserve System and the directors of the FDIC agree, as well as the secretary of the treasury, even an insolvent bank can be kept open.

6. See table 8-1 in chapter 8 for a list of more than fifty major episodes of bank insolvencies since 1974.

CHAPTER 4: ALTERNATIVE VIEWS OF THE DECLINE OF BANKING

1. By high or low profitability I mean high or low in relation to the risks that a bank takes.

2. It should be noted, however, that finance company lending continues to differ from bank commercial lending. Finance companies tend to specialize in "good collateral" lending and leasing, while banks tend to make unsecured commercial loans (Becketti and Morris 1994; Remolona and Wulfekuhler 1992).

3. Theoretical studies have argued that banks can produce information about potential borrowers and can monitor borrowing firms more efficiently through their superior ability to enforce loan covenants (Diamond 1984; Boyd and Prescott 1986; Thakor and Bhattacharya 1991). In addition, empirical studies have found some evidence of bank uniqueness (James 1987; Lummer and McConnell 1990; Himmelberg and Morgan 1995).

4. Typical loan covenants may require firms to maintain a minimum net worth or working capital, or may restrict dividend payments and indebtedness.

5. It should be recognized, however, that commercial mortgage lending accounted for much of the growth in banks' real estate lending during the 1980s. Even so, there is no reason to believe that banks have a par-

ticular informational advantage with respect to commercial mortgage lending. They are only one of several financial intermediaries that make such loans, and they have recently suffered large losses as a consequence of making those loans. If these are the fruits of the comparative advantage banks purportedly enjoy, they are indeed bitter ones.

6. Himmelberg and Morgan (1995) find, however, that bank loans continue to be "special" for a small subset of borrowers: all low-quality, business borrowers.

7. The joint production of liquidity services and opaque business loans may even be an inferior technology because it requires substantial and costly government regulation to ensure systemic stability. Those regulatory costs may outweigh the advantages of the joint-production technology.

CHAPTER 5: MUTUAL FUNDS AND FINANCIAL STABILITY

1. This figure understates the magnitude of the transaction-balance services provided by mutual funds because many nonmoney market mutual funds, such as bond funds, also provide check-writing facilities.

2. The Community Assets Management's fund is the first MMMF to "break the buck." Shareholders are expected to get back only ninety-four cents on the dollar, making the fund's losses equal to about 6 percent of its assets. Those losses were derivatives-based: the fund held about a third of its assets in interest-sensitive secured notes created from a variety of U.S. government agency securities (Wayne 1994).

3. It is notable that the Community Assets Management's fund catered to large institutional investors: its shareholders were 112 community banks, primarily in Colorado.

4. D'Arista and Schlesinger propose bringing mutual funds under banklike prudential regulation, among their other recommendations.

5. There is no widely accepted definition of the commonly used term *systemic risk*. A recent report (Bank for International Settlements 1992) defines a *systemic crisis* as: "A disturbance that severely impairs the working of the financial system and, at the extreme, causes a complete breakdown in it. Systemic risks are those risks that have the potential to cause such a crisis. Systemic crises can originate in a variety of ways, but ultimately they will impair at least one of three key functions of the financial system: credit allocation, payments, and pricing of financial assets."

6. Moody's assigns Prime-1, Prime-2, Prime-3, and Not Prime short-term ratings according to an issuer's capacity to meet its short-term debt obligations. The fact that few issuers with the highest rating have ever defaulted should be viewed with caution. As faltering companies move

closer to default, it is common for Moody's to reduce their commercial paper ratings. Thus, immediately before default, it is not surprising that many defaulting companies have a low rating.

7. Similar recent bailouts kept MMMF shareholders from incurring losses because of derivatives-associated losses.

8. That regulation applies only to taxable MMMFs. In late 1993 the SEC proposed that similar restrictions be placed on MMMFs that hold tax-exempt securities.

9. Owing to the defaults in 1989 and 1990 and to the amendments to Rule 2a-7, MMMFs significantly reduced their holdings of lower-rated commercial paper. In late 1989 they held an estimated $25 billion in lower-rated paper that amounted to about 8 percent of their total assets. By June 1991, they held only about $1 billion of lower-rated paper that amounted to less than .5 percent of total assets (Collins and Mack 1993, 7).

10. For an assessment of the effects of Rule 2a-7, see Collins and Mack (1994).

11. Although recent innovations, such as the securitization of loans and the development of an efficient federal funds market, have enhanced the liquidity of some bank assets, the fundamental opaqueness and nonmarketability of bank assets still exist.

12. There have been many historical episodes of depositor panics. The most recent case of a bank run was in Venezuela when the nation's second largest bank collapsed in January 1994. The bank's failure caused a run on eight other banks and triggered Venezuela's biggest financial crisis in memory. To rescue the banks and prevent a financial panic, the government spent more than $7 billion, equivalent to about 16 percent of the country's 1993 gross domestic national product. The crisis also caused a sharp deterioration of the country's currency, the bolivar, and a run on the central bank's reserves that forced the government to impose price and currency controls and to suspend constitutional guarantees (de Cordoba 1994).

13. It is widely believed that banking is vulnerable to contagion effects (Corrigan 1982, 1987; LaWare 1991, 344; Gorton 1989; Calomiris and Gorton 1991). Not all scholars, however, believe that banking is especially susceptible to runs and to industry contagion (Kaufman 1992). My approach in this chapter is to accept the proposition that banks are vulnerable to runs and then to compare other intermediaries such as mutual funds with banks to determine whether they too are subject to runs.

14. See Form N-1A (the registration statement for open-end management investment companies), Rule 482 under the Securities Act of 1933, and Rule 34b-1 under the Investment Company Act of 1940.

15. There are some assets held by mutual funds for which a ready secondary market may not exist. Examples may be some local government bonds or the stocks of very small companies.

16. See section 22c of the Investment Company Act of 1940. Mutual funds are permitted to use pricing services to estimate prices for assets for which a deep and active secondary market does not exist, such as some municipal bonds. But the boards of directors of MMMFs have the ultimate responsibility for making those value determinations.

17. The transparency of mutual funds' assets is, of course, still not perfect. Mutual funds may change the composition of their portfolios between reporting dates, although most mutual funds do not make large changes between reporting dates. Also, for some mutual fund assets, such as municipal bonds, the quality of the publicly available information about the issuers may be poor, and the secondary markets for those assets may yield poor estimates of market value.

18. Gorton and Pennacchi's sample of events, however, is small, so it is unclear whether their results can be generalized. In addition to the Gorton and Pennacchi study, there have been several studies of the Penn Central crisis in 1970 that do find some evidence of contagion in the commercial paper market (Mishkin 1991; Schadrack and Breimyer 1970). Today's commercial paper market is, however, considerably different from the one that existed in 1970, so the results of those studies are probably not indicative of what would happen today.

19. See SEC Rule 2a-7. SEC regulations limit a fund's average portfolio maturity to ninety days.

20. SEC Rule 2a-7 imposes restrictions on the assets that MMMFs can hold. Those restrictions do not apply to tax-exempt MMMFs.

21. We can view those regulations as prudential regulations, not unlike those applied to banks.

22. These data can be found in Presidential Task Force on Market Mechanisms (1988). Chapter 5 of that study also notes that only 5 percent of owners redeemed or exchanged their stock mutual funds in the month after the market break, and by May 1988 only 15 percent of fund owners reported having taken any actions to redeem or exchange any type of mutual fund.

23. It is not, of course, obvious that direct owners of equity would be as likely to sell their stock as would mutual fund shareholders. The disparity in the propensity to sell would have to be quite large, however, to alter the conclusion that mutual funds had a dampening effect on October 19.

24. Although the average holding period for long-term funds, implied by the redemption rate, has ranged between 2.8 and 3.6 years in the 1990s, those figures are not necessarily inconsistent with the above survey evi-

dence because they reflect both institutional and individual holding periods. It is well known that institutions commonly have much shorter holding periods than do individuals.

25. Unpublished survey conducted by the Investment Company Institute in April 1994. The survey also indicated that the most frequent action taken by those shareholders was to purchase mutual fund shares.

26. See Guide 4 to SEC Form N-1A. In the case of MMMFs, the staff of the SEC has indicated that such funds should limit their investments in illiquid securities to less than 10 percent of assets. The SEC's definition of *illiquid* assets appears to be "assets that cannot be sold in seven days at approximately the price used in determining net asset value (the 'seven-day standard')" (SEC Release No. 33-6990, 34-32116, IC-19399, April 7, 1993). See also Smythe (1992).

27. In support of the bill, Senator Christopher Dodd, Democrat of Connecticut, said:

> It [FDICIA] also includes a provision I offered to give the Federal Reserve greater flexibility to respond in instances in which the overall financial system threatens to collapse. My provision allows the Fed more power to provide liquidity, by enabling it to make fully secured loans to securities firms in instances similar to the 1987 stock market crash (Dodd 1991, S18619).

For a review of that legislation, see Todd (1993).

28. That legislative authority is contained in the Emergency Relief and Construction Act of July 21, 1932, Public Law No. 72-302, which is reproduced in *Federal Reserve Bulletin*, vol. 18, August 1932, pp. 520–27. The critical section 210 of that act (sec. 13(3)) is at p. 523. The Federal Reserve Board's circular authorizing emergency discounts under section 13(3) for six months beginning August 1, 1932, is at pp. 518–20.

29. Instances in which the Federal Reserve has activated its emergency lending authority include the Penn Central Railroad failure in 1970, the Continental Illinois failure in 1984, the Bank of New York computer failure of 1985, the Ohio thrift crisis in 1986, the Texas bank failures in 1987 and 1988, and the Bank of New England failure in 1990.

30. Another episode in which the Federal Reserve acted as lender of last resort in aiding nonbanking firms was the Penn Central crisis in 1970. For a description of the actions taken by the Federal Reserve in that instance and an analysis of their impact, see Calomiris (1994).

31. In subsequent discussion in this book I use the term *banklike prudential regulation* to refer to that set of regulations.

32. While not stated explicitly, that proposal would presumably extend some form of deposit insurance or federal guarantee to all institutions that provide liquidity balances to households and businesses.

33. For an elaboration of this thesis, see Kaufman (1995).

34. A derivative is a financial instrument whose performance is derived, at least in part, from the performance of an underlying asset price or index of prices. The term *derivatives* commonly includes forward contracts, futures, options, swaps, and structured notes. In addition, participations in pools of mortgages are often thought of as derivatives instruments.

35. A fund's registration statement must provide disclosure about all significant fund investment practices and risks, including those relating to derivatives. In addition, investments in derivatives must be consistent with the fund's stated investment objectives and policies, with its name, and with its risk profile as set forth in the fund's prospectus, sales materials, or other disclosure documents.

36. SEC regulations require that a fund's investments in derivatives not be inconsistent with its "name" (Investment Company Act of 1940, sec. 35(d)). Perhaps for that reason as well as others the SEC staff recently stated that structured notes such as inverse floaters are not eligible investments for MMMFs (Barbash 1994).

CHAPTER 6: FINANCIAL INTERMEDIATION AND MONETARY POLICY

1. Turnover is measured as the ratio of total debits to an account over a year divided by the average yearly balance of the account.

2. See table 6-2 for the components of M2. Also, the most comprehensive turnover measure of debits is used for MMMFs: both asset exchanges and redemptions.

3. Friedman updates the Feinman and Porter (1992) chart on the relationship between M2 velocity and the opportunity cost of holding M2 (the difference between the weighted-average return paid on the various components of M2 and a weighted-average return on short-term market instruments not included in M2).

4. Rigorous statistical tests of the relationship between M2 and GDP provide mixed results with respect to the structural stability of the relationship. When I estimated a first-difference regression equation of GDP on a distributed lag of M2 and short-term interest rates for the 1969 to 1995 period, I found that a structural shift in the M2-GDP relationship occurred subsequent to the mid-1980s. But when I estimated a similar regression using logarithmic values (or rates of change) of those variables, I did not find a significant change in the structural relationship. Thus, econometric tests of the structural stability of the M2-GDP relationship are sensitive to the model and statistical methodology used.

5. We may also adopt a new monetary policy aggregate to replace M2 that will have a stable relationship with either aggregate economic activity or price inflation.

6. This is true regardless of whether the regressions are estimated in level or logarithmic form.

7. In Canada, for example, banks are no longer subject to legal reserve requirements.

8. See, for example, the symposium, "The Monetary Transmission Mechanism" (*Journal of Economic Perspectives* 1995).

9. Alternatively, households are not indifferent between holding money and other financial assets because of market imperfections at the household level. Specifically, all financial assets cannot be used for transactions purposes to the same degree.

10. In this case, therefore, the market imperfection is at the firm level, rather than at the household level: firms are not indifferent between borrowing from banks and borrowing from nonbank lenders.

11. For an empirical analysis of the importance of the credit channel of monetary policy, see Romer and Romer (1993).

12. Considerable empirical work has been done on the monetary transmission mechanism, but the issue remains a contentious one. For a review of that work, see Ramey (1993). In general, the results of those studies confirm the view that "money" is an important element of monetary policy; they find only weak support for the "bank credit" view. I think, however, it is fair to say that nothing is settled. There are many critics of those studies.

13. Depressed economic conditions also may have played an important role in bringing down interest rates in the 1990 to 1992 period.

CHAPTER 7: OTC DERIVATIVES MARKETS AND FINANCIAL FRAGILITY

1. A derivatives instrument (or transaction) is a bilateral contract or payments exchange agreement whose value derives, as its name implies, from the value of an underlying asset or underlying reference rate or index. Some derivatives, such as futures contracts, are exchange-traded; others, such as forward contracts and swaps, are traded only in OTC markets. While derivatives transactions may cover a broad range of underlyings, the bulk of OTC derivatives transactions are based on foreign currencies and interest rates. See table 3-15 in chapter 3.

2. A swap transaction is a bilateral contract that obligates the parties to the contract to exchange a series of cash flows at specified intervals known as payment or settlement dates. The cash flows of a swap are either fixed or floating and are calculated for each settlement date by multiplying the quantity of the underlying—the notional—principal by specified reference rates or prices. Interim payments are generally netted, with the difference being paid by one party to the other. Except for cur-

rency swaps, notional principals are not exchanged but are used only to calculate the payment streams.

3. Both in the United States and in foreign countries, banks are the dominant OTC dealers.

4. For example, the recent bankruptcy of the British investment bank Barings PLC might have resulted in substantial losses for both clearing associations and end-users.

5. Other risks are legal and operational. Legal risks occur because of the possibility that a contract will not be legally enforceable. Operational risks occur because of inadequate systems and controls, inadequate disaster or contingency planning, human error, or management failure.

6. Another example of credit exposure arising from a swap is the following. Assume that, under an interest rate swap agreement, a firm receives fixed-interest payments and pays floating rates. At the inception of that swap, the market value of the firm's position in the swap is zero. If, subsequently, interest rates decline, the firm will receive more than it will pay, so the firm will have a valuable or profitable position in the swap. That value, created by the change in interest rates, is the firm's credit exposure, or the loss to the firm if its counterparty defaults. That credit exposure can be measured by what it would cost the firm to replace the swap on the same favorable terms in the event its counterparty defaulted on future payments. That cost is referred to as the swap's "replacement cost."

7. Other types of OTC derivatives also exist. For example, "structured" debt and "hybrid" debt instruments are contracts that combine straight debt instruments with one or more attached derivatives to create payoff features different from either of the component parts. Thus, the reported sizes of OTC derivatives markets are very likely understated.

8. An interest rate swap is a contract under which two parties exchange net interest payments based on an agreed-upon nominal or notional principal. In its simplest form, a swap consists of a series of payments made at six-month intervals, where one party's payments are variable and are based on whatever the current interest rate happens to be (for example, they are based on the six-month London Interbank Offered Rate), while the other party's payments are based on a predetermined, fixed interest rate, such as 5 percent. The notional principal is never exchanged. By convention, interest rates in swap contracts are typically set so that the swap has a zero market value at inception. Subsequently, as market interest rates change, the required swap payments will change, which will change the market value of the swap. It will become an asset for one party (or be in-the-money) and will become a liability (or be out-of-the-money) for the other party.

9. The GAO (1994, 34) also reports that about 22 percent of the swaps outstanding are between dealers, as opposed to between dealers and end-users.

10. These include both their swaps and forward contracts.

11. Most banks have gross credit exposures in their loan portfolios that substantially exceed their total equity. See table 7-6.

12. The GAO report references the Group of Thirty (1993, 131–32). The Group of Thirty study, in turn, relies on a survey referenced by Swaps Monitor Publications, Inc. (November 1992). In its citation of the Group of Thirty study, the GAO report (1994, 36) incorrectly refers to the largest worldwide dealers (U.S. or foreign) as being only U.S. bank dealers.

13. This figure is not comparable to the $17.6 trillion that the GAO reports as being the total size of the derivatives market in 1992. The $8.7 trillion figure for the eight dealers includes some double-counting, which is eliminated in arriving at the total market figure of $17.6 trillion. Specifically, a $100 million notional swap between Citicorp and J. P. Morgan & Co., Inc. is counted in the total for the two dealers as $200 million because it appears in the accounts of both dealers. In contrast, in the GAO's $17.6 trillion estimate for the size of the total derivatives market, the same swap is counted as only a $100 million swap.

14. That figure, like the figure for the eight dealers, includes some double-counting.

15. It is noteworthy that, on average, only 10.97 percent of dealers' total net derivatives-related credit exposures were with other derivatives dealers (GAO 1994, appendix III, 157, 167).

16. The danger of imposing regulatory-mandated capital requirements is that over time those requirements can turn out to be *lower* than the market would demand in the absence of regulation. In other words, counterparties may come to rely more on government regulation and the associated implicit government guarantees than on the firm's capital and internal management.

17. The failure of Barings PLC is a vivid example of this.

18. The credit exposure to capital ratio is calculated by using risk-based capital (tier 1 plus tier 2 capital). See footnotes to table 7-6. Table 7-6 was compiled by the Office of the Comptroller of the Currency, Washington, D.C., 1995.

19. These proposals are similar to those made by the Financial Economists Roundtable (1995) in an October 1995 press release.

CHAPTER 8: FINANCIAL REGULATION FOR THE 21ST CENTURY

1. See my earlier discussion of bank crises in chapter 5.

2. A proposal for privatizing deposit insurance and banking regulation is the "cross-guarantee" scheme. (See H.R. 5227, introduced by Representative Tom Petri, a Republican from Wisconsin.) In that scheme each bank and thrift would be required to obtain a cross-guarantee contract for all its deposits and nondeposit funding. The guarantors would be a voluntary syndicate of other banks and thrifts, which would act much like an insurance underwriting syndicate. The syndicate would charge a risk-based insurance premium and would be responsible for specifying safe operating practices for the insured institutions and for monitoring insured institutions. That proposal, as well as other private insurance schemes, raises the question of who will guarantee the private guarantors in the event of a systemic failure. For a supporting view of that proposal, see Ely (1995).

3. U.S. banks must maintain minimum levels of capital depending on the composition of their asset portfolios and their off-balance-sheet risks. Capital requirements are stated as a percentage of weighted risk assets, where the weights reflect the riskiness of the various assets or the off-balance-sheet obligations that the bank is holding. Regulators may also require banks to exceed minimum capital requirements if their risk exposure warrants it. U.S. banks must simultaneously meet three capital standards: total capital must be at least 8 percent of total weighted risk assets (the total capital ratio); core capital must be at least 4 percent of total weighted risk assets (the core capital ratio); and core capital must be at least 3 percent of average total assets (the leverage ratio). Core capital (often referred to as "tier 1 capital") is defined as common stock plus surplus, retained earnings, noncumulative perpetual preferred stock, and minority interests in the equity accounts of consolidated subsidiaries less goodwill. Total capital is defined as core capital plus supplementary (or "tier 2") capital, where supplemental capital includes subordinated debt and intermediate-term preferred stock up to an amount equal to 50 percent of core capital, and an allowance for loan losses up to 1.25 percent of total risk-based assets.

4. Those so-called section 20 securities affiliates now account for about 15 percent of the assets of all broker-dealers registered with the SEC.

5. More specifically, the term *firewalls* has been loosely applied to a variety of legal and operational restrictions imposed by statute, regulation, or order. Besides insulating the bank from affiliate risk, they are also intended to prevent practices regarded as potentially unfair or risky between a bank and its affiliates and their customers and to prevent financial or other abuse of the bank by its affiliate.

6. Another example occurred in October 1987, when the stock market crashed. A securities subsidiary of the Continental Bank, First Options, incurred substantial losses and was in danger of violating its capital requirements. To prevent that from occurring, Continental Bank made

loans of about $130 million to First Options in violation of its legal lending limit. At the insistence of regulators, that violation was corrected the next day, when the parent company took out the bank. For additional examples, see Whalen (1995). Although there is little evidence that firewalls have not worked in recent years, they have also not been tested by widespread insolvencies.

7. A mechanism for doing that already exists. Part 5 of the regulations of the Office of the Comptroller of the Currency gives the office the authority to authorize activities considered incidental to the business of banking. The OCC has recently used that authority to permit banks to expand their nonbank activities through operating subsidiaries. The office's actions have been supported by recent court decisions. See *NationsBank of North Carolina, N.A. v. Variable Annuity Life Insurance Company*, 115 S. Ct. 810.

8. The recent collapse of the British investment bank Barings PLC, brought on by an inappropriate derivatives trading strategy coupled with poor internal controls, is a good illustration. For another example of what can happen when using derivatives, see Edwards and Canter (1995).

9. FDICIA of 1991 instituted a capital-based supervision mechanism that directs regulators to impose various sanctions on banks that fail to meet the risk-based capital requirements. The law requires regulators to establish five capital categories based on the amount of capital a bank has: well-capitalized, adequately capitalized, undercapitalized, significantly undercapitalized, and critically undercapitalized. For example, banks are considered to be undercapitalized if their ratio of total capital to weighted risk assets falls below 8 percent and both their core capital and leverage ratios fall below 4 percent. They are considered to be critically undercapitalized if their ratio of core capital to average total assets falls to less than 2 percent. If a bank becomes undercapitalized, regulators are directed to take various actions to reduce risks and restore the bank's capital levels. Significantly undercapitalized banks face a number of sanctions: mandatory recapitalization through the sale of voting shares, acquisition by a bank holding company, restrictions on the interest rates they can pay on deposits, restrictions on transactions with affiliates, forced divestiture of nonbank subsidiaries, and restrictions on executive compensation.

10. In the absence of transparency, regulators may engage in either under- or oversupervision. They may demand insufficient supervision so as to please banks or excessive supervision to minimize their political risk.

11. In any case, a first step toward improving public disclosure would be to make public the nonproprietary section of bank examination reports.

12. Functional regulation, of course, still leaves open the question of who will determine the kind of activity or function in which an institution or a firm is engaged. For example, what constitutes a "securities activity"?

13. For a discussion of the Federal Reserve's ability to lend to nonbank financial institutions to maintain financial stability, see the discussion "Can the Federal Reserve Still Be Effective as Lender of Last Resort?" in chapter 5.

14. For an analysis of the effectiveness of the current early intervention criteria, see Jones and King (1995).

15. For some suggested ways of improving the early intervention criteria, see Jones and King (1995).

16. Some scholars argue that there are important synergies between deposit-taking and making loans. As a consequence, they argue that core banks should be allowed to make opaque loans because of the associated deposit-taking efficiencies. The evidence that such synergies exist, or are important, is weak. Whatever synergies may have existed in the past also have been diluted by changes in the financial structure. See the discussion "The Theory of Declining Bank Uniqueness" in chapter 4.

17. The primary bank regulator, of course, would still be responsible for valuing the bank's investments in any nonbank subsidiaries or affiliates.

18. Privatizing the payments system is another way to eliminate those subsidies.

19. Collateralization could also be used to guarantee longer-maturity, fixed-term deposits by matching such liabilities with low-risk assets having the appropriate maturities and by marking such assets to market as described above.

20. This assumes that reforms are adopted that either eliminate large overdrafts on the Fedwire system or correctly price the risks associated with such overdrafts. See my discussion in the preceding section.

21. In particular, to prevent the market value of even short-dated Treasury bills from falling below the redemption value of the bank's par value deposits when interest rates rise, the bank would have to post collateral assets with a value somewhat greater than 100 percent of the value of its deposits—say 101 percent of its deposits. That additional sum is in effect analogous to the initial margins required by private clearing associations in futures markets. Or, alternatively, it can be viewed as a form of capital requirement that collateralized banks would have to meet by holding additional collateralizing assets. Since collateralized banks will be holding very short-dated assets and will be subject to daily variation margin payments, very little capital will be needed.

22. Such custodial arrangements are widely used in the mutual fund industry.

23. This system would be similar to the present mutual fund industry, where investment companies are allowed to operate both MMMFs and general purpose mutual funds. Shareholders place their funds with different mutual funds depending on the risk they are willing to take.

24. As with MMMFs, the profitability of collateralized banks will come from their ability to charge a fee for the service they provide. Presumably, the service they provide will be sufficiently valued by depositors to earn them a normal profit. If not, there is no reason for such banks to exist.

25. Some critics of collateralized banking assert that such a system would facilitate government allocation of credit by enabling government regulators to determine which assets are acceptable for collateralization purposes. That has not occurred with respect to MMMFs, however. Further, if it so desires, government through bank regulators already has the power to redirect the allocation of credit by altering existing bank regulations.

26. See the discussion "The Theory of Declining Bank Uniqueness" in chapter 4.

27. They can be expected to pay lower yields on deposits because of the costs associated with providing payment services.

28. Uninsured institutions would not have to be given access to Fedwire clearing. Alternatively, they could be given such access if certain reforms were made. See my discussion in the preceding section.

29. For a discussion of the feasibility of private insurance, see Ely (1994).

30. In chapter 6, I discuss the issue of monetary policy effectiveness and conclude that this also is not a problem.

31. Many mutual funds groups now offer investors over a hundred different choices.

32. An example of that is the so-called Leach Bill (H.R. 1062), which appears to be the favored reform bill before Congress. A major objective of the Leach Bill is to replace section 20 of the Glass-Steagall Act with a new regulatory framework allowing affiliations of full-service banks and securities firms without product or volume limits. To accomplish that the present Bank Holding Company Act would be extended to encompass a larger universe of securities and financial companies, thereby extending and perpetuating the current cumbersome and costly regulatory structure. In particular, the bill adopts the restrictive notion that nonbanking activities can be conducted safely only in subsidiaries of a holding company, rather than in the bank itself or in bank subsidiaries, and that restrictive and costly firewalls must be used to wall off nonbanking activities from the bank. The bill also continues to restrict the financial activities of bank (or financial services) holding companies to activities deemed by the Federal Reserve to be "financial in nature" (which does not include, for example, insurance activities) and continues to prohibit affiliations with commercial firms. Finally, the bill would rely on an expansion in the regulatory bureaucracy to control

institutional risk-taking by extending the jurisdiction of the Federal Reserve to encompass all aspects of the holding company's activities.

33. While there are currently implicit subsidies and guarantees extended to banks through the Fedwire system, there is no reason for those to exist. Indeed, the Depository Institutions Deregulation and Monetary Control Act of 1980 explicitly required the Federal Reserve to set cost-based fees for services performed, including daylight overdrafts. If the Federal Reserve would only do that, there would no longer be any Fedwire subsidies. See my recommendations earlier in this chapter.

34. Meltzer (1994) made a similar proposal.

Bibliography

Antilla, Susan. "In the Face of a Fund Panic . . . ." *New York Times*, June 27, 1993, sec. 3, p. 13.

Bacon, Kenneth H. "Banks' Declining Role in the Economy Worries Fed, May Hurt Firms." *Wall Street Journal*, June 9, 1993, p. A1.

Bank Administration Institute and McKinsey & Company, Inc. "Banking Off the Balance Sheet." New York: 1994.

Bank for International Settlements. "Recent Developments in International Interbank Relations." Report prepared by a working group established by the Central Banks of the Group of Ten Countries (also known as the "Promisel Report"). Basel: Bank for International Settlements, October 1992.

Bank for International Settlements and Central Banks of the Group of Ten Countries. "Public Disclosure of Markets and Credit Risks by Financial Intermediaries." Eurocurrency Standing Committee Discussion Paper, September 1994.

Barbash, Barry P. Letter from director of investment management, Securities and Exchange Commission, to Paul Schott Stevens, general counsel, Investment Company Institute, Washington, D.C., June 20, 1994.

Barth, James R., and Philip Bartholomew. "The Thrift Industry Crisis: Revealed Weaknesses in the Federal Deposit Insurance System," in James R. Barth and R. Dan Brumbaugh, Jr., eds., *The Reform of Federal Deposit Insurance*. New York: HarperCollins Publishers, 1992.

Barth, James R., R. Dan Brumbaugh, Jr., and Robert E. Litan. *The Future of American Banking*. Armonk, N.Y.: M. E. Sharpe, 1992.

Becketti, Sean, and Charles Morris. "Are Bank Loans Still Special?" *Economic Review* (Federal Reserve Bank of Kansas City) (Third Quarter 1992): 71–84.

Becketti, Sean, and Charles Morris. "Reduced-Form Evidence on the Substitutability between Bank and Nonbank Loans." Federal Reserve Bank of Kansas City, photocopy, 1994.

Benston, George J. *The Separation of Commercial and Investment Banking.* Oxford: Oxford University Press, 1990.

Benston, George J., and George G. Kaufman. "Risk and Solvency Regulation of Depository Institutions: Past Policies and Current Options." *Monograph Series in Finance and Economics.* New York University: Salomon Center for Graduate School of Business, 1988.

Bernanke, Ben S., and Alan Blinder. "Credit, Money, and Aggregate Demand." *American Economic Review* 78 (1988): 435–39.

Bernanke, Ben S., and Mark Gertler. "Agency Costs, Net Worth and Business Fluctuations." *American Economic Review* 79 (1989): 14–31.

Bernanke, Ben S., and Mark Gertler. "Inside the Black Box: The Credit Channel of Monetary Policy Transmission." *Journal of Economic Perspectives* 9 (Fall 1995): 27–48.

Bisignano, Joe. "Structure of Financial Intermediation, Corporate Finance and Central Banking." Bank for International Settlements, photocopy, 1992.

Black, Bernard S. "Agents Watching Agents: The Promise of Institutional Investor Voice." *UCLA Law Review* 39 (1992a): 813–93.

Black, Bernard S. "The Value of Institutional Investor Monitoring: The Empirical Evidence." *UCLA Law Review* 39 (1992b): 895–939.

Black, Fischer. "Bank Funds Management in an Efficient Market." *Journal of Financial Economics* 2 (1975): 323–39.

Bleakley, Fred. "Stock Drop Could Have Broader Impact Now." *Wall Street Journal*, February 28, 1994.

Blinder, Alan S. "Comment." *Brookings Papers on Economic Activity* 1 (1989): 111–14.

Board of Governors of the Federal Reserve System. *Federal Reserve Bulletin* (1982): 747–53.

Board of Governors of the Federal Reserve System. *Federal Reserve Bulletin* (1987): 286–89.

Board of Governors of the Federal Reserve System, Federal Deposit Insurance Corporation, and Office of the Comptroller of the Currency. *Derivatives Product Activities of Commercial Banks.* Joint Study Conducted in Response to Questions Posed by Senator Riegle on Derivatives Products. Washington, D.C.: Board of Governors of the Federal Reserve System, January 27, 1993.

Bosworth, Barry. "Institutional Change and the Efficacy of Monetary Policy." *Brookings Papers on Economic Activity* 1 (1989): 77–110.

Boyd, John H., and Mark Gertler. "Are Banks Dead? Or, Are the Reports Greatly Exaggerated?" in *The Declining Role of Banking.* Chicago: Federal Reserve Bank of Chicago, May 1994, pp. 85–117.

Boyd, John H., and Mark Gertler. "U.S. Commercial Banking Trends, Cycles, and Policy," in Olivier Blanchard and Stanley Fischer, eds., *NBER Macroeconomics Annual 1993*. Cambridge: MIT Press, 1993.

Boyd, John H., and Edward Prescott. "Financial Intermediary Coalitions." *Journal of Economic Theory* 38 (1986): 211–32.

Bradsher, Keith. "Bigger Role for Inflation Seen at Fed." *New York Times*, February 28, 1994, p. D1.

Brancato, C., and Patrick Gaughan. "Institutional Investors and Capital Markets." Center for Law and Economics, Columbia University, 1991.

Burnham, James B. "Deposit Insurance: The Case for the Narrow Bank." *Regulation* 14 (Spring 1991): 35–43.

"Business Bulletin." *Wall Street Journal*, June 12, 1986, p. 1.

Calian, Sara. "Bank America's Cost to Rescue 2 Funds Soars." *Wall Street Journal*, July 1, 1994, p. A2.

Calian, Sara, and Jasen Georgette. "Managers Prop up Money-Market Funds with Quiet Bailouts in Face of Losses." *Wall Street Journal*, June 10, 1994, p. C1.

Calomiris, Charles W. "Is the Discount Window Necessary? A Penn Central Perspective." *Monthly Review* (Federal Reserve Bank of St. Louis), (May/June 1994): 31–55.

Calomiris, Charles W. "The Motivations for Loan Commitments Backing Commercial Paper." *Journal of Banking and Finance* (May 1989): 271–77.

Calomiris, Charles W., and Gary Gorton. "The Origins of Banking Panics: Models, Facts, and Bank Regulation," in R. Glenn Hubbard, ed., *Financial Markets and Financial Crises*. Chicago: University of Chicago Press, 1991, pp. 109–74.

Collins, Sean, and Phillip Mack. "Avoiding Runs in Money Market Mutual Funds: Have Regulatory Reforms Reduced the Potential for a 'Crash'?" Board of Governors of the Federal Reserve System, photocopy, June 1994.

Collins, Sean, and Phillip Mack. "Has the SEC Reduced the Riskiness of Money Funds? An Assessment of the Recent Changes to Rule 2a-7." Board of Governors of the Federal Reserve System, photocopy, November 1993.

Cordoba, Jose de. "A Conglomerate Reels from Bank's Failure and Caracas Politics." *Wall Street Journal*, November 16, 1994, p. A1.

Corrigan, E. Gerald. "Are Banks Special?" *Annual Report*. Minneapolis: Federal Reserve Bank of Minneapolis, 1982.

Corrigan, E. Gerald. "Financial Market Structure: A Longer View." New York: Federal Reserve Bank of New York, January 1987.

Cutler, David M., James M. Poterba, and Lawrence H. Summers. "Speculative Dynamics and the Role of Feedback Traders." *American Economic Review, Papers and Proceedings* 80 (May 1990): 63–68.

D'Arista, Jane W., and Tom Schlesinger. "The Parallel Banking System," Briefing Paper. Washington, D.C.: Economic Policy Institute, 1993.

Diamond, Douglas. "Financial Intermediation and Delegated Monitoring." *Review of Economic Studies* 51 (1984): 393–414.

Dodd, Christopher. Statement in Support of Federal Deposit Insurance Corporation Improvement Act of 1991. *Congressional Record* (1991): S18619.

Eaton, Leslie. "Fear of Mutual Funds Flows: Relax." *Wall Street Journal*, October 30, 1994, sec. F, p. 13.

Eckhardt, J., and T. Knipp. "Metallgesellschaft: Neue Probleme in den USA." *Handelsblatt*, November 4, 1994.

Edwards, Franklin R. "Derivatives Can Be Hazardous to Your Health: The Case of Metallgesellschaft." *Derivatives Quarterly* 1(1995): 8–17.

Edwards, Franklin R. "Financial Markets and Managerial Myopia: Making America More Competitive," in George Kaufman, ed., *Reforming Financial Institutions and Markets in the United States*. Boston: Kluwer Academic Publishers, 1993a.

Edwards, Franklin R. "Financial Markets in Transition—or the Decline of Commercial Banking," in *Changing Capital Markets: Implications for Monetary Policy*. Kansas City: Federal Reserve Bank of Kansas City, 1993b, pp. 5–62.

Edwards, Franklin R. "Listing of Foreign Securities on U.S. Exchanges." *Journal of Applied Corporate Finance* 5 (Winter 1993c): 28–36.

Edwards, Franklin R., and Michael S. Canter. "The Collapse of Metallgesellschaft: Unhedgeable Risks, Poor Hedging Strategy, or Just Bad Luck?" *Journal of Futures Markets* 15 (1995): 211–64.

Ely, Bert. "Financial Innovation and Deposit Insurance: The 100 Percent Cross-Guarantee Concept." *Cato Journal* 13 (1994): 413–36.

Ely, Bert. "Financial Innovation and Risk Management: The Cross-Guarantee Solution." Paper presented at the Conference on U.S. Financial Structure in the Years Ahead: Domestic and International Issues, The Jerome Levy Economics Institute of Bard College. April 7, 1995.

Ely, Bert. "The Narrow Bank: A Flawed Response to the Failings of Federal Deposit Insurance." *Regulation* 14 (Spring 1991): 44–52.

Emergency Relief and Construction Act of July 21, 1932, Public Law No. 72-302. Reproduced in *Federal Reserve Bulletin* 18 (August 1932): 520–27.

Fama, Eugene F. "What's Different about Banks?" *Journal of Monetary Economics* 15 (1985): 29–39.

Federal Deposit Insurance Corporation Improvement Act of 1991. Section 473.

Federal Reserve Act of 1913. Section 13(2).

Federal Register 56 (February 27, 1991): 8113–30.

Feinman, Joshua N., and Richard D. Porter. "The Continuing Weakness of M2." Federal Reserve Board, photocopy, 1992.

Feldstein, Martin. "The Recent Failure of U.S. Monetary Policy." National Bureau of Economic Research Working Paper No. 4236, December 1992.

Feldstein, Martin, and James Stock. "The Use of a Monetary Aggregate to Target Nominal GDP." National Bureau of Economic Research Working Paper No. 4304, 1993.

"Fill That Gap!" *Euromoney*, August 1994, pp. 28–32.

Financial Accounting Standards Board. *FASB Status Report No. 267.* August 21, 1995.

Financial Accounting Standards Board. "Proposed Statement of Financial Accounting Standards: Disclosure of Derivative Financial Instruments and Fair Value of Financial Instruments." *Financial Accounting Series No. 136-B*, April 1994.

Financial Economists Roundtable. "Statement on Accounting Disclosure about Derivative Financial Instruments." *Financier* 2 (December 1995): 70–71.

Fons, Jerome S., Lea V. Carty, and Denis Girault. "Defaults and Orderly Exits of Commercial Paper Issuers." *Moody's Special Report.* New York: Moody's Investors Service, February 1993.

Friedman, Benjamin M. "Lessons on Monetary Policy from the 1980s." *Journal of Economic Perspectives* 2 (Summer 1988): 55–72.

Friedman, Benjamin M. "Ongoing Change in the U.S. Financial Markets: Implications for the Conduct of Monetary Policy." Paper presented at the Federal Reserve Bank of Kansas City's conference at Jackson Hole, Wyoming, August 1993.

Friedman, Milton, and Anna J. Schwartz. *A Monetary History of the United States, 1867–1960.* Princeton: Princeton University Press, 1963.

Froot, Kenneth A., Andre F. Perold, and Jeremy Stein. "Shareholder Trading Practices and Corporate Investment Horizons." Report prepared for the Time Horizons of American Management Project, 1992.

Fuerst, Timothy. "Liquidity, Loanable Funds, and Real Activity." *Journal of Monetary Economics* 32 (1992): 3–24.

Furlong, Frederick. "Changes in Bank Risk-Taking." *Economic Review* (Federal Reserve Bank of San Francisco) (1988): 45–55.

General Accounting Office. "Financial Derivatives: Actions Needed to Protect the Financial System." Report to Congressional Requestors, GAO/GGD-94-133. Washington, D.C.: Government Printing Office, May 1994.

Gonzalez, Henry. Remarks. *Congressional Record*, June 18, 1993, p. H3322.

Gorton, Gary. "Self-Regulating Bank Coalitions." University of Pennsylvania Working Paper, March 1989.

Gorton, Gary, and George Pennacchi. "Financial Innovation and the Provision of Liquidity Services," in James R. Barth and R. Dan Brumbaugh, Jr., eds., *The Reform of Federal Deposit Insurance*. New York: Harper-Collins Publishers, 1992a, pp. 203–24.

Gorton, Gary, and George Pennacchi. "Money Market Funds and Finance Companies: Are They the Banks of the Future?" in Michael Klausner and Lawrence J. White, eds., *Structural Change in Banking*. Homewood, Ill.: Irwin, 1992b, pp. 173–214.

Gorton, Gary, and Richard Rosen. "Corporate Control, Portfolio Choice and the Decline of Banking." Wharton School, University of Pennsylvania, photocopy, July 1994.

Gorton, Gary, and Richard Rosen. "Banks and Derivatives." Wharton School, University of Pennsylvania, photocopy, February 9, 1995.

Group of Thirty. *Derivatives: Practices and Principles*. Working Paper of the Systemic Issues Subcommittee, Group of Thirty, Washington, D.C., July 1993.

Grundfest, Joseph A. "Internationalization of the World's Securities Markets: Economic Causes and Regulatory Consequences." *Journal of Financial Services Research* 4 (December 1990): 99–100.

Hale, David D. "The Economic Consequences of America's Mutual Fund Boom." *International Economy* (March/April 1994): 24–64.

Hallman, Jeffrey J., Richard D. Porter, and David H. Small. "M2 per Unit of Potential GNP as an Anchor for the Price Level." Staff Studies 157, Board of Governors of the Federal Reserve System, 1989.

Hetzel, Robert L., and Yash P. Mehra. "The Behavior of Money Demand in the 1980s." *Journal of Money, Credit, and Banking* 21 (1989): 455–63.

Himmelberg, Charles P., and Donald P. Morgan. "Is Bank Lending Special?" Paper presented at the Federal Reserve Bank of Boston's conference "Is Bank Lending Important for the Transmission of Monetary Policy?" June 11–13, 1995.

Hooks, Linda, and Tim C. Opler. "The Determinants of Corporate Bank Borrowing." Financial Industry Studies Working Paper No. 1–93, Federal Reserve Bank of Dallas, May 1993.

Hubbard, R. Glenn. "Is There a Credit Channel for Monetary Policy?" Federal Reserve Bank of St. Louis, May/June 1995.

International Monetary Fund. "The Deterioration of Bank Balance Sheets." *International Capital Markets: Part II*. August 1993, pp. 2–22.

Investment Company Act of 1940. Rule 34b-1.

Investment Company Act of 1940. Section 2(a)(32).

Investment Company Act of 1940. Section 18(f).

Investment Company Act of 1940. Section 22(c).

Investment Company Act of 1940. Section 22(e).

Investment Company Act of 1940. Section 35(d).

Investment Company Institute. *Profiles of First-Time Mutual Fund Buyers.* Washington, D.C.: Investment Company Institute, Fall 1994.

Investment Company Institute. *Understanding Shareholder Redemption Decisions.* Washington, D.C.: Investment Company Institute, Winter 1993.

James, Christopher. "Some Evidence of Uniqueness of Bank Loans." *Journal of Financial Economics* 19 (1987): 217–35.

Jones, David S., and Kathleen K. King. "The Implementation of Prompt Corrective Action: An Assessment." *Journal of Banking and Finance* 19 (June 1995).

Jordan, Jerry L. "A Market Approach to Banking Regulation." Federal Reserve Bank of Cleveland, photocopy, March 1993.

Kane, Edward, and Haluk Unal. "Modeling Structural and Temporal Variation in the Market's Valuation of Banking Firms." *Journal of Finance* 45 (1990): 113–36.

Kareken, John H. "Federal Bank Regulatory Policy: A Description and Some Observations." *Journal of Business* 59 (January 1986), pp. 3–48.

Kashyap, Anil K., and J. C. Stein. "Monetary Policy and Bank Lending," in N. Gregory Mankiw, ed., *Monetary Policy.* Chicago: University of Chicago Press, 1994, pp. 221–56.

Kaufman, George G. "Bank Contagion: Theory and Evidence." Federal Reserve Bank of Chicago, Working Paper Series, No. 92-13, June 1992.

Kaufman, George G. "Bank Failures, Systemic Risk, and Bank Regulation." Federal Reserve Bank of Chicago, Working Paper Series, No. 96-1, January 1996.

Kaufman, George G. "FDICIA: The Early Evidence." *Challenge* (July/August 1994): 53–57.

Kaufman, George G., and Larry R. Mote. "Is Banking a Declining Industry? A Historical Perspective." *Economic Perspectives* (Federal Reserve Bank of Chicago) (May/June 1994): 2–21.

Kaufman, Henry. "Financial Derivatives and Their Risks." *Central Banking* (Autumn 1993): 32–44.

Kaufman, Henry. "Structural Changes in Financial Markets: Economic and Policy Significance." *Economic Review* (Federal Reserve Bank of Kansas City) (Second Quarter 1994): 5–15.

Keeley, Michael C. "Deposit Insurance, Risk, and Market Power in Banking." *American Economic Review* 80 (1990): 1183–1200.

Kindleberger, Charles P. *Manias, Panics, and Crashes.* MacMillan: London, 1978.

Kollar, Mark. "Congressman Sees Need for Safety Net." *Knight-Ridder Financial Products & News,* July/August 1994, p. 1.

Koretz, Gene. "Mutual-Fund Mania: Danger Signal for the Fed?" *Business Week,* January 7, 1994, p. 20.

Kroszner, Randall S., and Raghuram G. Rajan. "The Role of Firewalls in Universal Banks." Working Paper No. 103, Center for the Study of the Economy and the State, University of Chicago, November 1994.

Kuhn, Susan E. "The New Perilous Stock Market." *Fortune*, December 27, 1993, pp. 48–62.

Lakonishok, Josef, Andrei Shleifer, and Robert W. Vishny. "The Impact of Institutional Trading on Stock Prices." *Journal of Financial Economics* 32 (1992): 23–43.

LaWare, John. "Testimony" in U.S. Congress, Subcommittee on Economic Stabilization of the Committee on Banking, Finance and Urban Affairs, U.S. House of Representatives, *Economic Implications of the "Too Big to Fail" Policy: Hearings*. 102d Cong., 1st sess., May 9, 1991, p. 34.

Lewis, M. K. "Theory and Practice of the Banking Firm," in C. Green and D. T. Llewellyn, eds., *Survey of Monetary Economics*, vol. 2. London: Blackwell Press, 1991.

Litan, Robert E. *What Should Banks Do?* Washington, D.C.: Brookings Institution, 1987.

Llewellyn, David T. "Secular Pressures on Banking in Developed Financial Systems: Is Traditional Banking an Industry in Severe Decline?" photocopy, 1992.

Lummer, Scott, and John McConnell. "Further Evidence on the Bank Lending Process and the Capital Market Response to Bank Loan Agreements." *Journal of Financial Economics* 25 (1990): 92–122.

Marcis, Richard, Sandra West, and Victoria Leonard-Chambers. "Mutual Fund Shareholder Response to Market Disruptions." *Investment Company Perspective*. Washington, D.C.: Investment Company Institute, 1995.

Mauskopf, Eileen. "The Transmission Channels of Monetary Policy: How Have They Changed?" *Federal Reserve Bulletin* (1990): 985–1008.

Meltzer, Allan H. "Regulatory Arrangements, Financial Stability, and Regulatory Reform." *BOJ Monetary and Economic Studies* 12 (July 1994): 1–12.

Merton, Robert C., and Zvi Bodie. "Deposit Insurance Reform: A Functional Approach," in Allan Meltzer and Charles Plosser, eds., *Carnegie-Rochester Conference Series on Public Policy* 83 (June 1993): 1–39.

Minsky, H. P. "Financial Stability Revisited: The Economics of Disaster," in Board of Governors of the Federal Reserve System, *Reappraisal of the Federal Reserve Discount Mechanism*, vol. 3. Washington, D.C.: Federal Reserve Board, 1972, pp. 95–136.

Mishkin, Frederic S. "Anatomy of a Financial Crisis." *Journal of Evolutionary Economics* 2 (1992): 115–30.

Mishkin, Frederic S. "Asymmetric Information and Financial Crises: A Historical Perspective," in R. Glenn Hubbard, ed., *Financial Markets and Financial Crises*. Chicago: University of Chicago Press, 1991, pp. 69–108.

Mishkin, Frederic S. "Preventing Financial Crises: An International Perspective." New York: National Bureau of Economic Research, November 1993.

"The Monetary Transmission Mechanism: Symposium." *Journal of Economic Perspectives* 9 (Fall 1995): 3–96.

Mosser, Patricia C. "Changes in Monetary Policy Effectiveness: Evidence from Large Macroeconometric Models." *Quarterly Review* 17 (Federal Reserve Bank of New York) (Spring 1992): 36–51.

NationsBank of North Carolina, N.A. v. *Variable Annuity Life Insurance Company*, 115 S. Ct. 810.

Nugent, Thomas E. "Greenspan Hews to Price Rule." *Wall Street Journal*, February 23, 1994, p. A20.

Organization for Economic Cooperation and Development. *Banks under Stress*. Paris: OECD, 1992.

Osborne, Dale K., and Tarek S. Zaher. "Reserve Requirements, Bank Share Prices, and the Uniqueness of Bank Loans." *Journal of Banking and Finance* 16 (1992): 799–812.

Pierce, James L. *The Future of Banking*. New Haven: Yale University Press, 1991.

Pollack, Alex J. "Collateralized Money: An Idea Whose Time Has Come Again." *Challenge* (September/October 1992): 62–64.

Post, Mitchell A. "The Evolution of the U.S. Commercial Paper Market since 1980." *Federal Reserve Bulletin* (December 1992): 879–91.

Presidential Task Force on Market Mechanisms. "The Effects of the October Stock Market Decline on the Mutual Funds Industry." Report of the Presidential Task Force on Market Mechanisms, Study IV. January 1988.

Protzman, F. "When German Safeguards Fail." *New York Times*, February 28, 1994, p. D1.

Public Law No. 102–242. December 19, 1991.

Ramey, Valerie A. "How Important Is the Credit Channel in the Transmission of Monetary Policy?" *Carnegie-Rochester Conference Series on Public Policy* 39 (December 1993): 1–45.

Rasche, Robert H., and James M. Johannes. *Controlling the Growth of Monetary Aggregates*. Boston: Kluwer Academic Publishers, 1987.

Remolona, Eli M. "The Recent Growth of Financial Derivative Markets." *Quarterly Review* (Federal Reserve Bank of New York) (Winter 1992–1993): 28–43.

Remolona, Eli M., and Kurt C. Wulfekuhler. "Finance Companies, Bank Competition, and Niche Markets." *Quarterly Review* (Federal Reserve Bank of New York) (Summer 1992): 25–38.

Roberds, William, and Charles H. Whiteman. "Monetary Aggregates as Monetary Targets: A Statistical Investigation." *Journal of Money, Credit, and Banking* 24 (1992): 141–61.

Roe, Mark J. *Strong Managers, Weak Owners: The Political Roots of American Corporate Finance.* Princeton: Princeton University Press, 1994.

Romer, Christina D., and David H. Romer. "Credit Channel or Credit Actions? An Interpretation of the Postwar Transmission Mechanism," in *Changing Capital Markets: Implications for Monetary Policy.* Jackson Hole, Wy.: Federal Reserve Bank of Kansas City, August 19–21, 1993, pp. 71–116.

Schadrack, Frederick, and Frederick S. Breimyer. "Recent Developments in the Commercial Paper Market." *Monthly Review* (Federal Reserve Bank of New York) (December 1970): 280–91.

Schwartz, Anna J. "Real and Pseudo-Financial Crises," in Forrest Capie and Geoffrey E. Wood, eds., *Financial Crises and the World Banking System.* London: MacMillan, 1986, pp. 11–31.

Scism, Leslie. "Commercial Finance Firms Have New Rivals in Banks." *Wall Street Journal*, June 24, 1993, p. B4.

Securities Act of 1933. Rule 482 (Form N-1A registration statement for open-end management investment companies).

Securities and Exchange Commission. Release No. 33-6690, 34-32116, IC-19399 (April 7, 1993).

Securities and Exchange Commission. Rule 2a-7.

Sellon, Gordon H., Jr. "Changes in Financial Intermediation: The Role of Pension and Mutual Funds." *Economic Review* (Federal Reserve Bank of Kansas City) (Third Quarter 1992): 53–69.

Smythe, Marianne K. Letter from director, Division of Investment Management, Securities and Exchange Commission, to Matthew P. Fink, president, Investment Company Institute, Washington, D.C.: December 9, 1992.

Starobin, Paul. "Make 'Em Pay." *National Tax Journal* (July 24, 1993): 1856–60.

Stoll, Hans R. "Organization of the Stock Market: Competition or Fragmentation?" *Journal of Applied Corporate Finance* 5 (Winter 1993): 89–93.

Swaps Monitor Publications, Inc. *The World's Major Swap Dealers*, various issues.

Thakor, Anjan, and Sudipto Bhattacharya. "Contemporary Banking Theory." Indiana University, Working Paper No. 504, 1991.

Tobin, James. "The Case for Preserving Regulatory Distinctions." Paper presented at "Restructuring the Financial System," a symposium sponsored by the Federal Reserve Bank of Kansas City, 1987.

Todd, Walker F. "FDICIA's Emergency Liquidity Provisions." *Economic Review* 29 (3) (Federal Reserve Bank of Cleveland) (1993): 16–23.

Wall, Larry D. "Too-Big-to-Fail after FDICIA." *Economic Review* 78 (Federal Reserve Bank of Atlanta) (January/February 1993): 1–14.

Wayne, Leslie. "Investment Soars in Mutual Funds, Causing Concerns."
    New York Times, September 7, 1993, p. D1.
Wayne, Leslie. "Investors Face First Money Market Funds Loss." *New York
    Times*, September 28, 1994, p. D1.
Whalen, Gary. "Bank Organizational Form and the Risks of Expanded
    Activities." Office of the Comptroller of the Currency, Washington,
    D.C., April 24, 1995.
Wheelock, David C. "Is the Banking Industry in Decline? Recent Trends and
    Future Prospects from a Historical Perspective." *Economic Review*
    (Federal Reserve Bank of St. Louis) (September/October 1993): 3–22.

Index

Accounting practices, 146–47
Antilla, Susan, 74, 75
Assets, financial
 households' direct holdings,
  19f, 20–27, 46t, 53, 73
 proposed bank collateral, 168
 securitized, 34
 shift of households', 73–74
 transparent, 97
 valuation of banks', 154
Assets, transaction
 in definition of money, 101–2
 turnover rates, 102

Bacon, Kenneth H., 63
Bailouts, mutual fund, 74–75
Bank failures and losses
 Japanese, 41, 148
 major episodes of, 148,
  150–51t
 as threat to stability, 14
Bank for International Settlements
 (BIS), 123
Bank holding company
 banks and capitalized nonbank
  subsidiaries under, 157

regulation by Federal Reserve
 and SEC, 161
Banking system
 with changes in financial markets, 10–11, 177–78
 current regulation of U.S., 149,
  151–63
 declining bank uniqueness theory, 63–70
 effect of 1930s legislative
  reform, 6–7
 excess capacity theory of
  decline, 60–61
 factors creating unstable, 148
 fragility of Japanese, 148
 lender-of-last resort concept,
  163
 MMMFs and finance compa-
  nies as substitute for current,
  94–96
 proposed disclosure requirements, 160–61
 regulatory burden theory of
  decline, 61–63
 with regulatory monitoring,
  158–60

restrictions on securities activities (1930s), 6–7
risk-taking under current regulatory regime, 163–64
suggestions for more effective regulation, 164–67
Banking system, collateralized
advantages, 169–70, 174
barriers to implementation, 175
criticism of, 170–72, 174
effect of proposed, xiii, 149
in effort to change regulation, 177
proposed public policy related to, 175–76
regulation of, 167–69
Banks
actions to maintain profitability, 12
activity restriction and prohibitions for, 156–58
advantages offered by, 5–6
broker-dealer activity, 12
capital requirements of, 155–56
changes in operation, xii, 179–80
checkable deposits as source of funds, 5, 16f, 64, 66–67t
constraints of regulation on, 180
derivative trading, 133, 136–37t, 138
diminished lending advantage, 64, 65t
economic functions of, 4–5
eroded market share, 10–12, 21–23, 34
eroded profitability (1980s), 35f, 36–37
loan-loss provisions of U.S., 47, 50–51t
mergers and consolidation, 10–11
operation without FDIC insurance, 154–55
under regulatory regime (1930s legislation), 7

response to lagging profitability, 10–11, 36t, 38–41
susceptibility to runs, 82–83
traditional role, 10
use of firewalls, 156–58
vulnerability to depositor runs, 82–83
Banks, foreign
competition from, 34–35
decline of traditional banking, 42–47
as lenders to U.S. business, 34f, 68
loan-loss provisions, 47, 50–51t
noninterest income, 47, 48–49t
risk-taking, 40–41
Banks, traditional
consolidation in, 178
decline of financial intermediation services, 11–15
erosion of market share (1920s and 1930s, 1980s and 1990s), 15t, 47
protective legislation for (1930s), 6, 60–61
recent changes in, 15t, 47, 52–53
theories of decline in, 60–70
Bank-subsidiary structure, 157
Barth, James R., 62
Bartholomew, Philip, 62
Beckette, Sean, 68
Benston, George J., 71, 165
Bernanke, Ben S., 113, 114
BIS. See Bank for International Settlements
Bisignano, Joe, 2
Black, Bernard S., 59
Black, Fischer, 64
Bleakley, Fred, 2
Blinder, Alan, 103, 113
Bodie, Zvi, 167
Bond market, 88–91
Bosworth, Barry, 103
Boyd, John H., 11, 40
Bradsher, Keith, 117

Brancato, C., 54t, 59
Brumbaugh, R. Dan, 62
Burnham, James B., 167
"Business Bulletin," 55

Calian, Sara, 74
Calomiris, Charles, 87
Capital markets
   borrowing from, 178
   direct access to, 115
Capital requirements, bank,
   155–56
Carty, Lea V., 79
Central banks as lenders of last
   resort, 91–92
Commercial paper
   guarantees or lines of credit,
      28, 34
   held by money market mutual
      funds, 77–80
   issued by nonfinancial compa-
      nies, 27–28, 29t
Commercial paper market
   changes since 1970s, 87
   defaults in, 76–77, 79–80
   direct borrowing in, 28
   of money market mutual funds,
      28
   potential for run on MMMFs,
      86–88
Communications technology
   impact on trading practices, 55
   influence on financial interme-
      diaries, 8
Community Reinvestment Act
   (1977), 61, 62
Competition
   effect of regulation on, 60–61
   effect of regulatory constraints
      on, 180
   of finance companies with
      banks, 22–23
   with internationalization, 8–9
Competitive advantage
   of foreign over U.S. banks, 35
   of U.S. banks, 34–35, 68, 70

Costs
   of bank regulation monitoring
      system, 159
   of deposit insurance "safety
      net," 152
   estimates of present system of
      bank regulation, 162
Credit exposure
   of banks in derivatives markets,
      138, 140, 142–43t
   OTC derivatives markets,
      125–30
Credit market
   finance company loans to busi-
      ness, 23, 30–31t
   intermediation role of banks,
      10
   nonbank financial intermedi-
      aries in, 115
Cutler, David M., 81

D'Arista, Jane W., 34, 63, 71, 75,
   76, 82, 95
Deposit insurance
   legislation mandating risk-
      based (1989), 153–54
   in regulation of banks, 152–55
   as safety net, 71, 74
   See also Federal Deposit Insur-
      ance Corporation (FDIC)
Deposits, checkable
   as component of M1, 104
   decline in banks', 16
   issued by banks, 5, 13, 16f, 64,
      66–67t
   ratio of MMMFs to, 73–74
Derivatives
   firm losses related to, 120–21
   growth of markets for, 55,
      57–58t
   risk-sharing component of, 145
   used by mutual funds, 96–97
Derivatives markets, bank
   regulation of, 140–41, 144,
      145
   volume of contracts, 133,
      136–37t, 138

Derivatives markets, OTC
dealers' risks, 125–27
difficulty of regulation for,
140–41
factors in development of, 53,
55, 57–58t, 71
federal regulatory oversight of,
132–35
GAO report (1994), 121,
123–25, 127–33
Group of Thirty study of, 121,
129, 130
major dealers, 122t, 128f
participation of banks in, 138
recommendations for improvements, 146
regulation of nonbank dealers,
145
sources of risk in, 125–33
stable conditions in, 145–46
studies of, 121
total contractual amounts outstanding, 57–58t, 122t, 127,
128f
unregulated, 132
Diamond, David, 113
Disclosure practices
for derivatives users, 146–47
proposed requirements for
banks, 160–61
Disintermediation, 13

Eaton, Leslie, 74, 75
Eckhardt, J., 120
Edwards, Franklin R., 11, 55, 138
Ely, Bert, 171
Equity markets
with growth of institutional
trading, 53–55
pension fund holdings of corporate equity, 17–19, 54t,
88

Fair Credit and Charge Card Disclosure Act (1988), 161
Fama, Eugene, 64

FDICIA. See Federal Deposit
Insurance Corporation
Improvement Act, 1991 (FDI-
CIA)
Federal Deposit Insurance Corporation (FDIC)
market operation without,
154–55
regulation of bank holding
company subsidiaries, 161
regulatory function of, 152–55
Federal Deposit Insurance Corporation Improvement Act, 1991
(FDICIA), 62–63, 92–93, 153,
160, 163
Federal funds rate, 115–17
Federal Reserve
control of money supply by,
101, 108–9
as lender of last resort, 71, 83,
91–94, 98, 163
proposals to expand legal
reserve requirements,
110–11
regulation of bank holding
companies, 161
Feinman, Joshua N., 104
Feldstein, Martin, 3, 101, 104,
108, 110
Finance companies
commercial paper issues, 28, 34
lending competition with
banks, 28, 32–33t, 34, 68,
69t
regulation of, 62
Financial Institutions Reform,
Recovery and Enforcement Act,
1989 (FIRREA), 62
Financial intermediaries
advantages offered by, 5–6
assets held by (1990–1994),
11–12, 14–15t
economic functions of, 4–5
factors influencing changes in,
7–9, 11–35
nondepository, 42, 44–45t, 46t

See also Banks; Banking system; Nonbank financial intermediaries
Financial markets
with changes in asset flows, 21, 27
innovations in, 10
internationalization of, 34
prevention of instability, 145–46
threat to stability of, 148
tranformation of, 177–78
See also Derivatives markets, OTC
Financial systems
effect of legislative reforms (1930s), 6–7
fragility of Japanese, 148
market imperfections, 115
segmentation with legislative reforms (1930s), 6–7
Firewalls
for collateralized banks, 169
criticism of, 157–58
lack of confidence in, 161–62
as regulatory devices, 156–57
FIRREA. *See* Financial Institutions Reform, Recovery and Enforcement Act, 1989 (FIRREA)
Flow of funds, 20
Fons, Jerome S., 79
Friedman, Benjamin, 100, 101, 103, 104, 106
Froot, Kenneth A., 54
Fuerst, Timothy, 113

Gaughan, Patrick, 54t, 59
General Accounting Office (GAO)
study of derivatives, 2, 121, 123–25, 127–33
Gertler, Mark, 11, 40, 114
Girault, Denis, 79
Glass-Steagall Act (1933), 62, 71
Gonzalez, Henry, 138
Gorton, Gary, 20, 86, 87, 138
Greenspan, Alan, 117

Group of Thirty study of derivatives, 121, 129, 130
Grundfest, Joseph, 55
Guarantees, government, 167–72

Hale, David D., 2, 74
Hallman, Jeffrey J., 104
Hedging instrument reporting, 146–47
Hetzel, Robert L., 103, 104
Hook, Linda, 68
Household financial assets
corporate stock outstanding, 18f, 54
distribution of, 22–23t, 53–54
flows into pension and mutual funds, 19–21, 24–26t
net flow of, 24–26t, 27f, 53–54
shift to nonbank intermediaries, 21, 27, 53, 73–74, 97

Information
of bank depositors, 82–83, 85
of mutual fund investors, 84–86
Information technology
assistance to nonbank competitors, 34
ease of borrowing with, 27–28
influence on financial intermediaries, 8
Innovations, financial
accommodation of, 1–2
effect of, 8, 10, 42, 71–72, 114–15
factors in development of, 13, 16
See also Nonbank financial intermediaries
Innovations, technological, 8, 21–22, 34, 42, 55, 172–73
Instinet trading system, 55
Institutional investors
public policy issues raised by, 54–59
share of total stock outstanding, 54

as stockholders, 55, 59
Interest rates
    influence of Federal Reserve on
        short- and long-term,
        115–17
    in money view of monetary
        policy, 112, 114–15
Investment companies. *See* Mutual
    funds
Investment Company Act (1940),
    91
Investment Company Institute, 90
Investment funds. *See* Mutual
    funds

James, Christopher, 68
Jasen, Georgette, 74
Johannes, James M., 104
Jordan, Jerry, 162
Junk bond market, 34

Kareken, John H., 167
Kaufman, George G., 11, 74, 165
Kaufman, Henry, 2, 3
Keeley, Michael C., 36
Knipp, T., 120
Koretz, Gene, 71
Kroszner, Randall S., 71
Kuhn, Susan E., 71

Lakonishok, Josef, 81
Leonard-Chambers, Victoria, 89,
    90
Lewis, M. K., 64
Life insurance companies, foreign,
    42, 46t, 47
Liquidity services, banks, 5–6
Litan, Robert E., 62, 167
Llewellyn, David T., 2

M1
    demand for, 103–4
    as policy target, 104
    relation to GDP or inflation
        rate, 104
    relation to monetary base,
        106–8

M2
    components and changing com-
        position, 104–7
    as predictor of economic activi-
        ty, 104
    ratio to monetary base, 106–9
    relation to GDP, 104
Marcis, Richard, 89–90
Mauskopf, Eileen, 118
Mehra, Yash P., 103, 104
Merton, Robert C., 167
Mishkin, Frederic S., 93
MMDAs. *See* Money market
    deposit accounts (MMDAs)
MMMFs. *See* Money market
    mutual funds (MMMFs)
Monetary aggregates
    M1 as, 103–4
    M2 definition of money, 104
    relation to GDP and monetary
        base, 103–9
    substitutability between M1
        and other, 104
    See also M1; M2; Money sup-
        ply
Monetary policy
    credit view, 113–14
    effectiveness, 115–19
    money view, 112, 114
    See also Federal Reserve; Mon-
        etary aggregates; Money
        supply
Money
    characteristics of transaction
        assets, 101–2
    substitutes for, 114–15
Money market deposit accounts
    (MMDAs), 101, 102, 104
Money market mutual funds
    (MMMFs)
    bank-type services of, 16
    commercial paper issues, 28,
        29t
    cost advantages of, 62
    growth of, 13–16, 20–21, 28
    impact on banks of growth, 22
    portfolio losses, 74–75

potential for run with commercial paper default, 86–88
‘ ratio of checkable deposits to, 73, 74f
ratios to M1 and M2, 103–4, 106f
scenario with run on, 76–80
SEC regulation of commercial paper in, 80
Money supply
components of, 103–7
control by Federal Reserve, 101, 108–9
in credit view of monetary policy, 113–14
in money view of monetary policy, 112, 114–15
Moral hazard
of banks' *ex post* changing risk exposure, 153–54
with collateralized banking, 168, 170
in extension of regulation to nonbank financial institutions, 98–99
Morris, Charles, 68
Mosser, Patricia C., 118
Mote, Larry R., 11
Mutual fund redemptions
potential for destabilization of stock and bond markets, 88–91
scenario in stock and bond funds, 80–81
Mutual funds
bailouts, 74–75
collateralized investments in, 179
growth of, 15t, 17–20, 178
influence as major equity owners, 53
lack of insurance, 74
as sellers of securities, 81
share of intermediary assets, 15–17
susceptibility to runs, 84–86

in terms of household assets, 20, 24–26t, 73
transaction services of, 73
use of derivatives, 96–97
vulnerability to shareholder runs, 84–86
See also Money market mutual funds (MMMFs)
Mutual funds, foreign
growth of, 42, 44–45t
share of household assets, 42, 46t

Nonbank financial intermediaries
attempts to protect, 145
competitiveness of, 13, 16
functions of, 10
growth of, 178
as OTC derivatives dealers, 122t, 132
NOW (negotiable orders of withdrawal) accounts, 101, 104
Nugent, Thomas E., 117

Open market operations, 115–17
Opler, Tim C., 68
Organization for Economic Cooperation and Development (OECD), 2
Osborne, Dale K., 68

Parallel banking system proposal, 94–96
Pennacchi, George, 20, 86, 87
Pension funds
growth of, 15t, 17–20, 178
influence as major equity owners, 53
share of intermediary assets, 15–17
in terms of household assets, 20, 22–23t
Pension funds, foreign, 42, 46t
Perold, Andre F., 54
Pierce, James L., 167
Pollack, Alex J., 167
Porter, Richard D., 104

Posit trading system, 55
Post, Mitchell A., 228
Poterba, James M., 81
Profitability
    banks' response to erosion of,
        38–41
    erosion of banks', 12, 35t,
        35–38
Promisel Report, Bank for International Settlements, 121, 123
Protzman, F., 120
Public policy issues
    related to decline of traditional
        banking, 70–72
    related to institutional fund
        managers, 54–59
    related to proposed collateralized banking, 175–76

Rajan, Raghuram G., 71
Ramey, Valerie A., 104
Rasche, Robert H., 104
Regulation
    of bank derivatives dealers,
        140–41, 144, 145
    as constraints on banks, 180
    current bank regulatory structure, 151–63
    effectiveness of bank, 144
    for financial stability, 7
    monitoring and corrective
        action, 158–60
    with 1930s reform of financial
        system, 6–7
    out-of-date bank, 148–49
    proposal for parallel banking
        system, 94–96
    of proposed collateralized
        banks, 168–69
    restrictions on bank activity,
        13, 16, 156–58
    theory of bank decline wth burden of, 61–63
Regulation Q, 7, 13, 16
Regulatory system
    components of current, 151–63

with financial and technological innovation, 172–76
    inefficiencies and dangers in
        current, xii, 2–3, 144, 148,
        180–81
    oversight of OTC derivatives
        activity, 132–33, 134–35t
    proposed collateralized banking
        system, xiii
    proposed reforms for banking,
        163–67
Remolona, Eli M., 28, 55
Reporting requirements, proposed,
    146–47
Risk
    for derivatives dealers, 125–27
    measurement of derivatives',
        146
    OTC derivatives activity of
        banks, 138, 140, 142–43t
    OTC derivatives markets,
        125–33
    See also Credit exposure
Risk assessment
    by insured bank depositors,
        152–53
    with risk-based insurance premiums, 153–54
Risk exposure
    of OTC derivatives dealers, 144
    of proposed collateralized
        banks, 168
Risk-taking
    control of, 154
    under current regulatory
        regime, 163–64
    foreign banks, 39–41
    incentives for banks, 153
    risk-based capital requirements
        for banks, 155–56
    SEC regulations related to
        MMMF, 87–88
    by U.S. banks, xii, 10–11,
        40–41, 178
Roberds, William, 103
Roe, Mark J., 59
Rosen, Richard, 138

Schlesinger, Tom, 34, 63, 71, 75, 76, 82, 95
Scism, Leslie, 68
Securities and Exchange Commission (SEC)
    regulation of bank holding companies, 161
    regulation of mutual funds, 84–85, 90–91
    regulations related to MMMFs' risk-taking, 80, 87–88
Securities markets
    competition with foreign banks, 42
    decline in direct purchases, 23f, 53
    effect of globalized trading, 55, 56t
    legislative requirements for, 6–7
    separation from banking activities (1930s), 6
    trading activity, 54
Sellon, Gordon H., Jr., 54
Shleifer, Andrei, 81
Small, David H., 104
Starobin, Paul, 63
Stein, Jeremy, 54
Stock, James, 104
Stock market. See Securities markets
Stoll, Hans R., 55
Summers, Lawrence H., 81

Systemic crisis, financial system
    BIS definition, 123
    potential trigger for, 123–25
    risk cited by GAO report, 131–33

Thrift institutions
    decline in nonfinancial borrowing, 11, 13, 15t
    financial crisis in, 145
Tobin, James, 167
Trading
    in derivatives, 55, 57–58t
    effect of new systems, 55
    off-exchange, 55
Truth in Lending Act (1968), 161
Truth in Savings Act (1991), 161

U.S. Comptroller of the Currency, 161

Vishny, Robert, 81

Wall, Larry D., 94
Wayne, Leslie, 71, 75
West, Sandra, 89–90
Wheelock, David C., 11
Whiteman, Charles, 103
Wulfekuhler, Kurt C., 28
Wunsch Auction System, 55

Zaher, Tarek S., 68

About the Author

FRANKLIN R. EDWARDS is the Arthur F. Burns Professor of Free and Competitive Enterprise at the Graduate School of Business of Columbia University. The author of *Futures and Options* (McGraw-Hill, 1992) and the editor of *Regulating International Financial Markets: Issues and Policies* (Kluwer, 1992) and *Issues in Financial Regulation* (McGraw Hill, 1979), he has published more than ninety articles in professional journals. Mr. Edwards is editor of the *Journal of Financial Services Research,* associate editor of the *Journal of Futures Markets,* an advisory board member of *Managerial and Decision Economics,* and an editorial board member of the Federal Reserve Bank of New York's *Economic Policy Review.* Mr. Edwards has consulted for the General Accounting Office, the Federal Trade Commission, the Department of Justice, the Federal Reserve Board, the Comptroller of the Currency, and various financial institutions and law firms. He holds a Ph.D. in economics from Harvard University and a J.D. from New York University Law School.

www.ingramcontent.com/pod-product-compliance
Lightning Source LLC
Jackson TN
JSHW020017141224
75386JS00025B/574